Penguin Books
Seashaken Houses

'*Seashaken Houses* is more of a personal journey and meditative essay than a conventional history. Tom Nancollas has visited seven rock lighthouses in Britain and Ireland, from the relative tameness of Perch Rock on New Brighton beach to the godforsaken Fastnet, Ireland's most southerly point . . . an expert on the construction and weathering of these unique buildings'

Joe Moran, *The Times Literary Supplement*

'A selective and more personal account of eight particular rock lighthouses, in nine chapters. Each separate chapter, as well as addressing the particularity of one place and one history, tells a different part of the overall story – early efforts and failures, the changing design of the lights themselves, the life of the keepers'

Tessa Hadley, *Guardian*

'Nancollas is intrepid and persistent. His book is a first-hand travel guide to seven places you almost certainly have no chance of ever visiting'

Bella Bathurst, *Spectator*

'With compelling narrative and fascinating historical anecdotes, Tom shines a spotlight on these little known but spectacular structures'

Roma Agrawal

'Impassioned . . . much more than a geeky history, it also helps us think anew about buildings, about heritage, and even about family'

The Bookseller, Editor's Choice

'Intensely interesting'

Engineering & Technology Magazine

About the author

Born in Gloucester in 1988, Tom Nancollas is a writer and building conservationist based in London. After university, he joined English Heritage to work on church repair grants before moving on to the City of London and its historic townscape. Of Cornish ancestry, Tom maintained a love of seascapes during his work in the capital and became fascinated with offshore rock lighthouses, finding in them a new way of looking at buildings, heritage and, unexpectedly, family.

Tom Nancollas

Seashaken Houses

A Lighthouse History
from Eddystone to Fastnet

PENGUIN BOOKS

PENGUIN BOOKS

UK | USA | Canada | Ireland | Australia
India | New Zealand | South Africa

Penguin Books is part of the Penguin Random House
group of companies whose addresses can be found at
global.penguinrandomhouse.com.

 Penguin
Random House
UK

First published by Particular Books 2018
Published in Penguin Books 2019
001

Text design by Francisca Monteiro
Printed and bound in Great Britain by Clays Ltd, Elcograf S.p.A.

A CIP catalogue record for this book is available
from the British Library

ISBN: 978–1–846–14938–2

www.greenpenguin.co.uk

To Josephine

And to the memory of Jefferson Edward Jones, 1987-2018

Contents

*'In my seashaken house
On a breakneck of rocks'*

Dylan Thomas, 'Prologue', 1952

Introduction

Far out to sea, at nightfall, a seventeenth-century tower creaks on its foundations. Sea sloshes and prowls below the stone base while, above the weathervane, seagulls hang momentarily before dispersing.

A small ship leaves a harbour, carrying the tower's architect and a gang of carpenters. This lighthouse – the first rock lighthouse in the world – has been reported by sailors and its keepers as defective. It wobbles in heavy weather, leans slightly out of true and needs strengthening if it is to survive the winter gales.

As they sail, a storm develops. Though they have 13 miles to cover, south into the English Channel, there is no question of going back. I imagine the sea that evening looked like one of J.M.W. Turner's visceral marine paintings, rearing and rippling in great folds. Ahead, their destination comes into view on the darkening horizon. Though by now they are used to it, the sight still initially defies the eyes. A building in the sea, standing where one shouldn't, with a light shining at its summit.

The tower appears to be hovering on the waterline, but is actually founded on a submerged reef. All hands eye it nervously. Many ships have been dragged towards this maroon, barnacled reef, which is harder than concrete and puckered like blistered tarmac, then sunk, bubbling, down the fathoms to become crashed craft deep on the ocean floor. In such stormy conditions, the crew are heading straight for it, urgently navigating for the landing-place.

For four years this tower has shown sailors where the reef lurks. Upon completion, it was immediately hailed as an impossible achievement. So certain was the architect of his lighthouse's staying power that he proclaimed a desire to be inside it during the worst storm imaginable.

As they draw nearer, they begin to make out the extravagant form of the tower in more detail. On sunnier days, you can imagine fishermen disbelievingly appraising the design from their boats. A strong, cylindrical base. Sensible enough. But what about the upper stages, which seem to be wooden, octagonal and crazily decorated? What use are those ornaments where few can see them? Bent and curving ironwork and suchlike? How does the chandelier stay dry enough, out here? But, tonight, there is no time for questions. The architect is just glad the tower is still there.

Somehow, they manage a landing against the fast-running currents around the reef. They tie up the boat and hasten to the tower. In the gathering storm, its timbers creak as though shortly to rupture. At the door, the lighthouse keepers greet the men with wide eyes. Although there is a certain luxury to living this far out to sea (the tower features a gilded bedchamber and Latin inscriptions), this cannot save the drowning. Winds whip their hair and billow their coats as the intensity of the storm cranks upwards.

Over the next few days, havoc is wrought on land. Thunder booms incessantly behind the horizon. Surging wind presses men against walls, breaks carts against posts, fells wide-girthed trees, strikes down spires and chimneystacks, smacks open gates and shuts them again, races mill-sails until they ignite, clogs up rivers with ships, topples livestock in fields and batters the face of England. During the Great Storm, all believed the Apocalypse had come.

Out there, they got on with the work, hastily reinforcing and buttressing what they could. Abandoning protocol, even the architect himself hammered and sawed frantically by the last rays of daylight. But the next night, shortly before midnight, the tower's candles were seen burning for the last time. As the storm grew beyond all proportion, the building began to shake madly, quaking from side to side, the iron stanchions rooting it to the reef slowly loosening. Finally, with no question of escape, the lighthouse was pitched into the sea, decisively uprooted. To a man, all perished.

*

1. The first rock lighthouse,
English Channel, 1698

Nothing remained of this first rock lighthouse but mangled iron bars.

It is not easy to establish an enduring presence in an unstable medium like the ocean. Firm structures are seemingly incompatible with this fluid setting. Though our maritime pedigree is considerable, few traces of us linger out to sea. All too frequently, man-made things lose their buoyancy and plummet to the sea floor. Flotsam is ushered towards land and ground to pieces in coves until nothing is left, as though the sea is in a never-ending cycle of erasure.

Perhaps the allure of the sea is that it appears too restless to be permanently marked. As well as vastness, there is blankness, freely interpreted. Since the time of Francis Drake, and even before, it has offered us a majestic sense of possibility, thrusting Britain's horizons outwards through trade, war and global circumnavigations. Then, the sea was an unknown realm that could lead to new territories with resources to capture and markets to exploit. The ugly undertow to historic seafaring and exploration is now recognized, but in more recent times, with oil-spills and plastics, we have despoiled the sea in other ways.

Yet today the sea remains incompletely known, not all its depths having been plumbed or probed. There is still an essential, primeval thrill in casting off from land, the excitement of discovery and transgression, and perhaps the fear that we might not make it back. Since we developed the technology to fly, the air and then space have offered us the same experience. Whether sea or space, these realms into which we stray are exhilarating because we know we are trespassers: we are present in them on the strength of our artifices, not because we can inhabit them. Nowadays, though, we look more to altitudes and space for possibilities of exploration. Our maritime past is celebrated in ballads and fine reminiscences, but for many it is just that: a past.

I was raised between two seas, the Atlantic that thrashes the Cornish coasts and the more placid Irish Sea that shimmers far away over sand-flats from the Wirral peninsula. Though my immediate roots lie in Gloucestershire, in the Forest of Dean, west of the River Severn, school holidays alternated between these two coastlines. Now, I realize this bred in me not only a subconscious affinity with the sea but also the knowledge that the sea is a thing of various guises.

A quirk of the tidal flows around the Wirral means that when the tide is out, it's out. Rarely would we ever trudge the half-mile or so to paddle in its shallows; rarely, too, was the Irish Sea ever more than placid when seen from Hoylake sands in June. Nonetheless, there were chilling stories of this apparently meek, distant entity: how it could race in deceptively quickly, stranding the unwary on sandbanks, or drowning them in pulsating riptides below sheets of featureless water. I don't recall ever seeing any ship on it, either, though towards my adulthood they started building windfarms in Liverpool Bay.

Conversely, the Cornish Atlantic was and is a vital, unpredictable thing, easily willing to show itself in a state of high dudgeon, with storms and roaring waves common when we ventured to our ancestral harbour towns on the south Cornish coast. When we felt brave enough we entered it, but with the feeling that it could flip at any minute, and that all kinds of hidden things awaited our bare, questing feet on the sea floor: rocks, wreckage, slippery weed, sharp teeth and claws.

On this Cornish horizon, 12 miles out, there is a rock lighthouse. A faint yet distinctive grey pillar, just visible enough to whet the appetite. I remember it specifically as a fixed point in an ever-moving seascape. But, in truth, I was not exclusively fascinated with this inscrutable thing as a child. That would come later. On the horizon there was too much else to see.

Yachts put out into the bay on Sundays, tacking about to the blasts of a foghorn on the shore. Fishing vessels, too, were numerous and endlessly varied in their liveries and configurations. Some even flew Breton flags, having crossed over from France. There was a diving school, the black-clad frogmen enigmatically disappearing and reappearing in a certain patch of the water. Further out, on clear days, larger ships could be distinguished upon the horizon. Container ships coming and going in the main lanes were frequent sights, but most thrilling of all was the unmistakably lethal profile of a ship of war, a frigate or a destroyer, stealing out of the English Channel.

It was only when, based in London, I found myself working on landlocked townscapes that my thoughts returned to that distant tower on the horizon. When I was studying to become a building conservationist, I needed a dissertation subject. By then, I already knew my way around most historic building types – houses, churches, pubs, warehouses, banks, etc. – and wanted a more exotic focus. Partly as escapism, I decided to investigate something more extreme, more unusual, which would stretch the very meaning of the word 'building' and preferably be found only in unfamiliar places. Then I remembered what, as a child, I had seen from the shore.

Beyond the apparent finality of Britain and Ireland's coastlines – whether of the mainland or islands – are a series of outposts raised off perilous footholds of marine rock. Commonplace maps show them only indistinctly and digital maps show only their names. But for this indistinct plotting, or the occasional glimpse from a distant ferry, their existence is barely known to most.

Over a period spanning nearly four centuries, we undertook to build in the sea. Lofty stone towers arose on reefs positioned many miles offshore, ushered upwards by labourers clinging to scaffolds or dangling in harnesses. Waves frequently confiscated tools, flooded workings, dismantled masonry, shattered glassware. Men and materials were ferried exhaustingly to these places and back again. Such ordeals seemed to underline how buildings were things of the land, not the sea, and to transplant them there was a great struggle.

Despite the sea's instability, we have achieved permanence there. Between 1698 and 1904, a total of 27 rock lighthouses were constructed to mark the most dangerous hazards to shipping in the seas around Great Britain and Ireland. Of these, twenty survive today, a panoply of exquisite buildings that are the descendants of fabular prototypes. Taking the form of tall stone towers crowned with iron lanterns, they appear to rise, mirage-like, straight out of the sea, their circular foundations often unseen.

In fact, they stand on jagged sections of reef, left jutting up in the seas by geological schisms. An early, famous shipwreck illustrates their danger. In 1120, a royal vessel named the *White Ship* set sail for England from Barfleur in Normandy, carrying a group of Norman aristocrats including Prince William Aetheling, son and heir of King Henry I of England. This was the evening that Henry had concluded a treaty with France and, toasting the new peace, the party had delayed their departure in order to carouse on the beach. It was not until after dark that they eventually embarked. Remarkably, given the prestige of the passengers, the ship's crew had not kept themselves sober for the crossing but had quaffed enthusiastically. Navigating drunkenly in the darkness, one of the helmsmen ran them straight onto an (unnamed) submerged rock a little way offshore. The *White Ship* broke up and quickly sank, drowning Prince William and all but one of the people on board.

Losing the heir to the throne plunged Norman Britain into turmoil and altered the lines of succession of several major Anglo-Norman families. The wreck of the *White Ship* showed the profound influence a submerged rock could have on land.

Human error aside, navigation remained an inexact art for centuries to come. Relying on imprecise charts and rudimentary instruments, seafarers could not always be certain of their position on the sea. Unmarked offshore hazards presented an obvious threat. In daytime, white breakers might betray their presence, but they were invisible to a ship feeling its way through a dark night.

Some form of warning was evidently needed for such dangers, one that could be heeded both day and night. There are accounts, later in the medieval period, of bells being fixed to offshore reefs to be rung by the sea, their sound audible at all times. One such is the bell supposedly attached to a reef off the coast of Arbroath by an abbot of the town. But the open seas remained dark at that time. Mostly this was down to a lack of technological capability, but there was also a lack of impetus. Compared with the maritime boom of later centuries, there were fewer ships plying British waters, with correspondingly fewer possibilities of wreck.

From the seafaring and warfare of the Elizabethan period emerged a new maritime age, with busier seas and a greater risk of misadventure. A collection of navigational lights had been established on the coastlines of England, burning at first from an array of adapted or improvised structures: church towers, wooden posts, even bonfires on headlands. Later on, as the use of brick and stone in buildings became more widespread, these improvised beacons were replaced with bespoke coastal lighthouses. Naked flames guttered and smoked within their lanterns, according to the diligence of their local operators, who trimmed costs as they sought to run them at a profit (tolls were extracted at harbours from ships which had passed the light).

So much for the coasts. Out to sea, those ship-threatening reefs were at first marked with naïve, prototypical buildings. A tower designed in the Rococo manner, spiky with ornaments and weathervanes. A strange, spindly wooden tower on stilts. A barrel-like cone that resembled a ship in the form of a building. They looked laughably inept for their unforgiving locations, where the seas could run into mountainous proportions and galloping winds could hammer their elevations, yet they clung to their reefs like barnacles. Eventually, though, they were felled or replaced.

At the turn of the nineteenth century, Britain's seas were busier than ever before. Over the decades that followed, British colonies and possessions coalesced into an empire that sprawled across the world, aided by rapid technological advancements such as the larger, faster steamships able to chart any course, superior to the wind-dependent vessels of before. While Britain's waters were still festooned with masts and rigging, the character of shipping began to grow more iron-hulled and mechanical. Painted in 1838, J.M.W. Turner's *The Fighting Temeraire* perfectly captured the prevailing mood. It depicts a venerable old timber warship, whose 98 guns had been used with distinction at Trafalgar, being towed by a steam tug to the breakers' yard.

One by one, those dangerous reefs were neutered. As well as seafarers' lives, national prosperity hinged on safe passage through our shipping lanes, estuaries and ports. This was a forward-looking age, an age of improvement. Politics, public health, prisons and other sectors of life were reformed. Scientific breakthroughs were altering the way people perceived themselves in relation to nature. Such moods converged in our rock lighthouses, most of which were built in a flurry during the Victorian period and which were the proudest expressions of the way that navigation, and by proxy the sea, had been 'reformed'. And for the Victorians, it was not just about constructing an efficient machine. Each tower improved upon its predecessor.

A blueprint had emerged for a marvellous new kind of building, contrived by a new breed of civil engineer. Gone were the days of creaky, experimental structures, whimsically designed. Now, the rock lighthouses being built were all of a common type: formed wholly in stone, with complicated joints and tapering profiles, reminiscent of oak tree-trunks. Once just naked flames, the lights they now housed were equally refined, shot over vast distances by exquisite glassware.

So overwhelming are they to look at - soaring hundreds of feet into the sky, their heads in storms and their feet in seas - that their parentage is a source of wonderment. So is their resilience. The oldest of them still to operate on its reef has been there since 1811: over two centuries' worth of tempests and unimaginable exposure. Now, still fixed in the seascape, they carry torches - literally, in the case of their still-functioning lights - for a maritime history which is a vital part of the national sense of self.

This book will celebrate these singular buildings, the seas over which they preside and their lifesaving function, which today remains essential. But their noble simplicity of purpose masks a fascinating series of paradoxes and ambiguities. They stand between land and sea, strength and fragility, the defined and the undefined, the mythical and the real. They stand at the edges of our nation and the edges of our consciousness.

Water can find its way through a hairline crack between roof slates and drip patiently onto wooden beams until sodden and fatally weakened. It can splash out of clogged drainpipes and cascade down walls, saturating them so that their structural integrity dissolves into rot. And, in winter, it can freeze within the fabric it has infiltrated, suddenly fracturing stonework, brickwork, or rust-jacking ironwork. To be a building conservationist is, at times, to be fighting a constant rear-guard action against this liquid menace. Water is the nemesis of the built.

Positioned on cliffs or promontories, over 150 lighthouses stud the coastlines of Great Britain and Ireland. For the most part, they are entirely conventional buildings. Access to them is usually easy and safe, by road, cliff-path or harbour. Apart from their large light fittings, they are designed and constructed much like any other terrestrial building. Formed of brickwork, timber, occasionally some stone, they are vulnerable to water and require the same vigilance against damp, leaks and flooding.

Standing far offshore, the rock lighthouses are stranger conceits, surrounded entirely by water yet supposedly impervious to its effects. This is despite the sea rarely being tranquil enough to leave them alone. In fair conditions, waves bounce against their massive, drum-like lower parts, sending chance plumes of spray up to harass the windowsills. Fouler weather sends heavier walls of water over their fragile glass lanterns, usually held protectively out of the sea's reach. And in the heaviest weather, they shake.

All of it happens out of sight. Most of us only glimpse these buildings on distant horizons, and close encounters with them are rare. In this, they seem to share the mystique of the sea and its power to seduce us with fable and myth. Some of our most compelling myths come from there: the *Flying Dutchman*, the *Mary Celeste*, the drowned country of Lyonesse. After its functional role as a series of great transport conduits, the sea surrounds us like a great basin of otherness, forever lapping at the edges of our national psyche. There are countless stories of strange events, phosphorescent visions, odd experiences.

A favourite story of mine concerns the Scilly Isles, an archipelago south-west of Land's End. On Boxing Day 1927, a strangely rigged barge entered their complex waters and tacked assuredly towards Tresco, one of the islands. The barge's near-flawless navigation between the many rocky hazards here suggested to the Scilly islanders that one of their kind was at the helm, but they soon doubted this when the barge suddenly began to list sluggishly towards land. A lifeboat was dispatched and caught up with the barge just as it ran ashore on Tresco. Though it had expertly steered through this difficult stretch of water, the lifeboatmen found nobody on board except a canary singing merrily in its cage.

Strange stories, too, are told of the rock lighthouses by those who built and inhabited them. Uncanny sightings from their lantern rooms, eerie lights and inexplicably shimmering swathes of sea. Groanings and deep crashes emanating from their depths during the harshest storms. Ethereal music heard by their stonemasons in the deepest Atlantic. I became fascinated with these distant towers because it is as though the sea's quality of otherness has seeped into them. The stories of their construction seem near-mythical. For me, they stand easily alongside the more outlandish maritime mysteries, only they are stonily, uncompromisingly real.

Together with the stars, buoys, coastal lights and daymarks, rock lighthouses comprise the old, now failsafe system of navigation, of which they are the most thrilling components. At nightfall, eighteen of them still show their lights. In times when the open sea equated to outer space for most people, the rock lighthouses were like satellites fixed in that vastness, beaming out critical navigational instruction. As the limits of our consciousness have expanded, it is a tender irony that actual satellites compete with them for day-to-day navigational purposes.

Shipping, though diminished compared to its imperial peak, remains vigorous in our waters. In 2016, 20 million people were ferried to and from Britain across the sea (compared to over 250 million people through the air). That same year, 484 million tons of freight passed through our ports. While our individual links with the sea may have been severed, ships continue to bring us most of our necessities. Rock lighthouses keep providing an older form of warning light to guide this modern traffic. Seafarers' eyes still strain for them, though how many, or how often, it is impossible to say.

There can be few other buildings designed expressly to repel, to emphatically not be seen at close quarters. Although they flicker tantalizingly out of reach, they mark very real hazards to ships. As well as the sea's mystique, they share something of its visceral nature. Compared with older times, there may be fewer disasters at sea these days, but it remains highly dangerous.

In 2016 alone, the Royal National Lifeboat Institution saved over 500 lives in the seas around Great Britain and Ireland. Lifeboats were launched nearly 9,000 times that year, and one of the most extraordinary incidents was the rescue of a foreign yacht that had run aground on Skerryvore, a remote, godforsaken reef off the west coast of Scotland. Over an operation that began at midnight and concluded at eleven in the morning the next day, the crew of the lifeboat managed to save the yachtsman's life by towing him away from the reef in pitch-darkness, gale-force winds and huge swells. Not only this, but lifeboat crew successfully avoided losing their own lives. The coxswain was rightly decorated with a bronze medal for gallantry.

Skerryvore is also the name given to the rock lighthouse that stands upon that reef. Completed in 1844, it is a powerful presence, a colossal granite tower 156 feet high. Yet, that February night, it could only preside impotently over the scene unfolding below. There is a strange paradox to this. Shipwreck numbers fell dramatically when these towers were first raised upon their reefs. There can be no question that they have saved lives and made the seas safer. Yet they can only do so much, as if making the point that although we may feel we have mastered the sea over the course of the centuries, it really goes untamed. In several senses, mastery over the water will remain far beyond our grasp.

There is something about the prospect of a distant tower that grips the imagination hard and refuses to let go, especially when the circular tower stands over the water, squaring the mystery. Entranced by the stories and paradoxes of rock lighthouses, I pursued them doggedly through websites and books, then, more boldly, across sands, across seas, and even through sky. Access was difficult and relied on luck, improvisation and the generosity of my contacts.

The buildings may be sophisticated, but my experiences of them felt elemental. Out in the starkness of the sea, the basics – stone, air, water, light, dark, life, death – were just as vividly emphasized as engineering prowess. By achieving a home, a presence, in the most hostile of environments, the rock lighthouses provide a poignant insight into what it means to build and endure – and to bring light to places where previously there was none. Entwined with the stories of the houses is the story of their purpose – how lights were established and maintained in these liquid places, then improved, made crisper, more powerful, until certain sectors of sea were as brightly and safely lit as Grosvenor Square.

I hope this book draws your eyes offshore. It is an account of my journeys to some of the rock lighthouses, starting with the oldest one, the pioneer, and ending with the last to be constructed. I place emphasis on the journeys because they were, I feel, key to gaining an understanding of each building.

At the Eddystone reef, off the Cornish coast, a pioneering family of towers tells the history of them all in microcosm. Their role in the national story is illuminated by the Bell Rock in Scotland, while Haulbowline in Ireland, standing more ambiguously between realms, shows how even offshore structures can become political.

Redundancy and ruin seem stark prospects for buildings like these, where form and function are so closely intertwined, a question explored one night at the defunct Perch Rock near Liverpool. Conversely, lessons in light and its manipulation are found at a Thames-side experimental lighthouse in London. It is but a temporary detour inland.

Back in the seas, off Land's End, the notorious Wolf Rock reveals what it was like to make a home so far out to sea, while Bishop Rock off the Scilly Isles establishes a strange narrative of distance and time. Finally, the exquisite Fastnet lighthouse, off the Irish coast, reveals the vital inner lives of these buildings and their attendants today.

Those with prior knowledge will have realized that this book will not be an exhaustive account of the rock lighthouses around Britain. That has been done elsewhere. Rather, it is a highly personal view of seven buildings that seem to display characteristics that are common to them all. It will be, I hope, a new way of seeing these seashaken houses.

Now, far out to sea, at nightfall, this family of stone towers weigh heavily on their foundations. Their generators shudder away unwatched, filling the drum-like rooms inside their granite walls with diminishing degrees of noise. In some of their chambers remain handsome pieces of circular furniture, Victorian in origin, relics of the time when lighthouses were homes as well as lights. Itinerant engineers sometimes fold themselves into the curved bunks, or stow their belongings in the curved cupboards, but otherwise they lie empty now, and are dejectedly trussed with leagues of electrical cabling. Lights frisk on modern display panels, reacting to unknown stimuli. Throughout, the rooms smell of unstirred air, salinity and seagull guano. A magnificent glass apparatus revolves serenely in the lantern room at the top of each lighthouse, elegantly broadcasting the beam at night or catching the sun during the day. Waves crash mindlessly and continuously at their bases below, the surroundings empty of vessels, as they should be.

Not for long.

2. A binocular view of
the Wolf Rock, 2017

Eddystone (I)

Pioneering lighthouses

1698, 1708 AND 1759,
13 MILES OFF PLYMOUTH, DEVON

Imagine a time-lapse film of this patch of sea, reaching back three centuries and rewound at speed.

It would show four towers falling and rising upon the Eddystone reef: one disassembled, one combusting like a firework, one destroyed in a storm, their materials cycling back from stone to wood, their forms regressing from engineered simplicity to experimental folly, the types of ships darting around them devolving from diesel to steam to sail, until the time-lapse halts at the first Eddystone lighthouse of 1698, a thing of outlandish fantasy.

Henry Winstanley's lighthouse mirrored the man. Born around 1644, Winstanley spent his formative years in the febrile climate of the Restoration of 1660, when Charles II was restored to the throne after the Puritan interregnum of Oliver Cromwell. The mood of the time was colourful and flamboyant, a reaction to the monochromatic years of before. Winstanley's father was a steward at Audley End in Essex, a stately home appropriated by Charles II as a palace in 1666. Later becoming Clerk of Works at Audley (overseeing building projects there), Winstanley experienced first-hand the games, ornament and spectacle of the trend-setting Restoration court. He was an astute professional adept at seizing opportunities. He had gained architectural experience at Audley End, but his horizons were unconfined to one discipline. He designed a remarkably successful series of playing cards. His bizarre museum, Winstanley's Water-Works, just off Piccadilly in London, brimmed with whimsical contraptions, including a 'Wonderful Barrel' which served visitors hot and cold drinks from the same tap, early robots of his own devising and moving chairs that played tricks on the sitter.

From the profits of these spectacles, which drew large crowds, he became a ship owner. His first encounter with the Eddystone reef came in anger; by 1696, the reef had claimed two of his ships, incurring substantial losses. Tradition suggests that on receiving news of the second loss, a ship named *Constant*, he galloped from London to Plymouth to demand something be done to light the reef. Amidst feeble protestations from the authorities that it would be impossible, he decided to attempt it himself.

Until then, Britain's seas had been dark and entirely devoid of architecture. As well as symbolic redress for his losses, it's possible to see another motivation in Winstanley's decision to build a lighthouse on the reef. The Eddystone supplied the potential for the most remarkable spectacle of them all: an impossible building, housing a light where none had been shown before.

Lurking in a busy shipping lane, the reef stood in the approach to Plymouth, about 13 miles to the north. Since the sixteenth century, when Sir Francis Drake legendarily concluded his game of bowls on Plymouth Hoe before engaging the Armada, the port had been a resonant one in the national consciousness, a place from which seafaring pioneers such as Drake and later Captain Cook came and went. In 1620, the Pilgrims set forth from it in the *Mayflower* for America. In his biography of Winstanley, Adam Hart-Davis quotes the *Mayflower*'s captain on the then-unmarked Eddystone:

> a wicked reef of twenty-three rust-red rocks lying nine and one half miles south of . . . the Devon mainland, great ragged stones around which the sea constantly eddies, a great danger to all ships hereabouts, for they sit astride the entrance to this harbour.

Plymouth was then a thriving town, with much commercial and naval traffic bustling in the harbour. In the 1690s, the Royal Navy Dockyard was established to the west of the city. As its prosperity mounted, so the presence of the Eddystone on its approach caused greater and greater angst.

Eddystone (I)

In 1694, the Crown had granted a corporation named Trinity House a lease to build a lighthouse on the Eddystone. Originating as a medieval guild of boatmen, Trinity House was given jurisdiction over England's maritime affairs by successive Tudor monarchs. Today, it remains the only authority responsible for lighthouses around England, Wales and the Channel Islands.

But for centuries, this was an institution defined by its excessive caution. By the 1690s, it had built a few coastal lighthouses, but it was exceedingly reluctant to build rock lighthouses, despite its official role. In some instances, it even opposed proposals on the grounds that they might confuse or mislead the mariner. Perhaps a clue to this odd behaviour is found in its membership. A charitable organization run by old sea-captains is not exactly perfectly qualified to build a tower in the open sea, a project which calls for audacity, deep pockets and engineering nous.

Curiously, under a system that prevailed until the nineteenth century, Trinity House did not have a monopoly on lighthouse building: private individuals could directly petition the monarch for permission to build a lighthouse as a profit-making venture. Revenues came from tolls collected at harbours from ships that had passed the lights, calculated by the tonnage of the vessel and cargo. Their builders hoped that the enormous expense of these projects would be offset by equally enormous profits. Lighthouses were not always the product of altruism.

Trinity House attempted to delegate the immense task of building on the Eddystone to a local man, William Whitfield, but on paltry terms. Whitfield was invited to manage and finance the entire project of designing and building a lighthouse on the reef in return for only the first five years' worth of tolls it generated. Thereafter, he would have to share half of the profits with Trinity House, before the lease expired and they assumed full control. It was a canny attempt by the corporation to absolve themselves of the risk. Unsurprisingly, Whitfield demurred.

But not Winstanley. After striking a deal with Trinity House, in 1696 he set to work. There was then no such thing as a rock lighthouse. Apart from a few apocryphal stories of bells or other devices fixed to offshore hazards, there was no precedent for erecting a navigational aid, let alone a building, out in the open sea. Though he had some architectural experience, Winstanley would have to depend largely on his fecund imagination.

The result was a marvel. At the base of his lighthouse, a circular drum of masonry rose up for 16 feet, anchored into the reef with twelve iron stanchions. It formed the solid base for the rest of the tower, a hollow polygonal structure in two stages made of stone and timber, which housed the stores and living quarters. An external stair, reached by a ladder from the base, wound around this part up to an open woodwork gallery, ornamented with balustrades. Above, an octagonal lantern, glazed with small glass squares, was set into a leaded dome. Winstanley's 60 candles burned within. Atop was an extraordinary finial, a tangle of decorative ironwork with an ornamental weathervane.

Drama spliced the construction of the tower. As Britain was at war with France, Winstanley and his men risked being captured and ransomed by French warships, which at that time were frequently seizing ships sailing the Channel under a British flag. Indeed, during 1697, they were captured by a French privateer and taken to the court of Louis XIV. When he understood that they had been building a lighthouse, the king released them, grandly stating that he was 'at war with England, not with humanity'.

On 14 November 1698, the light first shone from a building that looked less like a lighthouse than a folly in a landscape, or a corner tower on a Restoration palace. There was more than a hint of the architecture of Audley End in the stylings of Winstanley's Eddystone. It may have been raised in the sea, but this was a building essentially terrestrial in design. Apart from the hefty iron anchors into the rock, few of its features seemed to have been created with the sea in mind. Waves would have broken around the circular base, but the polygonal section above offered five flat sides for them to strike against without losing their force. Even more vulnerable to being ripped off in violent gales were the many projecting parts of the tower – the external stair and the ornamental ironwork.

Nevertheless, the new lighthouse survived its first winter. In 1699, Winstanley embarked on a programme of strengthening and enlargement, bolstering the masonry at the base and reinforcing the whole tower with iron ties. In doing so, the lighthouse became even more flamboyant. As if he couldn't help himself, Winstanley added projecting rooms, platforms, Latin inscriptions (one of which proclaimed him as a 'Gent' of Essex), insignia and yet more ornamental ironwork. Inside, he dreamt up a 'very fine bedchamber with a chimney and closet, the room being richly gilded and painted and the outside shutters very strongly barred'. Some of these new features were ostensibly practical – hoists and chutes to transfer goods to and from the tower – but most were decidedly ornamental. This was a building not of the sea, nor the land, but simply of Winstanley's mind alone. It looked like what it was: a building with no precedents.

But unlike his other ventures, this was no conjuring trick: Winstanley's tower stood on the reef for four years, surviving four sets of winter storms. It proved that it was possible to build a lighthouse out in the open sea, on a reef exposed only at low tide. Somewhat hubristically, Winstanley had declared the hope that he might chance to be inside his Eddystone during the fiercest storm nature could muster.

On 26 November 1703, a storm of unprecedented ferocity hit England. Thereafter known as the Great Storm, it demolished thousands of chimneystacks, razed trees to the ground and set windmills spinning so fast that friction ignited their sails. According to Daniel Defoe, a witness, it ravaged coastal ports to such an extent that they looked as if they had been destroyed by an enemy. In the English Channel alone, thirteen Royal Navy ships were lost, mostly on the Goodwin Sands, with over 1,000 sailors drowned.

As alluded to in the Introduction, Winstanley and his men hurried to the lighthouse to strengthen it against these forces. But though his tower had the fortitude to endure nasty winter gales, it stood no chance against a storm of this magnitude. That night the tower was carried off, with its eccentric creator inside, and no trace of it was ever found. Elizabeth, his widow, was granted a pension by the Queen on the recommendation of Trinity House.

Nevertheless, seafarers had become accustomed to a light on the Eddystone. Prayers and stargazing were no longer the sole techniques by which they navigated this approach to Plymouth; a light – empirical, reliable, heartening – had been there to shepherd them. Winstanley's achievement had become vital for Plymouth's prosperity, but the reef remained unmarked for the next three years. Once again, Trinity House was exceedingly reluctant to take on the risk of building a lighthouse on the reef. It fell to a Captain John Lovet, another private citizen, to take up the challenge.

In 1706, Captain Lovet obtained a 99-year lease on the reef from Trinity House. His designer was John Rudyerd, a silk merchant from Ludgate Hill in the City of London. This was perhaps an unlikely figure to select for the job, but then so was Winstanley. Generally, early rock lighthouses had unlikely proponents: the first Smalls lighthouse off the Welsh coast (1776) was designed by Henry Whiteside, a maker of musical instruments. After all, this was the age of gentlemen amateurs, when the boundaries between professions were not clearly demarcated. If a playing-card maker could successfully design for the Eddystone, then so, in theory, could a silk merchant. Much depended on the audacity and ingenuity of the person in question. Very few details about Rudyerd's character have survived, but his design for the Eddystone suggests a sobriety absent in Winstanley.

Unlike its remarkable predecessor, Rudyerd's lighthouse was a more cautious building, created firmly with the sea in mind. The basic, circular form was of a steeply tapering cone, shorn of any external adornment, with nothing to give the waves any purchase. At the foundations, 36 wrought-iron anchors secured into the reef a solid base made of alternating layers of stone and timber. Above this were four decidedly spartan rooms for the keepers. Most strikingly, massive vertical timbers sheathed the entire structure, designed and installed by two master shipwrights and waterproofed like those of a ship. On 28 July 1708, the 24 candles in the lantern were lit for the first time.

Other than constant incursions of marine worms into the timber exterior, requiring its frequent renewal, Rudyerd's lighthouse was a success. The use of timber gave it the ability to flex with the action of the waves, while its streamlined form ensured heavy seas parted around it. During the first half of the eighteenth century, the Royal Dockyard at Plymouth was greatly expanded to accommodate more vessels, a decision in which Rudyerd's guiding light on the Eddystone must certainly have been a factor. But the timber throughout the structure also gave it a fundamental vulnerability.

On the night of 2 December 1755, watchers from land saw the Eddystone light burning with unusual brightness. A fire had started in the wooden lantern, caused not by the 24 candles but probably by a fracture in the stovepipe that passed through this room from the kitchen below. Accelerated by the many candles, timber and years' accumulation of spilled wax, the fire devoured the upper levels of the lighthouse, driving the keepers down through the structure to take refuge on the exposed reef outside. They huddled there for eight hours until ten in the morning, when a boat finally arrived to rescue them. Rudyerd's lighthouse burned ferociously for five days thereafter and was utterly destroyed.

There is a bizarre (and apparently true) story that a 94-year-old keeper named Hall gazed open-mouthed up at the inferno and somehow swallowed a globule of molten lead that had dropped from the lantern. No one believed him. Complaining of stomach pains, he survived only for twelve days.

On his death, the autopsy revealed a piece of solidified lead in his stomach, now in the collections of the National Museum of Scotland.

Both lighthouses were admirable attempts to solve the problem of placing a light out in the open sea. And had it not been for cataclysmic weather or poor maintenance they might well have lasted far longer. But in a sense, they were designs at opposite ends of the scale. Winstanley's was as architectural, as terrestrial, as a rock lighthouse could be; Rudyerd swung the other way, and made his so nautical it was virtually ship-like. Each raised different design issues that threatened their longevity. What was needed was something in the middle ground, a building that married the land with the sea.

Reared in landlocked West Yorkshire, John Smeaton is often thought of as the 'first' civil engineer, in the sense that his activities were recognizably those of the profession today. In contrast to Winstanley and Rudyerd's dabbling amateurism, Smeaton established a career designing canals, harbours, bridges and other interventions into nature. His was the era when technical and scientific advancements met the burgeoning Industrial Revolution. Smeaton was at the vanguard of an emerging breed of professionals who engineered infrastructure schemes to support the fast growth of the new industries.

But he didn't simply qualify in engineering (or 'engineery', as he called it); no courses of such study then existed. Instead, he found his calling through a talent for making things. Much influenced by a genius clockmaker of York, his teenage years were mostly spent in a self-built workshop. His parents had disapproved of his frequent dealings with tradesmen, and had attempted to steer him towards a legal career, which they considered to be more respectable. Nevertheless, his instinct to make was untameable, and he set up in London in 1748 as a manufacturer of 'philosophical instruments' just off Holborn. But his interests were wide and voracious. At 28, he had been elected Fellow of the Royal Society after conducting award-winning investigations into wind and wave power.

By March 1756, a syndicate led by a Robert Weston held

the lease on the Eddystone reef. After a recommendation from
the president of the Royal Society, Weston and the lessees
sought out Smeaton and persuaded him to design and build
the third Eddystone lighthouse. Examining models of the first
two towers, and seeing their mangled foundations embedded
on the reef, Smeaton learned what the third Eddystone lighthouse should *not* feature. Winstanley's lighthouse offered the
sea too many wave-holds to tear it down; Rudyerd's timber
structure was more compatible, but also more combustible.

Bold, simple lessons from nature informed Smeaton's
approach. He knew that a mature English oak, with its wide-
girthed base and tapering thickness, withstands the worst
storms. Though most of its leaves may be stripped away, the
tree itself is rarely torn down, anchored by its roots, weight and
low centre of gravity. Accordingly, the profile of his lighthouse
would be an elegant, tapering tower, wide at the base and slimmer at the top. With a circular ground plan, the smooth, curving walls would give the waves nothing to grip.

For weight and strength, Smeaton chose to build solely in
stone, but Trinity House, Weston and the lessees were aghast at
this decision. It was not only the expense and the nightmarish
logistics that it would entail. They found it inconceivable that
a stone building would survive out in the English Channel. In
their minds, stone was a terrestrial material used for fine buildings and it had no place in the open ocean apart from as ballast.
Surely wood, a material of proven compatibility with the sea,
would fare better? But Smeaton won them round. He persuaded them that weight would counteract weight: the heavier the
lighthouse was, he argued, the more capable it would be of handling the tremendous loads placed upon it by heavy seas and
high winds. Granite, locally available and extremely durable,
would be the ideal type of stone to pit against the sea.

Smeaton's masterstroke lay in his method of joining the
stones to one another, and the lighthouse as a whole to the reef.
Just as he drew the form of his lighthouse from an oak tree,
so a freshly paved London street provided the means of its
assembly. Conventional building methods were too weak for

such a hostile marine setting. Square or rectangular blocks of masonry would be awkward for a circular building. Mortar and iron pins would be fiddly and time-consuming to use for the whole structure and could not be guaranteed to hold the stones together as waves slammed into them. But ambling around London one day, Smeaton noticed how some kerbstones on a new section of pavement had been dovetailed together to prevent them from becoming dislodged. If the stones of his lighthouse were carved so that they interlocked with one another, he reasoned, the sea could not dismantle them.

From 1756 to 1759, between May and October each year, Smeaton's lighthouse rose incrementally. At Millbay in Plymouth, a quiet anchorage formerly owned by Sir Francis Drake, he established a mason's yard and jetty. Raw granite from Bodmin Moor, Cornwall, was here chiselled into the bespoke, interlocking stones of the tower. To carve the intricate shapes demanded talented masons and they carried Eddystone tokens, minted by the Admiralty, to signify their work and exempt them from military service.

Steam power had not yet become widely available in building or in sailing, so a significant share of the credit for Smeaton's lighthouse is due to a series of ex-tin miners whom he employed alongside the masons. These men shifted the masonry from the quarry to the mason's yard, from the yard onto a sailing boat (which they rowed if the sea was windless) and from the boat onto the reef. The total distance travelled from the quarry to the reef was nearly 50 miles and these blocks of granite weighed up to 5 tons each in their finished state. Like the builders of Stonehenge, their methods were ropes, pulleys and hard labour. In one respect, it was harder for Smeaton and his men, for they somehow had to transfer the heavy, precisely carved stones from a swaying vessel to a slippery reef.

They worked according to the weather, frequently losing fortnights' worth of building time to unruly conditions. The build had been stressful, but Smeaton led by example. He was involved at all stages, regularly pitching in with the masons on the rock at critical points. He was nearly shipwrecked, and was partially asphyxiated from inspecting too closely the forge where the iron lantern was being made. He paid his workmen well, because they constantly ran the risk of being washed away (on the reef) or being press-ganged into service by the Royal Navy (in the yard) as they worked. He was a great improviser: when they ran out of tin for the door hooks one day, he insisted on melting down all their auxiliary vessel's pewter cutlery – knives, forks, spoons, drinking cups – to keep to schedule. Presumably, dinner that night was eaten by hand.

The resistant gneiss of the reef had been shaped, blunting scores of pickaxes in the process, into a series of steps into which the earliest stages of dovetailed stones were firmly fixed. The lowest part of the tower was half-reef, half-worked stone until the sixth layer or 'course' of stones, at which point it became completely masonry. For extra security, the stones were pegged to the courses above and below with marble dowels and a layer of mortar. Between the fourteenth and 23rd courses the masonry pattern was recalibrated to incorporate the entrance door, passageway and spiral stair, as narrow as one in a country church tower. These lower courses made up the heaviest, fattest half of the structure, firmly set into the grudging Eddystone.

Above them were the four rooms of the lighthouse. Their circular walls were made differently: they were thinner, being one block of masonry thick and not dovetailed, but either pinned with iron cramps or encircled, at each floor level, by rings of iron chains. These floors were of dovetailed stone, forming a shallow domed ceiling in each room, quite beautiful and simple, but a system which produced outward thrust that was held tautly in check by the chains. Sir Christopher Wren had used such a system on a much grander scale at St Paul's Cathedral, to counteract the thrust of his dome.

(There are wider affinities: both Wren's cathedral and Smeaton's tower replaced buildings that were destroyed by fire; above the cathedral's south transept is carved the single word *Resurgam*, Latin for 'I rise again', a motto that could equally apply to the Eddystone lighthouses.)

A fine lantern crowned Smeaton's tower, and he undertook the dangerous job of screwing home its finial himself. On 16 October 1759, the candles in the lantern were lit for the first time. After a brief abeyance, thanks to Smeaton's ingenuity, the English Channel was a little safer once more. And from this point onwards, towers began to rise in other seas around Britain and Ireland, inspired by the blueprints of the Eddystone innovators. Winstanley had shown it to be possible; Rudyerd had demonstrated that it could be done again; Smeaton had illustrated how genius could take root in the sea.

Smeaton's tower was the most influential and all other rock lighthouses surviving today follow his essential principles. Against the wild contours of the reef had been placed a new type of building, made of precisely carved, interlocking stones, stamping order on disorder, laying a pioneering set of foundations.

3. John Smeaton's third
Eddystone lighthouse of 1759

Bell Rock

A nation's lighthouse

1811,
11 MILES OFF ARBROATH, SCOTLAND

> *The light will be exhibited on the night of Friday, the first*
> *day of February 1811, and each night thereafter, from*
> *the going away of daylight in the evening to the return*
> *of daylight in the morning . . . The bright light will, to a*
> *distant observer, appear like a star of the first magnitude,*
> *which, after attaining its full strength, is gradually*
> *eclipsed to total darkness.*

'Notice to Mariners',
early nineteenth century

It flashes white, once every five seconds, in a perfectly black seascape.

At night-time, from the harbour wall at Arbroath, the bright flash of the Bell Rock is like the blast of a distant shotgun. Up in the lantern, rays of light spring into a turning complex of glass prisms, which fuse them into a horizon-sweeping beam. A wrangling of space and time brings it to me as a flash, 11 miles away.

Most national monuments can be touched, knelt before, closely contemplated. There is usually a place before them for crowds to assemble. Few are built where they cannot be encountered, except in very rare circumstances. Few appear so differently at night to how they do in the day.

I was drawn here, to Scotland, to explore how a rock lighthouse could be unexpectedly totemic, a monument to a country from which it literally stands apart. It feels suitable that my first glimpse should be of the light, rather than the house. The three lost Eddystones may have been the pioneers, but the Bell Rock is the oldest working building to remain standing upon its reef.

Since it was first lit in 1811, it has been exhaustively observed, studied and celebrated, the subject of paintings and poems. It has sired legends and monumentalized people, a dynasty and ultimately a nation: Enlightenment-era Scotland. Far from being a lonely, utilitarian work of engineering, the Bell Rock is as intense an expression of national prestige as anything on land.

But these layers of meaning are subordinate to its essential purpose: a white flash, every five seconds, to deflect ships from danger.

Between flashes, I count off the seconds on my fingers. There have been a prodigious number of them since the light first burst into being on a cold February evening, over 200 years ago. While war, fire and misdemeanour have delivered their glancing blows, the light has never been fully quenched. This is mainly due to the staunch stone tower beneath it, holding the lantern protectively out of the sea's reach. The two are interdependent; the house enables the light, and the light justifies the presence of the house.

The beam can be seen from up to 18 miles away, illuminating a circular swathe of the North Sea, reaching out to a long stretch of the Scottish coastline. I wonder whether other eyes have lit upon the Bell Rock tonight. Russian cargo-captains, perhaps, or oil-tanker crews returning to Aberdeen, looking up from blinking instruments at an older warning light. Others, like me, might be watching from the shore, from rainy coastal paths or darkened windowsills. But for the moment, on the dark harbour wall, there is only the light and I.

The next morning, the lighthouse is the faintest of marks on the horizon when seen from the shore. It was constructed between 1807 and 1811 by an up-and-coming engineer, Robert Stevenson, guided by John Rennie, a more established engineer with a bigger portfolio of marine engineering projects. Other talents ably assisted them: from Francis Watt, a carpenter who devised an ingenious balance crane to lift the stones (the ancestor of modern high-rise cranes), to Bassey, a horse that hauled the stones of the lighthouse around the mason's yard. It was conceived and completed during the reign of King George III, and owes its proportions and refinements to the classical architecture of the Georgian period.

The story of the lighthouse, and the reef on which it stands, really begins with the primeval geology of the Scottish east coast. From Edinburgh up to Aberdeen, red sandstone cliffs march between ploughed fields and the North Sea, but this sandstone is unconfined to dry land.

After shelving down into the sea, an outcrop of it emerges 11 miles offshore, in a large sea-estuary traversed by ships entering the mouths of the rivers Tay (for Dundee) and Forth (for Leith and Edinburgh). Over 1,420 feet long and 300 wide, this is the Bell Rock, a triangular, submerged reef only fully exposed at the lowest spring tides. The dry redness of the cliffs out here is wetted and dulled to the colour of old blood. The reef stands squarely in the way of shipping routes into the large ports of the aforementioned cities. Captains making for those destinations have worried about it for centuries, and many went to such lengths to avoid it that they ran too close to the coastline and were wrecked there instead.

Known initially as the Inchcape reef, the first warning to issue from it was not a light, but a sound. A medieval bell, mounted on a timber post driven into the surface, was rung by the waves to alert passing seafarers to the danger.

Tradition declares it was the work of a clergyman based at Arbroath, a large town about halfway between Edinburgh and Aberdeen, built mainly of red sandstone from the nearby cliffs. Foremost among the town's red buildings is the spectacular Arbroath Abbey, founded by the Scottish king William the Lion in 1178. It was one of the richest and most influential monasteries in Scotland during the medieval period. In 1320, Abbot Bernard oversaw the composition of the Declaration of Arbroath, an early articulation of Scotland's right to freedom from the English meddling in its affairs. Nine years later, the Declaration had forced the Papacy to recognize Robert the Bruce as king of a Scottish nation independent from England.

Arbroath is the closest harbour to the hazardous Inchcape reef. As the engine of the local medieval economy, the abbey would have had a considerable interest in local shipping; it may well have been the enterprising Abbot Bernard who had the bell erected out there, to protect valuable cargoes endangered by the presence of the reef. But I wonder how successful this device would have been. The bell and post must have been substantial to survive the rougher waves and be heard over their noise; but what happened when the sea was placid? One of the reef's tell-tales is the sight and sounds of water breaking over its various parts. Little can be seen or heard of it in flat seas, and presumably the bell remained silent too.

Whatever its efficacy, in the end the bell was dismantled by an unnamed pirate, who suffered the comeuppance of being wrecked upon the reef. Afterwards the name, if not the device, stuck to the Bell Rock.

Of course, the abbey is now ruinous. As in England, the Scottish Reformation of 1560 led to the closure of the monasteries, and by 1580 the red stones of the abbey itself were being quarried for other buildings. Whether as invitations to prayer or as repulsions to ships, all its bells ceased to ring. Glittering candles, precious metals and jewels once burnished the nave and transepts of the large abbey church; now these spaces are roofless, open to the heavens. If blood-red when first cut, the abbey's red stonework is now as weathered and faded as the cliffs from which it was taken.

But the decline of the abbey did not mean the decline of Arbroath. It did well out of the Industrial Revolution, becoming a centre for jute and sailcloth production. In 1839, the harbour was rebuilt and expanded, stimulating the growth of its fishing fleet. But having boomed in one way or another up until the late twentieth century, when quotas constricted the fishing industry, Arbroath's fortunes are perhaps of a lesser hue today. Handsome red sandstone buildings remain on the High Street, but the trading seems sluggish, and many of the pubs have closed. Standing on elevated ground, the abbey still dominates the town when seen from afar.

Bell Rock

We gather on the quayside near the boat – a catamaran named *Ultimate Predator* – at nine o'clock in the morning. Its engines are already gurgling as James, the gruff, canny-looking skipper, beckons us to descend the ladder into the stern. For almost 50 years he has operated from Arbroath harbour, mainly as a fisherman but skippering boats for other purposes too. Despite the decline of the fishing industry, people from Arbroath haven't stopped going to sea. James's brother is a seafarer and his sons work on the oil rigs in the North Sea. His sister runs one of the pubs near the harbour. Beyond the harbour walls, the waters around Arbroath are pocked with flags marking crab and lobster pots. These are the principal catches landed here today, the quaysides stacked with the netted traps, the harbour steadily trafficked by the small boats taking them to and from the fishing grounds. Once upon a time, haddock was the town's main prize (and can still be purchased, smoked, as 'Arbroath Smokies'). Not so any more, says James, who says that fishing went a long time ago.

Eleven of us have chartered James and his boat. With me is my friend Roland, an industrial designer, furnished with cameras. A delegation joins us from the Signal Tower Museum, led by its manager, Kirsten. Finished in 1813, shortly after the Bell Rock, this was its shore-station, incorporating accommodation for the lighthouse keepers between their shifts and a signal tower for communicating with the offshore tower. Now, it is a museum dedicated to the Bell Rock lighthouse, which looms over the exhibits while being out of reach to its visitors. Kirsten and her colleagues are in the curious position of curating a building they rarely see: curating the *idea* of it, or the memory. She has only seen the lighthouse in the flesh once, but has amassed great knowledge of it despite having never landed there.

I wonder how it will be for her to see it again. None of us climb into the boat in an idle or neutral state of mind. Unlike most tourists, we all have some sort of foreknowledge of the Bell Rock, some idea of how it will seem up close. Motoring gently across the sheltered harbour water, we talk of what we expect to see. Seals lounging against the curving base. A glass optic turning serenely in the lantern. As we pass through battered seawalls, we surge forward with a lurch, and raise our voices over the engines. One of the crew tries to cast a cigarette butt over the side, but the quickened wind blows it back into the boat. He tries a few times more, as if making a point, despite a bin standing at his feet.

This morning, the North Sea is as smooth as polished stone, scored only by our boat's white wake. There is a beautiful simplicity about our course, and to the surrounding elements: placid water, nitrogen-cold sky, the ever-growing speck of the lighthouse, which rose upon this reef and has remained there. We traverse a straight line between the harbour and the reef, a journey measured only in time instead of twists and turns. I savour it, for later journeys to rock lighthouses will be more convoluted.

I watch the abbey recede from the stern of the boat, the upper gables and tops of walls still distinct against the skyline as we draw gradually out to sea. In particular, the remains of the south transept stand prominently above Arbroath's lower rooftops. Originally one of the shorter arms of the cruciform-shaped abbey, this part of the ruin contains a large, circular window opening, known locally as the 'Round O'. It's clearly visible to the naked eye, even 5 miles offshore. James tells me that sailors once used it as a navigational landmark. He points out other landmarks on the shrinking coastline – church spires, distinctive hills – that trawlers use to pinpoint themselves when out in the deeper sea. Though the boat's dashboard glimmers with digital instrumentation, it's somehow heartening to hear that medieval wayfinding remains a failsafe.

Steadying ourselves on the handrail, we move to the bows and look ahead. At first a tiny mark, the Bell Rock lighthouse grows out of the horizon in stages, like a shoot in soil. Binoculars are handed around; details coalesce as the lighthouse produces larger versions of itself. Through the eyepieces, I recognize the features familiar from photographs; the curved, dark base, where the masonry is exposed, the white-painted shaft of the tower above, the spatter of wave-marks, the projecting entrance platform and the lantern, netted to keep off the birds. As we draw closer, our anticipation builds.

Scotland prospered in the eighteenth century. Union with England in 1707 had abolished trade tariffs and given Scottish merchants access to colonial markets. With the removal of Scottish politicians and aristocrats to the centre of government in London, a burgeoning group of lawyers, doctors, clergymen, academics, scientists and representatives from other disciplines formed a new middle class in Scottish cities. Rigid medieval piety gave way to a strongly intellectual, rational outlook. Advancements in sciences and the arts came rapidly, unbeholden to aristocratic patronage, but instead fuelled by the principles of the Scottish Enlightenment, which promoted empiricism and progress for the benefit of society as a whole. Edinburgh, Glasgow and Aberdeen became intellectual foci. By the end of the eighteenth century, Scotland had five universities, while England possessed only two. As well as economic prosperity, union had given Scotland a more vivid sense of itself.

A fine expression of this prosperity and enlightenment is the Edinburgh New Town, a planned section of the city laid out in the second half of the eighteenth century. Planned by a 26-year-old architect named James Craig, it was arranged around a grid of streets and squares, the elegant uniformity of which stood in stark contrast to the rackety tenements of the Old Town around the castle. Newly rich merchants and intellectuals had not wanted to live in this backward part of town, which seemed to stand for all that Scotland had left behind. So, the New Town was built to provide residences that matched the quality of the city's new intellectual, commercial and civic life. As with elsewhere in eighteenth-century Britain, the architecture of Greece and Rome provided the template for the new buildings. Founded upon classical principles of harmony and proportion, this neoclassical Georgian style exactly matched the new enlightenment of its inhabitants.

At night, the elegant squares and thoroughfares were illuminated by the works of Thomas Smith, an ironmonger and lamp-maker. After an apprenticeship with a Dundee ironmonger, Smith moved to Edinburgh and established his own business at Bristo Street, just as demand surged for lamps and ironmongery for the New Town development. He manufactured the ornamental railings, grilles, grates and bootscrapers required, but also found time to innovate. Oil lamps then in use discoloured their glass housings with grime, weakening their illumination. To remedy this, he devised a system of reflectors – metal hemispheres covered internally with pieces of polished silver – that would ensnare the escaping rays of light and better define the beam.

Smith's reflectors would find application beyond the fashionable confines of the New Town. Until the late eighteenth century, the Scottish coastlines had been largely unlit, lagging behind the lights gradually freckling the English coasts. But as Scotland grew more prosperous and shipping increased along its dangerous coastlines, the need for lighthouses here became acute. So, in 1786, a Scottish lighthouse authority was formed with a similar remit to Trinity House of England. But while Trinity's origins were medieval and clannish, the Commissioners of Northern Lights were Georgian and clubbable, being a consortium of shipowners with their headquarters in the New Town.

A year after their formation, in 1787, the Commissioners of Northern Lights completed their first lighthouse at Kinnaird Head, 40 miles north of Aberdeen. Rather than build a new one, they had adapted a sixteenth-century castle on a headland bought from Lord Saltoun, the local landowner. Many of the commissioners would have lived or mixed in the New Town, probably enjoying first-hand the efficacy of Smith's reflectors. As a result, they employed him as their first consulting engineer, his first project the conversion of Kinnaird Head into a lighthouse. In a neat twist of fate, Smith went from lighting the streets to lighting the sea.

But year in, year out, the unmarked Bell Rock continued

to wreck ships. As Scotland's economy grew during the eighteenth century, and ships using the ports of Dundee and Edinburgh swelled in number, so did the toll caused by the reef. By
the 1790s, petitions from agitated captains and shipowners for
an aid to navigation had begun to pile up at the commissioners'
offices. In December 1799, a particularly powerful storm drove
many vessels from their moorings into the North Sea, forcing
them to try to seek refuge along the east coast of Scotland; in
their efforts to avoid the Bell Rock in these violent conditions,
many ended up wrecked elsewhere. Around 70 ships were
claimed by the gale. A Royal Navy officer and a Leith ironmonger ventured out to put up beacons on the reef, but each
iteration was immediately felled. Meanwhile, the commissioners procrastinated, complaining variously of the expense and
the impossibility of building a lighthouse there. By the beginning of the nineteenth century, Thomas Smith had built them
a total of nine coastal lighthouses around Scotland, but had yet
to tackle a wave-afflicted hazard such as the Bell Rock.

By this time encumbered with his flourishing New Town
business and work on the Northern Lights, Smith had taken
on an apprentice, his serious-minded, capable stepson, Robert
Stevenson. Robert's father, Alan Stevenson, had been a Glas-
wegian merchant but died of fever in the West Indies. In the
summer months, Robert worked with his stepfather on the
Northern Lights; in the winter, he attended lectures on math-
ematical and scientific subjects in Glasgow and at the University of Edinburgh. While a competent enough student, his
preferred classrooms were the churning seas around the splintered, rugged coastlines of Scotland. It was in these wild places
that he developed a flair for mechanics. With his stepfather
advancing in years, Stevenson was increasingly trusted to fit
lenses and build lighthouses on his own. In 1797, then 25 years
old, he succeeded Thomas Smith as consulting engineer to the
Northern Lights.

Three years later, he first set foot on the Bell Rock. Arbroath fishermen went there in calm seas to look for relics
from shipwrecks, and one day Stevenson and his friend James

Haldane accompanied them. After landing on the rock, the tides granted them a few hours of perusal, the fishermen scurrying off to search the crevices while Stevenson measured and sketched. He had been toying with the idea of a lighthouse on six cast-iron stilts, on the same principles as the first Smalls lighthouse of 1776. But this plan had been formed with inexact information about the Bell Rock's topography and immersion by water. Having now seen it with his own eyes, Stevenson realized that the rock became exposed enough at low spring tides to allow space for the foundations of a stone building. His friend Haldane agreed. While the fishermen gleefully carried off nearly 100 kilos of shipwreck scrap (anchors, stove-lids, door straps, and so on) from the Bell Rock, Stevenson left with the certainty that a stone tower could be built there.

After his first visit, Stevenson composed plans for a stone lighthouse inspired by Smeaton's designs for the third Eddystone lighthouse. Outwardly, there were a few small differences – Stevenson proposed an external winding stone stair around the base, and the tapering profile of his tower was more pronounced – while inwardly, there were more fundamental ones. Instead of dovetailing the solid, lower third of the masonry together for strength, Stevenson proposed standard masonry jointing with copper pegs: a potential weakening of Smeaton's formula. In the upper half of the tower, he designed strange rooms proportioned like upturned cones with the tips broken off, their ceilings wider than their floors.

On the basis of this early proposal, a bill was submitted to Parliament in 1803, requesting authorization of the work, a starting loan of £30,000 (over £2.5 million today) and authority to exact tolls from shipping using ports on the east coast of Great Britain to finance the scheme. It passed the House of Commons, but was opposed by the City of London Corporation, because the proposed finance taxed too extensive a stretch of coastline in which their business interests would be affected. The bill was withdrawn.

Perhaps discouraged by the defeat in obtaining parliamentary authorization for the lighthouse, the commissioners sought a second opinion on Robert Stevenson's scheme for a stone tower on the reef. Though he had their trust, he was a comparatively young engineer and had never before executed a project of this scale. So, they turned to John Rennie, who by this time had earned distinction on marine projects throughout Great Britain. His harbours, bridges and canals were distinguished by their careful planning and execution. And he could work on a vast scale: in 1806 he proposed the monstrous Plymouth Breakwater, a mile-long wall across Plymouth Sound to shield the harbour, which contains over 3.5 million tons of stone.

In January 1804, minds were further focused on the Bell Rock problem when HMS *York*, a 74-gun ship of the line, was wrecked on the reef. The complete loss of this sizeable warship with all hands aboard was not just a tragedy; it was an embarrassing dent in a supposedly invincible Navy. Had the reef been marked, the disaster would have been averted. That year, Rennie visited the reef with Stevenson and had no hesitation in supporting Stevenson's concept for a stone lighthouse.

A second bill was presented to Parliament in 1806, requesting authorization and the finance necessary to build the lighthouse. The loss of HMS *York* played heavily on the minds of parliamentarians debating the issue, who also exhaustively examined both Stevenson and Rennie; but this time, after a torturous progress through both Houses, the Bell Rock bill was passed and it received Royal Assent in July 1806. Reflecting upon events later, Stevenson remarked on his 'feelings of the greatest satisfaction' at this, though simultaneously brooding on the 'crowd of difficulties' which lay ahead.

They could begin. Still wary of the project's magnitude and Stevenson's youth, the commissioners decided to appoint John Rennie as chief engineer for the Bell Rock lighthouse, with Robert Stevenson subordinate to him as resident engineer, overseeing the daily execution of the project. Prior to starting, Rennie made important amendments to Stevenson's early designs. He refined the tapering profile of the tower so that its centre of gravity lay as low in the base as possible. In place of

Stevenson's original method of regular, mortared stonework for the solid base of the tower, Rennie insisted on dovetailing the sides of the masonry blocks together and securing them above and below with stout oak pegs, as Smeaton had done. These amendments brought the proposal more in line with Smeaton's Eddystone, a formula that had been proven to work.

The commissioners set up a floating light-ship, a captured Prussian ship renamed *Pharos* in honour of the great classical lighthouse at Alexandria. Three large copper lanterns were fixed to her three masts, and she was moored about a mile to the north-west of the reef, her lights first lit on 15 September 1807. Earlier that year, Stevenson had established a work-yard in Arbroath, and procured supplies of granite (for the exterior of the building) and sandstone (for the interior) from quarries near Aberdeen and Dundee. However, before they could start on the lighthouse, he had decided to build a temporary barrack on the reef, called the Beacon House, so that the workmen could remain there for up to four weeks at a time and wring the most out of their seasonal working schedule. The first of the workmen's tasks was to bore holes for the foundations of this odd home-from-home.

On Tuesday 18 August 1807, Stevenson and his workmen first landed on the reef. It was half past five on a perfect summer's morning, with a light easterly breeze. The waves lapped about quietly, but would not fully uncover the reef for another half-hour or so. While they waited, the excited masons were 'regaled with a glass of rum' by the ship's steward; by six in the morning, the tide was fully out and they got to work, cheeks flushed. They had two hours before it immersed the reef again, so they hacked quickly at the rock, their pickaxes sharpened by a makeshift blacksmith's forge. At eight, the tide rose, swamping their first marks on the reef. After waiting the whole day aboard their boat, the *Smeaton*, they managed a further two hours' work at the evening low tide.

After six days, twelve holes had been bored for the Beacon House. Until it was completed, the men lived in cramped conditions aboard the *Smeaton*, miserably seasick, which some overcame by chewing a particular kind of seaweed. Another difficulty in these early stages was the onset of neap tides, when there is the least difference between low and high water, meaning the reef was barely uncovered. Water sloshed about their heels as they hammered at it; the blacksmith could barely keep his forge alight. Nevertheless, for the most part, in Stevenson's account:

the rock had a more habitable appearance, from the volumes of smoke which ascended from the smith's shop; and the busy noise of his anvil; the operations of the masons; the movements of the boats, and shipping at a distance, all contributed to give life and activity to the scene.

But there were many dangers. On just such a day later on, in September, the *Smeaton* broke free from her moorings and drifted 3 miles away, just as the tide was starting to rise. The men were too busy working to notice. There were 32 of them, far too many to escape in the two small boats tied up at the reef that had brought them in groups from the *Smeaton*. Only Stevenson had seen what had happened. If the *Smeaton* did not come back and rescue them, they would all be drowned by the rising tide. Hoping desperately that it would return, he said nothing, and let the men work away obliviously. But, as the tide rose, the men downed their tools and looked to the empty swathe of sea where the *Smeaton* should have been anchored. When they realized what had happened, he wrote: 'not a word was uttered by any one, but all appeared to be silently calculating their numbers ... the workmen looked steadfastly upon the writer [Stevenson] ... in the most perfect silence'.

Just as he was about to address them, a boat was spotted. It was James Spink, the Bell Rock pilot, who had unexpectedly come out from Arbroath with letters for the men. Visibly sagging with relief, they piled into his boat and escaped, just as the water wallowed over the reef. But it had been a very narrow escape, too narrow for some. The next day, eighteen men would not go back.

By late October 1807, in the face of worsening winter weather, tools were downed for the year. The Beacon House had been finished, a curious twelve-sided wooden cabin on thick oak stilts sunk into the reef, further secured by thick iron chains. It provided a platform for the blacksmith's forge and the mortar gallery, a cook room above that, separate quarters for Stevenson and his foremen on the floor above, and finally the barracks for the workmen at the top. When Stevenson and his men returned to the reef next spring, ready to begin work again, they found the Beacon House had survived the winter storms completely intact, though a group of cormorants had taken up residence. Amazingly, this temporary wooden structure was to survive the entire building project, and five sets of winter storms, until it was dismantled in 1812.

In March 1808, some of the men moved in to start work in earnest on the lighthouse. Their next job was to form a smooth, circular foundation pit out of the hard, chaotic surface of the reef. Working between tides as they did the previous year, it took them four months to excavate a circular pit 2 feet in depth, 42 feet in diameter, and twice daily flooded by the sea.

In parallel to this, the mason's yard at Arbroath was hectic with dust and clinking chisels. Bassey, the Shire horse, dragged around vast chunks of raw stone from the quarries. The masons were dressing the blocks into their complex, interlocking shapes; despite the fiddly nature of the carving, and irregular supplies from the quarries, the first stones were ready by the beginning of July. So too was the foundation pit on the reef. On the 10th, Stevenson recounts, the foundation stone was:

> hooked to the tackle and lowered into its place, when the writer [Stevenson], attended by his assistants Mr Peter Logan [Senior Foreman], Mr Francis Watt [Head Joiner], and Mr James Wilson [in charge of the boats that landed the stones on the reef], applied the square, the level, and the mallet, and pronounced

the following benediction: 'May the Great Architect of the Universe complete and bless this building,' on which three hearty cheers were given, and success to the future operations was drunk with the greatest enthusiasm.

Stevenson published his exhaustive *An Account of the Building of the Bell Rock Lighthouse including Details of the Erection and Peculiar Structure of the Edifice* in 1824, thirteen years after the building was finished. With illustrations, the tome runs to over 640 pages of closely written text, describing every conceivable aspect of the building project, from the arrangement of the gears on the cranes used to lift the stones, to how, before addressing his men on the reef, Stevenson drank a handful of water from a rock-pool to overcome a dry throat. The thoroughness of the book reflects his thoroughness as an engineer. In an 1807 inventory of the Arbroath workshop, there is an exhaustive list of everything used to build the lighthouse, including eleven stone axes, 54 hammocks and five nail bores. Yet he was not just a bean-counter: the numerous toasts drunk at various stages of the Bell Rock's construction reveal a man attuned to ceremony and to his men's welfare.

The *Account* evokes the nineteenth-century building site with splendid engravings, showing the state of the structure at the close of each year's working season. At first the lighthouse rose slowly. An engraving of the reef in September 1808 shows it as a circular stone platform just 5 feet high, three broad layers or courses of masonry finished. Requiring the most stones, these broadest courses took the longest to complete. Men in hats and breeches swarm about, gesticulating, manipulating cranes and manhandling stones into place.

Possibly the only offshore railway in the world – raised on stilts over the tide – encircles half the base, helping the workmen to quickly move their burdens. Iron rails stretch from landing-places to the base of the lighthouse, with materials transferred from ships to little wagons pushed and pulled by the labourers. To see it operating must have been truly surreal:

here was a working railway (albeit without locomotives) regularly engulfed by the sea. After the tower was completed, the track was used as a causeway and much renewed in 1917. Remarkably, the railway tracks still survive on the reef.

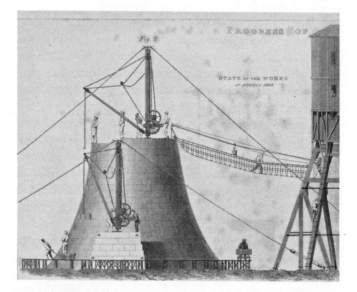

4. Construction underway
at the Bell Rock, 1809

Stevenson and his men were now well established in this exposed location. The engraving for 1809 shows a very efficient operation. Stones went by boat to the reef, by rail to the lighthouse, and by cranes up to the rising structure. A cat's cradle of chains, ropes, winches and pulleys criss-cross the building site. A rope walkway connects the Beacon House and the partially built lighthouse, avoiding the need to set foot on the reef, allowing work to continue even at high tide. You can almost hear the exertions of the men in hats and breeches, the spooling of chains through the winding mechanisms; the random hammering intermingled with the barking of seals. By August 1809, the solid base of the tower – and a third of the overall structure – had been completed.

Fewer stones were needed for the upper parts, where the rooms were located. By July 1810 the tower had grown to 80 feet high. The engraving for this stage of the works shows a cross-section of the nearly finished tower, built all the way up to the masonry wall on the balcony into which the large iron lantern would be fixed. A sturdy timber bridge is shown passing between the Beacon House and the lighthouse tower. A little bucket of mortar dangles precariously in mid-air. Stones were hooked and unhooked between four cranes, relayed from ground level all the way up to the balcony.

At the top stood the ingenious balance crane, for lifting the stones the final part of the way. It looked like an oversized cross with winding-gear at the intersection of the timbers. This, the world's first counter balance tower crane, was a fascinating by-product of the Bell Rock works. Much like modern high-rise cranes used to build skyscrapers, the balance crane was anchored to the top of the lighthouse, and lifted the heavy stones while balanced by adjustable counterweights along its horizontal beam. Francis Watt, the head joiner, had devised it along with the railway and the other cranes. Other than his 'zeal and intrepidity' noted by Stevenson, little is known of this remarkable problem-solver, but his inventions gave the project technical finesse, and reduced the wear on the labourers' muscles.

Vivid though these engravings are, they show a reef that is deceptively placid. In reality, the sea was forever lunging and recoiling, upsetting the work. In June 1809, it flooded the platform containing the blacksmith's forge and the mortar buckets, washing everything away. Strong gales rattled the Beacon House, throwing the men from their chairs or beds, straining everyone's nerves: 'They found their habitation extremely cheerless, while the winds were howling about their ears, and the waves lashing with fury again the beams of their insulated habitation.' Stevenson wrote this after losing one of the young smiths, Charles Henderson, who slipped off the rope ladder and drowned. He was one of only five fatalities during the lighthouse's construction; tragic, but a testament to Stevenson's meticulous planning, and the way he watched over his men.

In 1810, the workmen laid the 51st and 52nd courses of masonry in a thunderstorm, with lightning-bolts forking the sea, and waves walloping the base of the tower. Visitors to the reef must have found Stevenson and his men like a race of giants, as hardened as the reef on which they were living and building. Ostensibly busy with other projects, John Rennie visited the reef only twice between 1807 and 1811. As chief engineer, he shared the design of the lighthouse and made the decisions, but it was Stevenson who faced the daily hardships of the build with his men. In this sense, it was Stevenson, not Rennie, who sequestered this house from the sea.

As 1810 closed, the pace of the building accelerated and significant milestones were rapidly passed. On 30 July the last stone – the lintel of the light room – was laid, to much fanfare. On 15 October, they finished installing the iron lantern. And on 27 October, the last window of the Bell Rock lighthouse was glazed. Though, unusually, this last act had not been marked by any ceremony (by contrast, the screwing of a gilded ball to the top of the lantern, a few days before, warranted a seven-gun salute from a nearby ship), it was the point at which a masonry shell became a habitable building, sealed against the elements.

They had done it: an immaculate tower of granite and sandstone, 115 feet high, curving slenderly up from foundations covered twice each day by the tide. It contained (from bottom to top) a storeroom for provisions, a storeroom for fuel, a bedroom, a kitchen, a library and the lantern. It stood proud as a flagpole, robust as a buttress, and as poised as a sculpture against the scarred and ugly surface of the reef. On their return to Arbroath, Stevenson and his men were justly greeted as conquering heroes.

Two centuries on, we float languidly around the reef, admiring the finished building. The boat swivels on the currents,

**5. The Bell Rock
lighthouse, 2017**

the engines chatter quietly at the stern. Now and then, James
works the controls, adjusting our position to keep the lighthouse in view, getting as close to the reef as he dares. Both
the surrounding sea and the sky have fused in the same colour
blue. The sea is calm enough to hear the play of surf on the
sandstone knuckles and ledges. Seals stare menacingly at the
boat, affronted by our presence in their realm, while cormorants look haughtily into the middle distance. We have arrived.

A metal walkway on stilts – the converted remains of
Watt's railway – extends from the base of the lighthouse out
to a point on the reef where landing is possible in calm conditions. Bits of the red sandstone rise up above the waters, like
litter, not looking very threatening until you realize that the
reef itself is mostly submerged, its dark shadow visible for
some distance away from the lighthouse, the end of it marked
with a scrappy iron pole.

At its base, the curve of the lighthouse's profile is just
like that of a bell-mouth, echoing the peal of that first ecclesi-
astical warning nailed to the reef. Here, the dark granite blocks
are unpainted and their joints seem as precise as when they

47

were first laid. As it curves upwards into a shaft, the tower is painted a pure white, blotched in places by liquids cast from the windows (probably coffee and urine, from the time when it was inhabited), smoke damage (from a fire in the 1980s), and a big streak of green-black wave-spatter on one side. Where the paint begins, a little metal platform forms the entrance to the lighthouse, reached by an upward curve of rungs let into the stonework below. Six flights of windows march up the tower to the lantern gallery.

From base to upper parts, the proportions of the tower seem perfectly configured. Working as they did in the Georgian age, Stevenson and Rennie would have been influenced, consciously or not, by the vogue for the harmony and proportionality of classical design. Most rock lighthouses have a similar profile, curving upwards from base to apex, but the gradient of the curve changes with each one. Sometimes there is an abrupt transition between a sloped base and perpendicular upper levels. At the Bell, these proportions are smoothed by classical thinking. Indeed, I have to remind myself how extraordinary it is to find a Georgian building out here in the North Sea. Only a few of the surviving rock lighthouses were constructed in this age; the majority came later, in the Victorian period. Compared to these, the Bell Rock is a little smaller, more modestly sized, a testament to its construction in the age of sail, rather than steam. The more I look at it, the more it seems to radiate a sense of maturity, of its stones infinitesimally settling over time.

At the top of the lighthouse, your eye meets a form of circular cornice, gracefully moulded, with the balcony above, enclosing the domed lantern. Ranks of modern, rectangular metal cabinets are assembled on the balcony, with solar panels on one side. Another later addition is a huge net, tenting the lantern to keep off the birds. Within the lantern, the glass optic is smaller than expected, considering its range of 18 miles. It turns throughout the day and night, driven in Stevenson's time by clockwork, but now by solar-powered batteries: one form of light turning another.

By night, the Bell Rock exists as a warning, but at daybreak it becomes a monument. Skipper James leaves the wheelhouse to tell me of one occasion in 1995 when all the fishing boats in Arbroath motored out here *en masse*, anchoring near the reef and going in jolly boats to the lighthouse. Assembled before the Bell Rock were fishermen, local politicians, businessmen and other dignitaries; it sounds ceremonial, though he doesn't tell me the reason for the trip. But unlike most monuments, such gatherings are the exception. Our smaller type of excursion is commoner, yet the atmosphere in the *Ultimate Predator* is still reverential. In a sense, rock lighthouses are monumentalized by their unfamiliarity to most people. We're not quite sure how to behave in their presence, so reverence fills the void.

Roland and I set about recording the experience, with microphones, cameras, filming gear, taking trophies of our time with the Bell Rock. But photographs are inadequate to convey the sheer *presence* of the building. You need the roll of the boat underfoot, the contrast between the stillness of the tower and the motion of its surroundings. You must have journeyed out across the unstable sea to meet this profoundly stable masonry building. And you must be spliced with the cold and spray of the wind and surf, and be feeling only tolerated, out on a limb in a restive kingdom, and only then will the Bell Rock fully make sense, applying the shades of meaning eluding the camera lens.

Skipper James, of course, has seen it all before, and is watching our reverence with a smile playing on his lips. Realizing that he is the only one among us on the boat to have been inside the Bell Rock, I ask him about the interior. 'Remarkable,' he says, before returning to the wheel.

For the Victorian 'writer for juveniles' R.M. Ballantyne, the uppermost room of the Bell Rock lighthouse was a 'singular room in a very peculiar position'. In 1865, he spent two weeks living in this room, designed by Robert Stevenson as a library:

or 'Strangers' Room' as it is sometimes called, being the guest-chamber, [. . .] fitted up in a style worthy of a lady's boudoir, with a Turkey carpet, handsome chairs, and an elaborately carved oak table, supported appropriately by a centre stem of three twining dolphins. The dome of the ceiling is painted to represent stucco panelling, and the partition [. . .] is of panelled oak [. . .] sufficient to contain the bookcase; also a cleverly contrived bedstead, which can be folded up during the day out of sight. [. . .] The centre window is ornamented with marble sides and top, and above it stands a remarkable bust of Robert Stevenson, the engineer of the building, with a marble slab below bearing testimony to the skill and energy with which he had planned and executed the work.

Although Stevenson himself was less effusive about the interior, he did provide a few details of this library or 'Strangers' Room' in his *Account*. An antique bronze lamp, modelled on a Roman or Greek original, was suspended from the ceiling. The furnishings were by Mr Trotter of Edinburgh, a renowned cabinet-maker based on Princes Street in the New Town, who would have been in step with the latest fashions. The faux-panelling decoration of the walls and ceiling was the work of a local man, a Mr Macdonald of Arbroath. The whole room was fitted out by Stevenson's carpenters, James and Alexander Slight, who also produced the wooden patterns for the dove-tailed stones of the lighthouse.

In such a building, in such a place, this was an extraordinary room to find. Nothing like it had been provided in any of the six rock lighthouses preceding the Bell Rock (with the possible exception of Henry Winstanley's 'gilded bedchamber' in the first Eddystone). None of the Bell's predecessors contained more than four meanly furnished rooms, in which their keepers were miserably confined. By contrast, Stevenson's Strangers' Room was as smartly appointed as any drawing room in

6. The Strangers' Room, painted
by R.M. Ballantyne, 1865

the New Town. The message seemed to be: not only could the
Bell Rock tame the seas, but it could also civilize them.

Revealingly, the other rooms in the tower were more
plainly furnished, with simple but well-made oak furniture and
partitions. More trouble was taken with the Strangers' Room
because it was provided for the use of commissioners and
other visitors, or 'strangers' (these included the poets Walter
Scott, Robert Southey and, of course, Ballantyne). The lighthouse keepers were allowed to use it between times, for it contained a good library of books 'chiefly historical, with the best
voyages' for their edification. Otherwise, the rigid hierarchy
between commissioners and their employees was maintained.
Stevenson later remarked that the commissioners 'should neither sit at the fireside nor the table of a man whose duty [they
are] sent to look after'. Accordingly, when the commissioners

visited, they occupied this plush room while the keepers made do with their plainer quarters below.

In 1952, the painted stucco dome of the Strangers' Room was carefully restored, suggesting the mode of life at the Bell Rock had changed little since Stevenson's time. But just over a decade later, when the lighthouse was modernized in 1964, attitudes had completely changed. The light was converted from paraffin to electrical, requiring the installation of generators in the former storerooms at the base of the tower. The old kitchen became a storeroom; the bedroom above it was refurbished; and the Strangers' Room became a lost interior. Its fine, circular furnishings were butchered to make way for a modern kitchen and living area within that elegant space. With this, the Bell Rock lost its old shades of New Town style, and became more machine-like. The loss of this unique space was a tragedy, for it requires only a little ingenuity to let the old coexist with the new, even offshore.

The lost Strangers' Room served the priorities of its age, but it was also a statement of Stevenson's ambition. As construction was under way, it was clear that the success of the Bell Rock could be his vehicle for entry into the engineering establishment. The Strangers' Room provided a means for entertaining distinguished visitors such as Robert Southey and Walter Scott. When the Bell Rock was completed, Stevenson was feted in the parlours and periodicals of Edinburgh. He had started out there, an apprentice to his stepfather, Thomas Smith, fitting ironmongery to the crisp architecture of the New Town, illuminating those streets while learning to be an engineer. Then, he had flitted as a tradesman between the drawing rooms and front doors of the newly enlightened citizenry of Edinburgh; now, he had created a drawing room of his own, in the best style. Only, it was 11 miles out to sea.

From that apprenticeship too, he had learned how to innovate, how to wrangle more out of existing technologies. For the Bell Rock, he refined and perfected his stepfather's reflectors, those hemispherical mirror-plated discs for lighting the New Town. In the lantern of the Bell, he planned for

24 of them, on a revolving chandelier, each one a copper sheet hammered into a parabolic shape, coated in a silver compound. The principle was the same, but the light would be more brilliant. As the notice of the Bell Rock's completion put it: 'The bright light will, to a distant observer, appear like a star of the first magnitude.'

Both the Strangers' Room and the marvellous new light of the Bell Rock showed how far Stevenson had come from his early years in the New Town. The lighthouse had made his reputation, and he would go on to establish a dynasty of Scottish lighthouse engineers – his sons Alan, David and Thomas – who built rock lighthouses that equalled and surpassed their father's achievement. Of these, the most notable is Alan Stevenson's rock lighthouse on the Skerryvore reef, 12 miles off the west coast of Scotland. Called by his nephew Robert Louis 'the noblest of the deep-sea lights', this awesome tower outshone the Bell Rock in most aspects, from the Sisyphean problems of the build to the stellar quality of its optical apparatus, developed by Alan in collaboration with a French optical engineer, Augustin Fresnel.

But the limelight Stevenson enjoyed depended on his having sole claim to authorship of the Bell Rock. This was not the case. Though Stevenson undoubtedly is due credit for the execution of the works to such a high standard in near-impossible conditions, John Rennie played an essential, if more distant, supervisory role.

Rennie had made significant amendments to Stevenson's designs and, as chief engineer, provided the authorization for each stage of the works. But in Stevenson's *Account* of 1824, there is scant mention of this. Following the deaths of both men, an unseemly spat developed between their sons about the Bell's authorship. History sided initially with the Stevensons, but recent reappraisal has placed Rennie on a more equal footing. Important research by Professor Roland Paxton and David Taylor has conclusively demonstrated his contribution to the Bell Rock.

At stake, perhaps, was authorship of something more

than just a lighthouse. Though a testament to the personal abilities of the two engineers, there was a nationalistic subtext to the Bell Rock. It was proof of Scotland's ability to light the most dangerous seas of its coastlines, with a tower better than anything the English or Irish had made, on a reef just as treacherous as anything they had lit. Despite being in union with England, the Bell Rock played to Scotland's vivid sense of its new self. It had been designed and built by Scottish engineers, educated in burgeoning Scottish centres of excellence.

The previous evening, Kirsten had shown me around the Signal Tower Museum, and I had climbed up into the tower that gives the building its name, to discover fine, circular rooms with original Georgian panelling and woodwork still intact, the faintest echo of the vanished Strangers' Room.

Kirsten had arranged for me to speak at the museum and, for an unknown author on a rainy Friday night in March, the turnout was auspicious. People filled the rows of seats as we fiddled with the projector. Though there were only 25 in all, I felt nervous before the talk began. I was conscious that some in the audience would know far more about Rennie, Stevenson and the Bell Rock than I did. So, I gave it only a passing mention, talking instead of the English and Irish towers.

Afterwards, many shared their thoughts. They were a real cross-section of ages and professions. Most lived in Arbroath, but everyone had some connection to the place. All had a uniquely personal point of reference to the Bell Rock, too. One lady told me how she would watch the pulse of the light when she couldn't sleep at night. A former journalist spoke of his visit there, while manned by keepers, on one of his more extraordinary assignments. A scholar told me how an ancestor of his had skippered the boats that ferried the stones to the reef. An elderly man showed me an extraordinarily exact scale model of the lighthouse he had donated to the museum. I asked him how many visits he had made to the reef to get the details right. None, he replied with a twinkle, I did it from memory.

He did not mean his own memories, but those of others:

Stevenson's exhaustive (and, as it transpires, one-sided) *Account*, visitors' writings and imagery, the museum's exhibitions, and two centuries' worth of folklore. Through this corpus of recollections, the Bell Rock has, in effect, a hologram-like presence on land. Despite its great distance out to sea, so much data has accumulated about the lighthouse that one can know it well without ever visiting the reef.

People here have real pride in the Bell Rock, said Kirsten as we put away the chairs after the talk, even those who never come to the museum. They may not have any specific stake in the lighthouse, or even have seen it at close quarters. But that distant speck, that distant flash, means something. Arbroath is a totemic place for Scotland: it is where, in the fourteenth century, the nation first declared its independence from England. Five centuries after this, the Bell Rock first shone. With its expense, difficulty and requisite perfection, the erection and maintenance of a rock lighthouse was a building project to test a nation. Scotland passed. Despite the wrangling over its authorship, it emerged as a dazzling tribute to an ascendant Scotland, feted by locals and scholars alike.

But the Bell Rock has another, stronger meaning. A rock lighthouse is a symbol of tolerance and altruism, of assistance made available to those in need regardless of their nationality. Taken too far, nationalism can lead to division, but a rock lighthouse offers a message of fellowship. It is a type of building that is not introspective, but outward-looking. It may monumentalize an enlightened Scotland, but the Bell Rock itself enlightens the sea, which is indifferent to nationhood.

Haulbowline

A liminal lighthouse

1824,
CARLINGFORD LOUGH, IRELAND

> **Lough** *n. Irish form of* **Loch** *n. Scottish 1. A lake.*
> *1.1 An arm of the sea, especially when narrow or*
> *partially land-locked.*
>
> OED

Through the doorway, a rectangle of lough water shivers in the daylight. I linger in the granite lobby, adjusting to the gloom after the brightness outside. This room – cell, more like – is sparsely equipped. A red and white lifebelt hangs on one curve of unpainted stone wall; a broom is propped against another; a thick rope uncoils from its peg to the circular floor. On the dusty threshold, there is a knot of footprints. Very faintly, I hear my companions clanging around in the upper levels of the tower, which is now unused to their echoes. Few visit Haulbowline these days, but this was not always so: it has known priests, pilots, Royal Marines and, of course, lighthouse keepers.

I turn to the cast-iron ladderway, curving steeply upwards to the first level of the lighthouse. *Clung-clung-clung* goes the sound of my boots on each tread, reverberating noisily in the level above. I emerge into an utterly bare, round granite chamber, devoid of fixtures or furnishings, smelling of corrosion. De-manned in the 1960s, it has the air of a long-abandoned place. Flakes of paint are piled about the circular floor. Windows as small as those of a medieval stair-turret grudgingly admit daylight; saline residue obscures the glass, which hasn't been washed for a good while. Settled on one of the sills outside, a cormorant eyes me warily, alarmed at my movements, even though my companions passed here a few moments ago. Judging that I pose no threat, she turns back to her chicks.

On closer inspection, the walls and floor are not as featureless as they initially appeared. Faint outlines are printed into them, seemingly traces of fixtures and fittings long since removed. They might offer clues to the former use of this room, a subplot within the broader story of the tower. But I don't have very long to examine them: just three hours to find signs of life in these walls, before our vessel returns on the switching tide. I do not wish to be marooned here.

As well as marking places of danger, rock lighthouses mark places of transition. They stand between realms. Some are poised between national and international waters, or near the places where the continental shelf deepens to become the open ocean (known, thrillingly, as the 'abyssal plain'). Others, like Haulbowline in Ireland, were built closer in, on shores or in sea-loughs, between shallows and depths, just as the land ends and the sea begins.

Haulbowline stands in a giant body of water opening onto the Irish Sea: the Carlingford Lough. Born as a glacial fjord, this deep-water inlet spreads expansively between Northern Ireland and the Republic. Mountains loom on both shores, with field systems traced on the terrain at their feet, and ruins and smallholdings studding the surrounding landscape. It is huge, sparse scenery, which sometime around the tenth century drew the Viking settlers who named this place: Carlingford derives from their word *Kerlingfjorðr*, 'narrow sea inlet of the hag'. Certainly, a powerful charisma hangs in the air, and it's easy enough to imagine a water-deity dwelling here.

With a history that is the most fragmentary and incomplete of all the rock lighthouses, Haulbowline itself seems to stand between reality and myth. Key records of its design and construction have been lost, or never existed in the first place. The tower is oddly absent from books about rock lighthouses. References to it in archive material are veiled or incidental. No one I spoke with seemed to have heard of it.

From the sea at its eastern end the lough leads, via a canal, to the inland city of Newry at its western end. In the

eighteenth century, Newry became prosperous, and Carlingford Lough became the beginning and the end of a busy trade
route. But it was hard to navigate safely. Hazards lurk throughout. Ships had to stick carefully to a demarcated channel
through the lough. In 1821, the entrance was surveyed by Alexander Nimmo, a surveyor for the Commissioners of Irish
Fisheries. His wonderfully evocative sailing directions are as
follows:

> To enter *Lough Carlingford*, take flood tide and bring
> the *New Light House* [Haulbowline] on Little Hawl
> Bowling, between the Block House N.W.1/2W. and
> Green Castle N. Sail for the east side of the Light
> House giving it a birth [*sic*] of half a Cable, you will see
> N by W the Chapel of Killowen, a white house without
> chimneys over the point of Green Castle, keep which
> Chapel always outside of the little green moat on the
> point, to clear the Scar and Soldiers Point. When Bal-
> lagan Point opens west of the Block house steer to-
> wards Greenore Point and Carlingford Castle, you
> avoid Sheep Rock while the New Light is to the east of
> the Blockhouse, and the Old Light clear West of Green
> Island keeps you off the Shoals of the Earl Rock.

Numerous ships were sunk in the entrance by rocks and
shoals such as Little Hawl Bowling, the Block House, Sheep
Rock or the Earl Rock. Between 1798 and 1820 alone there
were over twenty shipwrecks, an alarming rate of attrition
that threatened the prosperity of the lough's ports. Across the
lough's entrance runs the Carlingford Bar, a shallow limestone
ledge covered in boulders and clay that could only be crossed at
high tide before a channel was cut through it later in the nineteenth century. In just two consecutive days in January 1821,
the sailing vessel *Hope* struck the Bar and sunk, followed by the
stranding of the *Friendship* there a day later.

Nimmo's survey gives a sense of the significant landmarks – 'Green Castle', 'a white house without chimneys' – on
which seafarers depended for safe passage in the daytime. At

night, however, the way in to the lough was totally unmarked. To safeguard the increasingly valuable traffic on this shipping route, a land lighthouse was constructed at Cranfield Point in 1803, on the northern side of the entrance from the sea. Though marking the lough's entrance on the coastline, this light gave no indication of the dangerous litter of shoals and rocks just inside. Only a year after the Cranfield Point light first shone, the sloop *Auspicious* was wrecked on the rocks underneath.

So, in 1817, a consortium of Newry merchants lobbied the Dublin Ballast Board (named from their duty to weigh ships' cargoes, and then responsible for all Irish aids to navigation) to replace this badly situated light – as it happens presciently, for gradual coastal erosion later swept it into the sea.

The Ballast Board were convinced and sent George Halpin, their Inspector of Works and Lighthouses, to design and build a new rock lighthouse in the lough's entrance. When Nimmo produced his survey in 1821, this 'New Light House' was under construction on Little Hawl Bowling, or Haulbowline as it is now known. This is an unusual name. I had first thought it sounded like a sailors' coinage, perhaps connected in some way to the old sea shanty 'Haul on the Bowline'. But instead, like the lough, Haulbowline has a name derived from Old Norse, supposedly meaning 'haunt of the eels'.

Though there were larger, more deadly-looking rocks, this comparatively little outcrop was one of the acuter dangers to passing ships, jutting closest to the navigable channel, so it was chosen as the site for the new lighthouse. The surface of the rock is 12 feet below the level of high water and only completely exposed at spring tides, when low tides are lower and high tides higher (when they 'spring' forth, rather than occurring only in spring).

Haulbowline was completed in 1824, and its fixed paraffin apparatus was lit on 1 September of that year. At the time, Haulbowline was the fifth masonry rock lighthouse to be built in British and Irish waters, after John Smeaton's Eddystone (1759), Samuel Wyatt's Longships (1795), Thomas Rogers's South Rock (1797) and Rennie and Stevenson's Bell Rock

(1811). Like the pioneering Eddystone and Bell Rock towers, it is built of granite with a tapering silhouette. In 1848, Robert Stevenson's son Alan referred to it as 'the most remarkable lighthouse on the coast of Ireland'.

But nothing is known of how this remarkable building was designed and erected. No original records survive for Haulbowline: no sheaves of drawings, costings, schedules of work, contracts, or testimony from the builder. There is no information about how the foundations were treated, the stone cut, the structure built or the interior fitted. Halpin was originally a master builder and some theorize that he dispensed with drawings and instead gave mostly verbal instructions to his contractors (this is not as unlikely as it sounds: in a recent episode of *Grand Designs*, a man restored a ruinous Irish castle with no architect and no drawings whatsoever, to the bafflement of Kevin McCloud). Another theory is that the records were lost when responsibility for aids to navigation passed from the Ballast Board to the Commissioners of Irish Lights in 1867.

All we have is Haulbowline itself. The earliest view I can find of the lighthouse is a drawing of 1895, by Captain The Hon. Vereker, R.N. From the deck of HMS *Seahorse*, the ship he commanded, he sketched the topography of the coastline and the lough's entrance. While very useful for navigational purposes, it tells me little about Haulbowline, which stands mutely in the lough water, as inscrutable as the mountains looming behind.

Today, it is the second-oldest working rock lighthouse in Britain and Ireland. But in stark contrast to the exhaustive documentation by the Stevensons of their rock lighthouses, Halpin and Haulbowline are unsung. Most later publications barely mention Haulbowline, and it is absent even from the essential work on lighthouses, Douglas Hague and Rosemary Christie's *Lighthouses: Their Architecture, History and Archaeology*, of 1975.

Certainly, the absence of original building records is a factor in this obscurity. But the reason could also be a quirk of geography. Firstly, Haulbowline is less prominently in the

Greenore   Light.   Church.

Lough Carlingford - Haulbowline

7. Haulbowline drawn from
HMS *Seahorse*, 1895

sea than other rock lighthouses, tucked just into the lough's mouth. This makes it easy to miss if only rock lighthouses in oceans are counted. Perhaps more significantly, since the 1920s it has stood on the Irish border, the eastern end of which runs through the lough. Unlike the Bell Rock, this lighthouse has a far more ambiguous nationality.

Between the 1960s and 1990s, Haulbowline was engulfed by both waves and the Troubles. During this period of guerrilla war, the border became an increasingly embittered fault line as conflict escalated between the British Army, the IRA and the Ulster Loyalists. Armed conflict is a pretty strong deterrent to lighthouse enthusiasts, and I was later to find that Haulbowline had not escaped unmarked. It has really only been completely safe to visit since the noughties.

In the absence of any documentary evidence about this building, it seemed especially important to get inside. I wanted to see what could be gleaned from the state of its walls, floors, ceilings, fixtures and fittings. Fortunately, Haulbowline's operators today, the Commissioners of Irish Lights, were very accommodating. Because the lighthouse's position in a calm lough enables an easy landing by boat, I could join a routine maintenance visit without any specialist training (required for

the helicopter access to other rock lighthouses). While Haulbowline has the brooding charisma of a forgotten thing, it remains a 21st-century navigational aid.

I begin my journey at Greenore, County Louth: a few terraces
of houses and a deep-water port on a small horn of land jutting
out from the south shore of the Carlingford Lough, near the
seaward entrance. In 1830, it was prosperous enough to build
a little land lighthouse, now disused, to guide ships into its harbour. It became a jumping-off point from Ireland to London in
1873, when the London and North-Western Railway opened a
ferry link to their rail network. This stopped operating in the
1950s, but freight traffic swiftly replaced it: in 1963, it became
the first port in the Republic of Ireland to handle shipping containers. These replaced mismatching cargoes of all kinds with a
uniform 'unit' of cargo that could be swiftly and easily handled
in ports across the world.

It is this port from which I will embark for Haulbowline, and for a now-sleepy place it has a somewhat exotic past.
In February 1964, a 702-ton former Danish passenger ferry
was moored here and converted into a radio ship at the behest
of Ronan O'Rahilly, a maverick impresario and Soho busi-
nessman. Formerly known as the *Fredericia*, she would later
become infamous as the MV *Caroline*, host vessel for the pirate
radio station Radio Caroline. Anchored in the seas off Felix-
stowe with a cohort of rebel DJs, her subversive broadcasts
broke the monopoly of record labels and the BBC during the
Swinging Sixties.

But when I arrive on a Monday morning, Greenore seems
not to have swung for a long time. The lights are out in all the
houses. With its stilled cranes and gantries, the port seems to
lack the crackle of one plugged into a healthy trade route. Following my instructions, I linger in a deserted car park to meet
a man named Mick O'Reilly.

Arrangements for this visit had been a little clandes-
tine. The previous day I had travelled as far as Carlingford, a
Norman town on the south side of the lough, where I awaited

confirmation that the weather-dependent visit to Haulbow-line would proceed. I didn't then know who I would be meeting, or where. Reception in the town was poor, and I began to worry that the call wouldn't come. It was after eight o'clock in the evening, while sat in O'Hare's pub worrying at a Guinness, that I saw a voicemail had reached me. A male voice gave terse directions to the Greenore car park. The man repeated Mick's name and left me his phone number, and the line clicked dead.

As it turns out, Mick O'Reilly is an amiable, bespectacled Irish lighthouse technician. We shake hands and he opens the car boot, extracting a hi-vis jacket and a black case with wires peeping from it, equipment for testing the lighthouse's electrical system. We'll be out there for a few hours, he says in a soft brogue, and did I bring a sandwich? Ham and mayo, I say, patting my pocket.

I mention some of the reasons for my visit and he nods vaguely, lighting a cigarette, before another car pulls up nearby. Tony emerges, a boyish, fifty-something house painter, who like me is a visitor. It transpires his grandfather was one of the lighthouse keepers, and Tony wants to see what his workplace was like. Together we sit on the low wall above the shingle and Mick points out our destination. The dark figure of the tower is unmistakable in the lough. I feel a bolt of excitement. Though small at this distance, it seems to have just as much presence as the Mourne Mountains lining up on the shore to the north.

Our transport, the *Mourne Mist*, arrives early. She catches the eye instantly on the water, painted in the bright orange and blue colours of a lifeboat, though that is not her purpose. As the local pilot boat responsible for escorting deep-sea ships into the lough, she needs to be obvious to spot, especially from the lofty bridges of container ships and oil tankers. We watch her approach from the half-empty car park above a strip of shingle beach. A little way out she cuts her engines and stands off from the shallows, while a dinghy detaches itself from her gunwale and makes for the beach.

As it noses into the shingle we walk down to meet it, pebbles slipping and scrunching underfoot. A weather-beaten man in nautical gear descends from the prow: Sean Cunningham, the pilot, who knows the draughts and shallows of the Carlingford Lough better than anyone else in the vicinity. He is from Greencastle, on the northern shore, and his family have been pilots on the lough since the 1880s. He eyes me questioningly as I shake his hand, probably wondering why this Londoner should wish to see the tower. From the dinghy we board the *Mourne Mist*, and then motor out towards the lighthouse.

Though it's generally sunny the breeze is sharp, so I stand with Sean in the shelter of the wheelhouse, talking of his family. His three brothers are Carlingford pilots, as was their father, William, who started the job during the Second World War, and who himself was descended from pilots that appear on record in the late nineteenth century. I marvel at this accumulation of vital knowledge, presumably written down nowhere and passed on through the family. As we talk of Haulbowline he fishes out a set of keys. Ever since the keepers left the lighthouse, his family have acted as its attendants, visiting intermittently to check on its welfare. I mention how it will be the first rock lighthouse I have entered, and he grins. I swept it out for you last week, he says, and there's nothing left inside. It was gutted long ago.

Mick and Tony lean wordlessly over the gunwale, drinking in the view. There are no other vessels nearby and we seem to have the lough to ourselves. On both shores the landscape looks bare. The feeling of emptiness is strong, as though the place has been hollowed out, which of course it has: through successive famines, waves of emigration and unrest. Fittingly for a glacial fjord, it feels like past events have sloughed, glacier-like, across the landscape.

Haulbowline, I hope, won't be as empty as Sean implied. Even bare interiors can still hold valuable clues to past occupation: indentations or discoloration in walls, outlines on ceilings or floors, stray relics in overlooked niches. But at the same time, without evidence of human habitation, it would be much harder to resurrect the place as it was.

*

We approach the lighthouse from the west, passing to starboard an outcrop I recognize as the 'Block House' named on Nimmo's survey: a large expanse of seaweed-strewn rock. Seals sprawl on it like grey sacks, belching and tumbling into the waters.

Haulbowline stands ahead. Over the centuries, gentle weathering has given the grey granite the texture of elephant hide. At the base, the splayed profile of the tower is interrupted by a large square concrete landing-platform. Above, a granite entrance platform cantilevers over the sea, accessed by a scarlet ladder with a scarlet crane bolted to the adjacent stonework. Small, square windows are recessed in diagonal lines all the way up the lighthouse, as though illuminating a giant spiral staircase inside. At the top, a scarlet criss-cross of ironwork forms a circular balcony on a granite overhang, enclosing the white, domed cage of the lantern.

As I was to find with other rock lighthouses, Haulbowline seems to stand between identities. In one sense, it is a working navigational aid, marked on Admiralty charts and GPS systems, but in another it has the feel of a ruin, a brooding air of abandonment. I have encountered no other buildings that produce these twin impressions of use and disuse, centrality and marginality. The tower appears shuttered up, like a relinquished outpost and a relic of a time when we grappled more actively with the sea.

In general design, it is very similar to the Bell Rock, which Halpin must have visited, or he must at least have corresponded with its creator Robert Stevenson. Certainly, it was an uncommon building project in the 1820s, and these were the only two men in the country with the relevant experience. Stevenson himself visited all the extant rock lighthouses he could find before embarking on his own project at the Bell Rock. For such difficult projects, it seems only natural to seek out the hard-won experience of others.

Studying its profile again, I notice that Haulbowline's tapering silhouette is not exactly the same as Stevenson's Bell Rock tower but more like a vernacular version of it, Halpin's own interpretation of the design. Had he drawn inspiration from a visit to that building, and then only sketchily remembered what he had seen when he set to work back in Ireland? Abruptly Sean cuts the engine, and the boat slows to a crawl, easing alongside the landing-platform. I leave my speculations in the bottom of the boat for now, and scramble with the others up the corroded ladder to the entrance.

Sean isn't coming with us. After some to-ing and fro-ing hauling Mick's equipment up from the boat, the *Mourne Mist* eases off from the landing and executes a graceful about-turn towards the lough's interior. As we watch her shrink to an orange speck in the distance, I realize it's strange to be out in the water without moving. Motion is the sea's central characteristic, and movement – via boats, rafts, swimming – has been our primary way of engaging with it. Ever since Winstanley's Eddystone tower of 1698, rock lighthouses have introduced a different kind of interaction. We began to be present in the sea without moving, inhabiting fixed points.

The green doors to the lighthouse are bolted and padlocked, and the paint on them is peeling. Weathered signs warn sternly against carrying naked lights inside, so Mick and Tony have a last cigarette on the entrance platform. We have the run of Haulbowline for three hours, the slightest taste of what it means to occupy this outpost. Mick puts down his bag and rummages in his pockets for the keys.

Up the iron stair, and I emerge into a drum-like chamber on the first floor that is larger than I was expecting. But then, it is completely bare. The circular walls were once painted light blue, but granite walls poke through the paint in many places with a chequerboard effect. At a point on the wall there is a narrow indentation, a slot that seems to run up into the rooms above. Perhaps this held a flue from a long-vanished stove. For some reason, the stone floor was once painted red, around the marks of things no longer there: two large rectangular imprints with holes at their corners. I stoop for a closer look, then climb halfway up the nearby stair for a different perspective. Possibly two generators once stood here on rectangular plinths, bolted down to prevent them trembling over the floor as they operated.

The second floor is much the same as the first: bare and drum-like, with tattered paint on the walls and similar rectangular imprints on the floor. Another engine room? I see the narrow slot on this wall too and assume it runs all the way up the lighthouse. These rooms are like once-inhabited caves, the stonework reasserting itself against the civilizing paint, flakes of which lie in heaps upon the floor. I begin to notice dark brown blotches at numerous places on the walls. The close air in these rooms smells not of organic decay but of reacting elements: salt, metal, stonework, paint pigments. Without regular ventilation to alleviate the saline damp, something ferrous rusts within the stonework. This might be a clue to Haulbowline's construction: the stones – at least of the walls – might be pinned together with iron bolts, rather than dovetailed.

I climb the ladder to the third floor. Up here is a brighter, cleaner room than the caves below, closed off by doors from the rooms above and below. Three large white containers with brass taps at their bases partially line the wall. A small brass plate reads:

1964 / TANKS TO BE DISMANTLED AND PAINTED EXTERNALLY EVERY TEN YEARS / UNIVERSAL FABRICATORS (DUBLIN) LTD.

That this floor was used to store fuel is clear enough, but the tanks seem disused, and with the absence of generators I wonder how the lighthouse is now powered. A chipboard chest of drawers built against the curved stair compartment is clearly a later addition.

There is a third blue door in this room, not leading to the floors above or below but instead set into the circular wall away from the ladders. Light streams through glazed panels above the doorknob. Momentarily I'm confused – halfway up the tower, the door seems to lead nowhere except a sheer drop into the sea. I pull it open to find something utterly unexpected.

Behind the door is a white-painted iron room projecting

out from the lighthouse, supported on a granite balcony, roofed over with a dome. Its walls consist of six large rectangular panels arranged into an angular semi-circle. Five of these have big square windows with a splendid view of the sea, while one is a blank panel. In contrast to the unornamented granite of the lower floors, this room is surprisingly decorated. At the centre of large square panels below the windows are cast-iron relief mouldings, covered in layers of paint, but just about distinguishable: a harp, a globe, a sextant, a ship, a map and compass, an anchor and figures which the thick layers of paint make indistinct.

There seems to be a thin iron door in one of the six sides of this room, painted and rusted shut. After some difficulty, I manage to release the two bolts and spring it open. It leads to an extremely narrow walkway above the sea enclosed by a railing composed of criss-crossing iron poles, like bamboo. It reminds me of the Chinese-style (chinoiserie) decorative fashions first popular in the eighteenth century and still in vogue in the early 1820s when the tower was constructed. The symbols I had seen inside the room appeared on the exterior too, alongside six iron hand-holds cast in the shape of serpents, or dragons, again Chinese in style.

We had not seen this projecting room from the *Mourne Mist* because it had been hidden on the seaward side of the tower as we approached from the land. As far as I knew, no other rock lighthouses have such a feature, their deep-sea locations too volatile for such projections to survive storms. But I could see how it had been possible at Haulbowline because, in the lough's relative calmness, the tower does not face the tall, powerful waves that assault the others.

Far more mysterious is the room's original purpose. Much time, money and thought would have gone into the careful proportions and elaborate detailing, clearly designating it as an important space. But of a specific function there were no signs, only symbols. A fishing-stand? A platform for offerings to Norse deities? More prosaically, a watch-room?

The cast-iron ornaments could at least reveal something

about the elusive George Halpin. He had known enough about architectural fashions to work in the chinoiserie style, suggesting he was not just a master builder, but had some training as an architect. An element of whimsy now colours the vague picture I have of him, a man delighting in symbolism and ornamentation. But it was still difficult to say for whom he had designed the room. Had it been a place for visiting dignitaries, like Stevenson's library at the Bell Rock? To employ fashionable decorative styles suggests someone would appreciate them, but it seems unlikely the lighthouse keepers were connoisseurs. I can think of no convincing answer, so close the door and head upstairs to discuss it with the others.

On the fourth floor I encounter a table, chairs, cupboards and chest of drawers, indicating this was the keepers' living room. A laminated modern sign proclaims it as the mess room. It has the peeling paint and exposed granite walls of the first few floors, but the worn domestic furniture gives it the particular eeriness of homely things disused. The furniture is all mismatched and from different periods. The cupboards are bare but for a *Ship Captain's Medical Guide* of 1952, several ring-bound folders and a large bundle of white cloth. Unfurled, this turns out to be a flag, a red saltire on a white backdrop with illustrations of Haulbowline either side and lightvessels above and below. The folders hold photographs of the now-empty rooms looking starkly mechanical, cluttered with pipework and cabling. These images don't look old, but they are undated. One of the windows is covered by some kind of shutter, and next to it is an iron pole with a large empty bracket, as though something once hung there, since removed.

I draw back a wooden chair and repose in a dust-cloud. Over the table from me the fireplace yawns emptily, the surrounding granite wall painted black to hide soot stains. I eat my sandwich looking around the room, wondering whether I've missed anything. My eye alights on the mantelpiece, where there is gathered a container of incense, a small plastic vial of holy water, and two depictions of Christ: a small, painted statuette and a framed icon. Whereas the other objects in

**8. A panorama of the
mess room, 2016**

the room seem to have randomly accumulated here and there, these religious artefacts look like a deliberate ensemble. On the icon's reverse, a moisture-smudgred ink inscription reads:

Haulbowline Lighthouse
Consecrated on this date by the Rev Canon Denis
Cahill, PP [parish priest], Kilkeel
24.10.1958 Signed D. O'Donnell, P.V. Whelan,
[two more names too blurred to decipher]

Consecrated?

Suddenly the door behind me bangs open and I nearly drop the thing. Tony appears, on his way down for a cigarette on the entrance platform. I show him what I've found and he recalls an old story his grandfather told him. This was not consecration in the sense of establishing a place of worship, but what we would now call an exorcism. In the 1950s there came reports from its keepers that Haulbowline was haunted. They had become increasingly nervy at unexplained clatter-ing and rattling in vacant rooms and shimmers of light play-ing strangely on the lighthouse's walls. This must have been really alarming when there was no means of escape. I shiver, fascinated, and think again of the Norse meanings of the place-names, the hag's inlet, the haunt of the eels.

Irrationally, I speculate about the causes of this haunt-ing. Perhaps whatever spirits were thought to dwell in the lough were affronted at the tower's presence in their realm.

Perhaps they had been held at bay by offerings from that projecting room I found below, and by the 1950s this vital function had been forgotten and the offerings had ceased, rousing them again. Such speculations may be fanciful, but I relate them because they were woven by the strange atmosphere in that lighthouse. Tony says he's sure there was probably a simple explanation, but doesn't look altogether convinced.

That a rock lighthouse might be haunted seemed surprising at first, pointless even. Such occurrences do depend on human presence and grisly events, and as far as I knew these had been minimal at this lighthouse. But then, a lot depends on the character of a building and the feelings it arouses inside people. Even just for a few hours, to be marooned in this sequence of dimly lit, circular granite chambers is an affecting experience. And old Haulbowline is as lonely and out-of-the-way as the archetypal haunted house. The consecration seemed like proof that human superstitions can survive, and even intensify, offshore. I wonder if the same thoughts occurred to Rev Cahill, who was ferried out to the lighthouse from nearby Kilkeel on the northern shore. As I sit in the mess room I think of his presence here before me, clad in priestly robes, murmuring prayers while the keepers fix their eyes upon the floor.

Later, I learned that the lighthouse had been no stranger to tragedy. On 3 November 1916, 97 people died when two steamships, the *Retriever* and the *Connemara*, collided early in the morning while trying to pass one another in the lough's navigable channel just to the north of Haulbowline. Both ships were sailing with dimmed lights to evade German U-boats operating in the vicinity. Hurricane-force winds and the narrowness of the channel had made it impossible for their skilled captains to maintain an even course. The Haulbowline keeper on watch saw the dangerous proximity of the ships and fired warning rockets, but the fearful wind and tides caused the *Retriever*, laden with coal, to smash into the *Connemara*, which was carrying passengers. The sea rushed eagerly into an enormous tear in the *Connemara*'s port side. She sank too quickly for her passengers to escape, her white-hot boilers blowing up on contact with the freezing sea.

When the sun rose and the sea had calmed, the shores of the lough were harrowing in the extreme. Corpses, dead animals and wreckage were strewn everywhere. The *Connemara*'s exploding boilers had mutilated and burned many of the bodies. There were 58 of them; the remaining 39 were washed ashore along the lough over successive weeks, as though dripfeeding the horror to the communities there. Haulbowline's keepers had watched helplessly as the carnage had unfolded; it is very likely that some of the unfortunate passengers came to rest at their front door. The sole survivor was a crewman on the *Retriever*, who could bring himself to speak about the incident only decades later.

A few years after it had been consecrated, on 17 March 1965, Haulbowline was de-manned and converted to automatic operation. It was the first such rock lighthouse in Britain and Ireland to have its keepers permanently withdrawn.

Over 50 years later, signs of their presence have mostly weathered away. The mess room is the only place in the tower where ordinary furniture lingers. Above, the fifth and sixth floors revert to the cave-like appearance of the first and second floors. Instead of traces of machinery, the sole features of these bare rooms are blocked fireplaces in each one, suggesting they were living quarters. Based on what I know of other rock lighthouse configurations, I guess the fifth floor was used as a bedroom and the sixth floor, directly under the lantern, as an office or service room. Faint imprints on the walls locate vanished fixtures without identifying what they might have been. Flakes of paint and stone have been randomly shed from the walls, effectively pixelating the surviving evidence.

I push on upwards. After the juicy details of symbolism and hauntings, it's as though Haulbowline has curtly silenced itself.

At the summit of the lighthouse, in the lantern room, the archaeological character of all the previous floors vanishes. Daylight shines from 360 degrees through the copious glazing.

An iron roof curves up to a point overhead, like a circus tent. The walls below the glass have been recently painted white and the room feels used. I find Mick pottering around, connecting wires to half-open metal cabinets. The generous proportions of the room are interrupted by an iron gantry at mezzanine level by which the light source is accessed. This modern light is comically small, the LEDs contained within a glass cylinder about the size of a cake tin. The lantern frame around it feels too big, designed in an age when technology had been larger. When representatives of Trinity House visited Haulbowline in April 1869, they found 'a fixed light with twenty 25 inch reflectors placed on a circular frame' practically filling the lantern room.

Haulbowline's light flashes white every ten seconds during hours of darkness. Mick tells me the small size of the fitting today is due to the lighthouse's position in the lough. Rather than sending out strong beams of light over miles of open seas, Haulbowline's warning needs only to be visible from the lough's entrance and the waters of the interior. The little fitting has a nominal range of 10 nautical miles, in contrast to the much further reaches of those, like the Bell Rock, that stand far out in the open sea. Everything it needs to run can be comfortably housed in the lantern room, emphasizing the redundancy of the six floors below. Over 111 feet high, this stone tower, weighing many thousands of tons, suddenly feels preposterously over-engineered for the small light it now houses. But then, perhaps the old work and the new encapsulate the different ambitions of the ages that produced them.

Mick is able to explain a few of the features I had noticed on my climb. The narrow slot in the walls had accommodated the weighted chain attached to the clockwork mechanism originally installed in this lantern room. Exactly the same configuration had been used by Stevenson at the Bell Rock, and it deepens my certainty that he and Halpin must have met or corresponded. I had been correct about the presence of generators in the lower floors – they had run there until the lighthouse was converted to solar power in 2011. The undated photographs in that folder had shown the starkly mechanical interior before this.

As for the remarkable projecting room, Mick knows it as the 'half-tide room'. Originally, a light had been shone from this room at high tide, signalling to ships that the water depth was sufficient for the Carlingford Bar to be safely crossed. One keeper on watch, eight lamps and eight 25-inch reflectors were kept in the room for the purpose. Though a slightly more prosaic explanation than my speculations about sea-gods, I could see why the half-tide room had been decorated with ships, sea serpents, sextants and other nautical symbols. Shining with light when the tide was at flood, extinguished when it was on the ebb, the half-tide room was intimately linked to the rhythms of the sea. It might have been a straightforward task, but it says a lot about Halpin that he felt the need to give it an almost ceremonial housing.

In 1868, a wider and deeper channel was cut through the Carlingford Bar, allowing ships into the lough without having to wait for high water. With this, the half-tide room became redundant, and I like to imagine the keepers repurposing it as an extravagant fishing-stand.

The time of our departure draws nearer. Tony joins us in the lantern room, and we reflect on the success of the visit. For Mick, it was simply another day at the office; he found no short-circuits or alarming faults in the workings of the lighthouse. Tony had seen everything he wanted in the first half an hour or so, passing the rest of the time on the entrance platform or in the lantern room, gazing out at the sea. He doesn't say so, but I sense that the deserted state of the lighthouse made it harder for him to evoke his grandfather's time here.

As Mick packs away his equipment, I spot an orange and blue speck from the lantern: the *Mourne Mist*, heading our way. We descend through the lighthouse, sealing the rooms behind their doors. It's high tide now, and the seal-clad hazards we could see from the boat are covered by water. Sean hails us from the *Mourne Mist*. There is no lingering: we climb down into the boat, the engines growl and we pull away. Sean asks from the wheelhouse whether I had found what I had expected. No, I reply, something better. Though unknown to me then, it would not be the last time he and I would meet.

> **bowline** n. Naut. a rope attaching the weather
> side of a square sail to the bow / a simple knot for
> forming a non-slipping loop at the end of a rope.
>
> *OED*

I came away with the feeling that Haulbowline had told me some fine stories but had given away few of the incidental day-to-day details that make you feel as though you properly know a place. With the sea shanty nagging in my memory, further research revealed that a 'bowline' is not only a rope, but also a kind of knot. These twin meanings seemed to sum up the lighthouse very well: on one hand, a straightforward navigational aid, on the other, a past that remained difficult to fully untie.

Luckily, I later found that there is a particular phase of history in which Haulbowline is frequently mentioned. Though all original papers relating to the lighthouse seem to have been lost, it appears frequently in another cache of archive material: declassified government files about the Carlingford Lough during the Troubles. So, a few months after my visit, I spent hours among yellowing papers in the National Archives at Kew, looking for the lighthouse.

On 6 December 1921, the Anglo-Irish Treaty was signed following a ceasefire between the IRA and the British Army. It was the end of the Irish War of Independence, a vicious conflict ignited by Sinn Féin's (the governing Irish republican party) declaration of Irish independence in January 1919. There had been much brutality; particularly infamous were the British auxiliaries, the 'Black and Tans', veterans of the First World War notorious for civilian attacks. The 1921 Treaty ended British rule in what is now the Republic of Ireland, which would be governed by an autonomous Irish Free State formed in December 1922. Britain continued to occupy Northern Ireland and by 1925 a border between two new countries had been plotted, straggling irregularly from Lough Foyle in the north to the Carlingford Lough in the east.

Haulbowline was just over one hundred years old when the border came into existence, a profound shift in its circumstances. Northern Ireland remained in British hands on the lough's northern shore, while the fledgling Irish Free State had sprung up on the southern shore. Standing in the waters between the two, the lighthouse now occupied a volatile zone between two bitterly opposed nations. Almost immediately the shores resounded with gunfire.

At Greenore on the south shore, where I had embarked for the lighthouse, a garrison was established by the Irish Free State in the early 1920s. For machine-gun practice, they aimed at a concrete pillar mounted near the shingle beach, where we had waited for the *Mourne Mist*. The garrison must have been staffed with clumsy marksmen, because in 1923 ship captains were complaining to the Parliament of Northern Ireland that ricocheting bullets were endangering their vessels. I did not see bullet holes in Haulbowline's granite flanks, but then I had not been looking for them.

Calm prevailed around the lough until the late 1960s, when unrest broke out in Northern Ireland. A moribund Unionist government had been in power for nearly 50 years, ineptly managing the sensitivities between Protestants and Catholics, and most likely actively discriminating against the latter. Strife escalated; a civil rights march in Derry was broken up by police with batons and water cannon. There was outrage at this, and riots erupted elsewhere. British security forces were unable to keep control of the situation. The situation became so bad that in 1969 the army were sent in, occupying and partitioning Belfast and Derry. This was the beginning of the Troubles, a guerrilla conflict that would last for nearly 30 years.

Declassified Ministry of Defence papers of the time state that:

> Carlingford Lough has long been a traditional route
> for smuggling live-stock, food and dutiable goods

from the Republic into Northern Ireland. Since the start of the present IRA campaign in 1969, a number of intelligence reports have suggested that this route has been used for smuggling arms, ammunition and explosives into Northern Ireland, and that the option to use this route again is always under consideration by the PIRA [Provisional IRA].

Established in 1972–3, Operation INTERKNIT was the British government's attempt to stop terrorists smuggling arms and explosives across the lough. Haulbowline features frequently in the paperwork. Units of Royal Marines patrolled the waters in one of two Royal Navy ships, HMS *Vigilant* or HMS *Alert*. They had powers to stop and board vessels on certain grounds, including those carrying 'suspicious looking cargoes', 'shore-hugging' or 'sailing without lights at night'.

One of these was a private yacht, unnamed but numbered '183L', boarded on 8 June 1974. It had been borrowed by a man named William Sweetman, who was sailing it from Greenore to Dun Laoghaire, a port near Dublin. By his account (later published in *The Irish Times*), he was sailing in Irish waters on the south side of the navigable channel through the lough, on the other side of the border beyond British jurisdiction. Nevertheless, the Royal Marines held him at gunpoint and searched his vessel despite his protests that he was in southern, Irish waters. Sweetman claimed the unprovoked search was desultory and really made as a show of British force. To cap it all, the Marines hinted darkly at 'consequences' if he were found there again.

Outraged, Sweetman went to the British minister responsible for Northern Ireland and demanded confirmation of the exact course of the border through the lough. If he was within his rights in southern waters, then he called grandly for an 'energetic protest at this armed incursion and arrest in Irish territory and at the threat of future molestation'.

The Navy's version of events differed. According to it, Sweetman's vessel left Greenore and kept to the south side of the lough until it passed into what the Navy considered to be Northern Irish waters. They challenged him when he was 940 yards to the north-west of Haulbowline, but he doggedly continued down the lough's main navigable channel, heading for the sea. After the Royal Marines warned him via loudhailer that they would forcibly divert him if necessary, Sweetman reluctantly cut the engines, and he was boarded by the Marines after passing Haulbowline, 690 yards to the east. His borrowed yacht was searched, and found to be clean, by a single soldier who did not unlimber his weapon.

Haulbowline had come to be a critical orientation point in these territorial squabbles. A border should be clear and linear, but on the Carlingford lough the situation was confused. It remains so today; there is no official line drawn through the lough delineating the north and south waters. As well as standing between nations, Haulbowline stands between definition and vagueness. From the declassified MoD papers, William Sweetman cuts a slightly comical figure, but he illustrates the uncertainty on both sides about the true course of the border under water. I began to see the lough itself as a kind of swollen borderline, its waters a shadowy no-man's sea in which only force prevails.

At this time Haulbowline stood newly automated, its rooms mothballed, its lantern mechanically quenched and re-kindled, no longer a house, now just a light. It was even more lonely and out-of-the-way than before; only its attendant and Irish Lights technicians intermittently visited the place. In such a climate of ambiguity and acrimony, it wasn't long before the lighthouse itself came under suspicion. As part of INTERKNIT the Royal Marines landed at Haulbowline, broke down the doors and raided the uninhabited tower for smuggled weapons and explosives.

Or at least, that is what I deduce from an official complaint made by the Commissioners of Irish Lights to the Ministry of Defence in June 1974. They alleged that forced entry had damaged some of the lough's lights, and that HMS *Vigilant*'s commander had been 'high-handed' with Haulbowline's local attendant, who held the keys. But according to the *Vigilant*'s commander, 'the attendant [to Haulbowline] had been most co-operative with respect to searches of lights – to the extent that he had handed over his keys so that they could be copied . . . His wife, however, was not so disposed and on one occasion berated a search party saying that they "could not tell her husband what to do".'

The scene leapt vividly from the page: a tense stand-off between a furious Irish housewife and a heavily armed set of Royal Marines, with an anxious lighthouse attendant between them, sweating to keep the peace. I felt as though it was one of many similar flashpoints up and down Northern Ireland during that guerrilla conflict, though perhaps the only one that hinged on a rock lighthouse. Fortunately, the report of this incident struck a conciliatory note, concluding that: 'The Commander . . . will make his peace with Mr Cunningham [Haulbowline's attendant].'

As the Carlingford Lough pilots also acted as Haulbowline's attendants, the man referenced could be William John Cunningham, who had been a lough pilot since the 1940s. Or, it could be his son Sean, who by the time I met him had been a lough pilot for over 40 years, and would have been in his late twenties/early thirties in 1974. As he had ferried me to Haulbowline in the first place, I prefer to think that it was Sean Cunningham whom I encountered again in this top-secret government file.

I cast my mind back to the moment when we descended the ladder from the lighthouse into the *Mourne Mist*. From the wheelhouse, Sean had called over his shoulder to ask whether I had found in Haulbowline what I had expected. A story stranger than fiction, would be my answer to him now.

Perch Rock

A ruined lighthouse

1830,
AT THE MOUTH OF THE RIVER MERSEY, WIRRAL

> *'Three years!' I cried. 'Were you shipwrecked?'*
> *'Nay, mate,' said he - 'marooned.'*

> Robert Louis Stevenson,
> *Treasure Island*, 1883

We wrestle with zips and buckles in the sandstone courtyard, piling our bags on the uneven flagstones and impatiently looking at the sea from the ramparts. 'If anything happens out there then you'd better call the coastguard,' says my companion, the wind ruffling his hair, as we stand on the shore of the Irish Sea, about to spend the night in the abandoned Perch Rock lighthouse. I assume that he's joking.

Doug is an inscrutable man who owns this lighthouse and a nineteenth-century fort on the New Brighton shoreline, jutting out into Liverpool Bay. He runs the fort as a small museum of local history and military artefacts. Its collection is appealingly random, from old photographs of defunct Merseybeat groups to a complete reconstruction of the *Titanic*'s radio room. In this homespun operation, he takes the roles of museum owner, director, curator and painter-decorator. Various associates of his lend a hand; with one of them, Jimmy, Doug met us at four o'clock on a Friday afternoon, when the fort's visitors had all gone home. They had been repairing parts of the roof and were sticky with asphalt and sealant.

Jimmy distributes paper cups of coffee he has conjured from a kitchen in the fort's old holding cells. Perch Rock is one of the only rock lighthouses you can reach on foot, after the tide has left. The sea here doesn't go out at once, but in several haphazard channels, unwrapping the beach in muddled stages, with the area around the lighthouse left to the very end. We had watched it recede from the promenade on the journey here, which, devoid of people, had that pitch of melancholy found in seaside places in the off-season. Once a glitzy seaside resort, New Brighton in February is now something of a last resort, the ornamental promenade benches vacant save for nonchalant seagulls.

At this northern latitude, the February sky is like silver nitrate and the air seems to get weightier as the day turns. We notice that the lighthouse stands in the firing line of the fort's gun emplacements. Both were built at the same time, in the late 1820s, so this was either incompetence or dark comedy on the part of those responsible, the military and the Liverpool port authority. Or indecision: according to Doug, they couldn't decide between a lighthouse bristling with guns or a fort with a massive light fitting, so they built both instead. As the afternoon thickens and darkens the lighthouse is eventually left in a bowl of water by the retreating tide. The path across the sands to it from the fort is finally clear.

I have brought along my friend Michael, a Limerick poet and photographer, who was amused by the thought of camping out in the sea. Jimmy – genial, stooping and fifty-something – has never been inside the tower so will briefly visit with us; he recalls observing it as a baby from a pram on the promenade, back in the time when it was still operational.

Michael, Jimmy and I are sheathed in waders like flyfishermen, because to access the tower we have to wade through the water around the base. The four of us walk quickly across the sand, Doug coming only as far as the edge of the water to help us with the bags. I had been corresponding with him for a while before he suggested that I spend a night in the lighthouse. He seems surprised that we took him up on the offer, and greets us a little uncertainly, alternately cracking jokes about pneumonia and awkwardly offering us a Thermos for the slow hours of the night. He has suggested we give the place a clean, so we go armed with brooms, brushes and a bucket.

Seagulls drop their cries like tacks as Michael and I lead

the way towards the tower looming ahead. Doug and Jimmy bring up the rear in a murmur of Scouse. From a distance, the pool around the tower looked trifling, almost a puddle, but it proves a lagoon at closer quarters. I go in first, an oak ladder heavy on my shoulders, and the water suddenly grips my legs, midriff and chest, forcing pockets of air out of the waders. It is a queer sensation, like being vacuum-packed, and I hope there are no forensic tears in the rubber. Close up, the tower is abruptly colossal. Marine encrustations beard the black base, which is splayed like a trumpet. There are barnacles, mussels and cockles up to the high-tide mark and the stone shaft thereafter is painted a jolly white.

The entrance to the tower is about 30 feet above us. We need the ladder because the gunmetal rungs in the stonework only begin at head height. I prop it against the base underneath them. Behind, Jimmy and Michael are wading towards me holding bags above their heads, water encircling their chests; silhouetted in the gloaming they could be soldiers negotiating a swamp. The boots of my waders slip a bit as I climb and I focus intently on the passing rungs.

We find the door into the tower leaning from its hinges, the floor of the small platform matted with guano and silt. Dirty stone steps leer ominously and disappear beyond. A telltale whimpering betrays pigeons in the room above, which will need to be chased out. Jimmy comes up next to join me on this inconvenient ledge, and I wave him on up the stairs to find a rope with which to haul our belongings into the tower. Seconds after his legs disappear from view a pigeon rockets out of the opening like a bullet, nearly dislodging us. All the while, Doug stands in the windy shallows wearing a hi-vis jacket, calling up to us snippets of lighthouse trivia. Did we know the barnacles on the base of the tower originate from New Zealand, having hitched a ride on a ship's hull? Or that the lighthouse keepers here were drunks, regularly leaving the wicks untended? As the light fades he becomes a patch of luminosity against the dark sands, sending up facts while we heave up our consignments. Doug and Jimmy finally slink away as daylight putters out, calling luck to us across the sands, and promising to relieve us the next afternoon at low tide.

The stairs emerge in the centre of the first floor, where decay flexes in the air. Both this and the entranceway have been abandoned for a long time and the surfaces are layered with guano and shadow. It was once a small kitchen, water cistern and lavatory, but is now no place to linger. A trapdoor seals it off from the room above, a portal that leads to a startling discovery. We find ourselves in a circular living room, kept just as it was abandoned, nineteenth century in décor and with unmodernized fittings. A bustle of cupboards lines a quadrant of the curved wall and an iron stove squats next to a low bench underneath a series of shelves. An iron column pierces the room and a square wooden table. Within this tube dangles the weights and chains that turn the clockwork mechanism in the lantern room two storeys up. An elegant solution, though likely too rust-frosted to move now. A Bible, tea lights, a cracked glass ashtray, a framed keepers' eulogy, pictures of ships and old mugs ornament the room. It's an extraordinary scene, a late-Georgian moment stilled and sealed up.

Michael's waders turned out to be punctured and quickly took on water, leaving him fearful of trench foot, while I found that barnacles had slit my knuckles during the ascent. In the aspic of the living room we rest, pulling from the whiskey bottle, taking stock and saying little. The incoming sea pulses gently, and from far onto shore the sounds of civilization can dimly be heard. The living room slumbers as it has done for 40 years, bar intermittent pigeons, and the air sparkles with dust caught in the half-light from the windowpanes. Two of these are nailed shut, but the third – covered by a wooden hatch – we manage to spring open, and the room seems to shiver in response.

Today, the Perch Rock lighthouse stands apart from all the others by being redundant and close to shore. The hazards it marks are not obvious because its surroundings have changed since it was built, and the rocks that are visible are Ozymandian,

**9. The River Mersey seen from
the Perch Rock living room, 2016**

half-covered by the sand and lying close to the promenade –
there is a meekness to them compared to some of the other hazards described in this book. To founder in this location would
require a really savage gale, or an incompetent seaman, one
feels. But until the late nineteenth century, when the promenade was built out from the shore, these rocks were lonelier,
encircled by sea and more threateningly in the mariner's path.
Navigation around them into Liverpool was complicated by
fog, irregular currents and shifting sandbanks.

So the tower perches on the threshold between land and
sea. Built between 1827 and 1830, it is the fourth-oldest rock
lighthouse to survive. But all of these have lost most of their
original fittings, making the Perch Rock the only lighthouse
tower to retain its simple, late-Georgian interior. This rarity
value is enhanced by its intactness. Unlike other lighthouses,
the Perch Rock was hardly updated during its working life. Its
conversion to automatic operation in the 1920s was low-key.
Many towers suffered from their conversion to electrical or
diesel power and subsequent automation and de-manning,
their nineteenth-century interiors mostly gone as a result. The

fact that it was decommissioned and sealed before it could be tampered with makes this tower fascinating.

Perch Rock is one of two redundant rock lighthouses, the other being the Kilwarlin lighthouse of 1797, standing wave-invaded and slimily defunct in the middle of the Irish Sea. Designed by Thomas Rogers, a clever if erratic optical engineer, this tower fell out of use because it was built in the wrong place, too far from the hazard it was supposed to mark. In 1877, it was extinguished and replaced with a lightvessel in the correct location. Ignominiously, a century later, thieves made off with its lantern, leaving it forlorn and bollard-like in appearance.

Contrastingly, the Perch Rock suffered redundancy as a result of new technologies rather than its position. It was decommissioned in 1973 because the Mersey approaches had been more cost-effectively marked out and Liverpool's maritime prosperity had begun to wane. Today, more than ever, the progress in wayfinding and navigation seem to place the continued life of rock lighthouses under scrutiny. In capacity and convenience, technology advances at a mercurial pace. Are such vast navigational warnings still necessary when a tiny smartphone is capable of charting a course?

Patterns of seafaring have changed, too. The twin miracles of flight and satellite navigation have put considerable distance between us and the water, rendering us passive users of it instead of active participants in it. In her investigation of modern seafaring, Rose George writes convincingly of our national 'sea blindness', in which we no longer comprehend, or are interested in, the traffic and activity out in the open ocean. For many of us, the sea is now abstract or imaginary rather than real, yet there is nothing fictional about our economic dependence on it. The shipping industry continues to be the main source of all our consumer goods. From smartphones to sweetcorn, '99% of everything' we consume comes by boat. Sailors and seafaring are as important as ever.

Where does this leave rock lighthouses? Redundant buildings are compelling because they hold twin senses: of regret, at the loss of their function, and of anticipation, of what the future might hold for them. But where a building's form is so closely married to its function, a different use can be hard to specify. Rock lighthouses are so particularly designed for their purpose, so thoroughly *themselves*. To assemble their interlocking granite pieces is to complete one puzzle; to consider their post-navigational future is to be faced with another.

Before the light goes completely we worm our way through the upper reaches. Above the living room we find our resting place for the night: three semi-circular bunks stacked atop one another, curved at the back like segments of orange, veiled with drawstringed curtains. There are still mattresses and blankets on these bunks, looking suspiciously inhabited for a moth-balled room, as if the lighthouse keepers left only moments ago. There is a resilient homeliness here that comforts with one hand and unsettles with the other. Abandonment salts a place, shuttering it in morbidity, rigging the psyche to flinch at even the most workaday sights.

We come to the uppermost stage of the tower. Jaunty and ochre-coloured from a distance, the lantern from within is a handsome structure, a slender, octagonal iron frame hatted with an ogee ceiling, curving up into a point in the style of a circus big top. But corpses – some fresh, some polished to the bones – litter the floor: for years this has been a bird-trap. All that is required is a single smashed pane of glass and the entire lantern begins to work along the same principles as a lobster pot. The birds fly in and cannot get out again. This is an inversion of a problem common to many lighthouses, especially those standing under migration paths, which experience a high rate of attrition; birds rocket towards the light, smash into the glass and drop dead off the rail. One school of thought reckons the light disorientates them, another that it tempts them in. But without a light here, the creatures do not thud at high speed into the lantern; rather they enter it willingly. It is an odd, macabre sight, a return to the rank atmosphere of the lower levels through which we scuffled earlier, death – but with more light.

The room must have been clean and charming in its heyday, before it was quietly enclosed by decay. As originally designed, lighthouse lanterns were airy, gleaming places, the proud lenses and metalwork kept hospital-clean. They were the most important rooms in the towers. Just a suggestion of grime would unbalance their tense sophistication; here on Perch Rock, there is far more than a suggestion. Nevertheless, we can still discern the room's graceful form. At shoulder height, an iron gantry encircles the space to form a mezzanine supported by iron colonnettes in a classical style. Excitingly, the majority of the nineteenth-century lantern apparatus has been left intact, with only the lens missing. At the focal point of the room, a rectangular iron cabinet holds the clockwork mechanism for turning the glass optic: the lighthouse's heart, now rusted into a tangled artefact of cogs and gears. These would have been turned by those weights dangling in the iron tube running through the living room. This ruined lantern is probably the only one to survive with its original machinery *in situ*, because the light is often the first thing to be modernized, upgraded to electrical or diesel power. Here, this never happened.

Fresh air enters through a crack in the balcony doorframe. We stoop through, picking our way among the carcasses, emerging onto a circular stone ledge underneath the lantern frame. The encircling rail splays alarmingly outwards. Seizing it, we shuffle to the seaward edge and look out at the Irish Sea, inkwell-dark with the suggestion of advancing storms. From this prospect we could be on any rock tower, with only the sea in the furthest reaches of the eye, but on the landward side it could only be the Perch Rock. Many lights speckle the mainland, almost within grasp, revealing their location by their hue. Those of New Brighton have the suburban flicker of a thousand distant television sets. The lights of Liverpool shine as if Brylcreemed with city glam. On the opposite jaw of the Mersey, the Crosby dockyards shine sombrely from gantries, cranes and the bridges of ships awaiting departure.

*

Preceding the stone lighthouse in which we stand was a wooden thing called 'the Perch' that marked the hazard from the late seventeenth century. Early aids to navigation could be alarmingly primitive and the Perch was nothing more than a wooden tripod holding aloft a small brazier. Though relatively stout, it was frequently batted away by high rollers coming in off the Irish Sea. Other threats to it were man-made: wreckers would often disable it to harvest the goods washed ashore from distressed ships. As Bella Bathurst relates in *The Wreckers*, these characters reputedly plundered even the corpses that came ashore, gnawing at their digits to get at the jewellery, an accusation made in the 1834 Parliamentary Commission that revealed the full scale of the problem. Such methods resulted in bounty like that of the *Elizabeth Buckham*, which lost a cargo of rum and coconuts off this coast in 1867. According to Bathurst, the goods were immediately enjoyed, and the newly established Wallasey police force spent that evening dragging bibulous and unconscious wreckers off the sands before the tide came in and drowned them.

As a result of its calamitous coastline, the Wirral developed a string of lighthouses early on. One of the oldest surviving land-towers in Britain stands at Leasowe (1763), further west down the coast from the Perch Rock. Different lighthouse customs applied in this area: the peninsula had an unusually high proportion of female lighthouse keepers, for example, far more than any other part of the country. At Leasowe the keeper in charge until 1908 was Mrs Williams, a matriarch whose six children scurried up and down the ladders in the building and, I like to think, helped to keep the light. The Wirral was never under the jurisdiction of Trinity House, who would have implemented the all-male operation seen elsewhere. The Corporation of Liverpool, on the other hand, had no particular qualms about families inhabiting and operating their lighthouses. This seems to have resulted in reliability and stability: when the ribald behaviour of the all-male Perch Rock keepers started to cause problems, the Corporation considered staffing the tower with a family because the formula had worked so peacefully elsewhere. In the end, this came to nothing and the tower remained the only lighthouse on the Wirral garrisoned solely by men.

Through successive patching and replacement, the old-fashioned Perch stood until the early nineteenth century. The tower that replaced it was finished in 1830, designed by John Foster Junior, an able Greek Revival architect who is today undeservedly obscure. A splendid account of this man is given by Hugh Hollinghurst in *John Foster and Sons: Kings of Georgian Liverpool*. His family rose to prominence in Liverpool through his father, John Foster Senior, a carpenter's son who became master builder to the Corporation of Liverpool when the town's affairs were booming and it was hurriedly developing the infrastructure of a major seaport. For a while it seemed as though Foster Senior would be to Liverpool what Thomas Cubitt was to London – he exploited his position as Surveyor to the Corporation to gain a monopoly on building in the town, controlling the distribution of work. The pricing and quality control of works were easily fiddled, and some suspect his prosperity resulted from fraud on an enormous scale, although nothing was ever decisively proven. Entrenched ideas of class may well have played their part in this suspicion: here, after all, was a self-made man with purchase in society.

Hollinghurst relates how Foster Senior was briefly known as the 'King' of early-Georgian Liverpool and his son, John Junior, consequently enjoyed a gilded childhood. But while the father was by all accounts horny-handed, blunt, calculating, marinated in graft, his son was romantic, idle, cheerful and given to dreaming. It was intended that he too would enter the building trade, but in a capacity yet to be determined. So, in his early twenties, like many others of his pedigree, he left England for the Grand Tour. But fortune intervened for him in the form of the Napoleonic Wars. Europe – the traditional circuit – was too unsettled, so Foster travelled to Greece and the Balkans instead.

There, ancient Grecian architecture captivated him and he later became a key figure in the transmission of it back to

England, where it gained traction in the early nineteenth century as an architectural movement known as the Greek Revival. One of Foster's advantages was that he had actually visited the ruins and, with fellow acolytes, swarmed about them, measuring, sketching, drawing, observing and groping for the essence of the things. His letters home gush with youthful zeal. With fellow antiquarian C.R. Cockerell, he discovered several important sites, among which was the celebrated Temple of Apollo at Bassae, and published texts on them. He considered these ruins superior to those of the Parthenon at Athens, enthusing to his father about the 'most sublime effect' in the depictions of centaurs' limbs. But there was an uglier side to all this. Taking advantage of Greece's disorganized and unsophisticated administration, Foster and his companions stripped the temples at Aegina and Bassae of their marbles. They lost the bidding war for the marbles of Aegina to German archaeologists, but in 1815 secured those of the latter for England after the intervention of the Prince Regent. The act was comparable to Elgin's removal of the Parthenon marbles (both sets of sculptures reside in the British Museum) and perhaps reveals a harder, calculating edge to Foster. With this and other successes abroad, his reputation began to develop as an antiquarian and also as a socialite; between 1810 and 1811 he had wintered in Constantinople with Lord Byron.

When the tour was done, he came back to Liverpool in 1816. This was a somewhat meek return for someone whose star was ascending, possibly linked to his parentally unauthorized marriage to an Italian girl in Turkey. Or he may simply have wished to return to a place where, through his father's patronage, he could build in the Greek style unstintingly. Ultimately it was Liverpool's gain. Though many are lost today, his buildings brought to the city the new Hellenism then gripping London, Edinburgh and Bath.

To my mind, the two survivors that speak most eloquently of Foster's abilities are the Oratory standing at the foot of the Anglican Cathedral and the Perch Rock lighthouse. They are contemporaries, the former completed in 1829 and the latter in 1830. Built as a mortuary chapel, the Oratory is a neat little building, a convincing essay in the Greek Revival style Foster had helped to popularize. Correct in proportions and chaste in ornament, it shows very well how his time in Greece had advanced his understanding of classical architecture. He built this gem as he was overseeing what must have been a co-lossal workload – the construction projects at Liverpool Docks and the lighthouse and fort at Perch Rock were simultaneously underway. This Oratory was possibly a scheme with which he could divert himself during the other, more prosaic works.

Given Foster's classical proclivities, the design of the Perch Rock lighthouse is unusually straightforward. In fact, perhaps inevitably, the tower is a near-exact replica of Smea-ton's Eddystone. It is surprising that Foster chose to use this style verbatim, without classicizing it or adding flourishes to align the design with contemporary thinking. Perhaps he didn't have time to do anything more, occupied as he was with other projects at the time. Moreover, rock lighthouse towers were then experimental technology, and this design was known to work. Glamour may also have been a factor: the Eddystone tower was viewed as a minor miracle of building, an expression of England's conversance with the sea worth imitating. That Foster could build something so strikingly different to the Ora-tory is a testament to his architectural dexterity.

But the more I compared them, the more I realized that the Oratory and the lighthouse share deeply rooted classical traits. Ultimately derived from Greek and Roman designs, classical architecture is fundamentally concerned with pro-portional, harmony and symmetry. All three of these charac-teristics are present in the Perch Rock lighthouse. Such traits had a practical benefit in helping to counteract the volatility of the surrounding seas. More philosophically, the classical style is about expressing order where previously it did not exist, and a rock lighthouse standing in an unruly ocean is an exquisite expression of this idea (whether or not the sea was actually tamed). For Foster, Smeaton's design must have sat agreeably with the classical principles he had learned in Greece, which governed his work as an architect. Standing at the entrance to the Mersey, the Perch Rock demonstrated Foster and Liverpool's burgeoning enlightenment to incoming vessels, just as the Bell Rock had done for the Scottish national story.

Part of my fascination with visiting rock lighthouses has to do with the sensation of being temporarily marooned. With the character of Ben Gunn in *Treasure Island*, Robert Louis Stevenson planted this act in the public consciousness in 1883 as a 'horrible kind of punishment common enough among the buccaneers'. Robert Louis was a member of the Stevenson dynasty of lighthouse builders. *Treasure Island* is perhaps thrown into new light when we reflect that its author was himself temporarily marooned many times on remote hazards while building lighthouses for the family firm, before he went on to writing as a living.

I had an early brush with being marooned offshore at Hoylake, a town that is home to my mother's side of the family, around 20 miles along the Wirral coast from the Perch Rock. Bunched half an hour's walk out on the shoreline near my grandmother's house are the Red Rocks, outcrops of red sandstone on which nothing lives except the people who walk out to them and picnic at low tide. You have to pick your moment carefully because the tide races in deceptively quickly, sheeting the level sands in water in the time it takes to eat a sandwich and realize you're stuck.

When I was about ten years old, my family and I walked out there for a picnic. I vividly recall looking back to the shore and my guts knotting at the distance we had covered, feeling a queasy thrill at this gamble, at the potential for being outflanked by the sea. Nevertheless, we sat cross-legged and enjoyed the views and our sandwiches. After what seemed like a few minutes somebody noticed that water was coiling around the base of our rock. Disbelievingly we scrabbled back to shore, water sloshing threateningly at our heels.

The particular horror of marooning, at least by its dictionary definition, is that it is deliberately done to someone.

But what might it mean to be self-marooned? Keepers of rock lighthouses had chosen a career that effectively marooned them on the lighthouses for their timetabled shifts, and often for longer when bad weather foiled reliefs. There is an undeniable romance to living out in the wild, beyond society. There is the threat of uncertainty too, but perhaps that is where the romance lies.

At about six in the evening I hear an exclamation from Michael, who is standing at the living-room window. He rests his whiskey on the masonry sill and indicates the sight beyond: a tide far advanced up the beach, encircling the lighthouse and cutting us off from the land. That queasy thrill returns; we are stranded. Solemnly we toast the spectacle, with the sense that our visit to the tower has really begun. For the next 24 hours we are beyond society. Of course, this is a little fanciful, for we have the moon to retract the water and let us off again tomorrow and our phone signal lassoes us to the mainland. But although we are not true castaways, even at this modest distance there is a primitive feeling of isolation, a compressive anxiety that for some reason we might not make it back.

Unlike their deep-sea tower colleagues, who were often marooned for months at a time, the Perch Rock lighthouse keepers nipped to and from the shore at low tide, enjoying an uncommon measure of freedom. Much valuable research about the keepers is presented in John and Diane Robinson's *Lighthouses of Liverpool Bay*. Born into a family of Lancastrian weavers, Samuel Appleton was appointed the first Head Keeper in 1830 and lit the tower on 1 March that year. He had been a sailor, though his journeys around the world are not recorded. At the time of his appointment he was in his thirties and living somewhere in the city. He seems to have been reluctant to move into or even closer to the Perch Rock, a fact which may be explained by the decadent character of the nearby coast.

Among lighthouse keepers he is unusual in being a regular commuter, for he neither lived on or near his station nor made cross-country journeys to new postings like the others.

Before each shift, he would take the ferry across the Mersey to Egremont, a small dock halfway down the Wirral peninsula. From there he walked for 2 miles to the northern shoreline, waited for the tide to retreat and waded out to the lighthouse.

The idea of a commuting lighthouse keeper fascinated me, so I decided to retrace his steps a few months before our stay. Boats no longer cross the Mersey along Appleton's old route, so I compensated by standing first on one side of the river and then on the other, looking at his points of embarkation. Over the water from the Liverpool Docks lies Egremont, with its two-up, two-down houses, its crowns of trees badging parks and its squat church towers. A respectable promenade girdles the whole thing. The view in the other direction, towards the city, is a sharp contrast. The Liverpool waterfront and the instruments of its fortune are proudly advertised and behind it the city swells away over the horizon. Though ruptured by modern development, the towers of the cathedrals and the Three Graces (the Royal Liver, Cunard and Port of Liverpool buildings symbolizing Liverpool's past maritime successes) speak with old power on the skyline.

From Egremont he would have walked due north through the former townships of Wallasey and Liscard. I trek along the Seabank Road, the descendant of the road that used to run from Egremont to the coast, and find it quietly suburban, with ribbons of two-storey red-brick houses lining the street. Crenellated towers pierce the roofline here and there: St James', All Saints' and the old water tower at Gorse Hill. The character of this place is pitched between respectability and dishevelment. I pass a burly red sandstone church with a weed-ridden forecourt, the worn, ornate railings of a public park and a small parade of shops. After a while the road slopes gradually and a prospect of the sea emerges. The distant tower of the Perch Rock lighthouse strikes a weird note in the sober landscape of regular roofs and terraced houses.

In Appleton's time much of the Wirral was sandy heathland, with a few buildings lining the roads. Until the construction of the fort and lighthouse there was little in terms of infrastructure and the population was sparse: even in the early nineteenth century a census recorded only 201 people. Most were in some way associated with the sea, their boats drawn up on the beach rather than on any formal quayside. Dotted around the heathland were small, unkempt buildings serving as homes or inns. The inhabitants were clannish and uneducated; some interbreeding was suspected. Until the fort was erected, the police and the army were far away, over the Mersey in Liverpool, so the place was effectively lawless. One particularly infamous house was Mother Redcap's, thought to have been operating since 1595. A cottage-cum-public house with many guises, it earned notoriety under the management of Poll Jones (the 'Mother' of the name), who provided a safe house for the smugglers and aforementioned wreckers prolific along this coast. It was demolished only in 1974.

This landscape remained fallow until the mid nineteenth century, when Liverpool's fecund shipping industry began to require better protection from privateers (pirates licensed by a foreign state) and the hazards lying offshore. Liverpool had overtaken nearby Chester, whose River Dee had silted up, as the principal centre for shipping in the north-west. A better road was made from Egremont to the fishermen's cottages and boats at the end of the peninsula. In the late 1820s, the lighthouse and fort were constructed. An intimidating sandstone triangle, the fort was located to cover the approaches to the Mersey and deal with the increasing problems of piracy generated by the merchant traffic moving in and out of Liverpool. Appleton would have paced along this new road, seeing at the distant end of it the new red bulk of the fort and the white needle of his workplace.

These things were at the vanguard of the change that would soon more widely envelop the locality. Potential was spotted by James Atherton, a wealthy Liverpool merchant, who purchased 140 acres of the township down to the coast and built villas in the 1830s and 1840s, spaced well apart so that they did not interrupt each other's views. He then went on a publicity blitz: local papers described 'the sea bathing rendezvous par excellence of Lancashire people of note', 'a most agreeable and desirable place of resort to the Nobility and Gentry of all the neighbouring counties'. The speculation was christened New Brighton.

The population climbed, but the experiment in gentility was thwarted, and the area's previously seedy character begat full-on decadence. The name stuck, but little else. Atherton, the driving force, died suddenly in 1838 and the development halted. New Brighton slowly became known for day-trippers instead of the anticipated 'people of note' and an infrastructure of piers, funfairs, donkey rides and other entertainments developed to serve them. Edifices like the New Brighton Tower were raised, which on completion in 1900 was 121 feet higher than Blackpool Tower and the tallest structure in the country. It was dismantled shortly after the First World War because the owners could not afford to repair it. At the turn of the century one publication sniffily remarked 'if truth be told, we fancy few readers would care to be recommended to New Brighton, except Liverpool people'.

With the day-trippers came sleaze to the seaside. A cluster of shanties and cafés known as the 'Devil's Nest' was the central corrupting influence, like the plughole in a basin. Originally a string of cottages housing the builders of the lighthouse and fort, it quickly degenerated into beer shops, brothels and gambling dens. Successors to the Mother Redcap opened establishments along the 'Ham and Egg Parade' – Doug had told us earlier that it was known as a place where you could get a cup of tea and a woman for a penny. The author of *Three Men in a Boat*, Jerome K. Jerome, wrote a startled editorial about the advances he received there in 1894 in *To-Day*, a paper he founded.

The bawdiness was inflamed by the soldiers garrisoned at the fort and by Appleton's colleagues, many of whom were feckless and drunk all the time. His two subordinates, John Williams and William Flockheart, were dismissed for being drunk in charge of the lighthouse on several occasions, and a third, Matthew Curwen, managed *nine years* of misdemeanours before his dismissal. The lantern and fog bell were neglected and on several occasions abandoned by keepers enjoying their shore leave in pubs and brothels. Appleton himself appears to have been a tense, introspective character who took no part in these pleasures. The striking thing is that all this went on so close to the tower. On one side of the balcony rail lay the sea; on the other, a decadent hinterland.

We feel Appleton's disapproving shadow later on that evening as we smoke a cigar with difficulty on the balcony, huddling against the cold masonry. It's windy up here, as the earlier forecast of strong weather suggested it might be. Long, dark ships pass out of the Mersey, moving slowly and firmly over the sea as if ironing it. Few of their captains can be scanning the seascape for our tower, but we watch their every movement like voyeurs. From most rock lighthouses, the view is monochromatic, the endless sea roaming like a savannah out of eyeshot, but there is plenty to see from this tower. At this junction of the Mersey with the Irish Sea, the waters bustle with vessels even today.

The great shipyards of Birkenhead were another reason for the bustle, lying directly over the river from Liverpool on the Wirral peninsula. Notable among them is the yard of Cammell Laird, formed in 1903 by the merger of two ironworks opened in the early nineteenth century. This was a centre for British shipbuilding comparable to Glasgow or Newcastle and came to specialize in the construction of iron-hulled and eventually wholly metal vessels. Peak production ran from the 1820s until 1947, during which time over a thousand vessels were launched from the Birkenhead slipways.

From the windows of the tower Appleton and his colleagues would certainly have seen the maiden voyage of the infamous HMS *Birkenhead*, launched in 1845 as the steam frigate HMS *Vulcan*, but later renamed and converted to a troopship. One of the first iron-hulled ships built for the Royal Navy, the vessel was wrecked in 1852 off the coast of South Africa while transporting troops to fight in the eighth Xhosa War, a now-obscure conflict. Hugging the coast - a perilous but faster progress - *Birkenhead* was carrying around 640 men, with some officers' wives and children also on board, when she struck an uncharted rock, broke her back and began to founder. As there were not enough lifeboats for everyone on board, the troops were ordered to stand fast on deck while the women and children were gathered into the lifeboats. According to legend, they did this in cinematic silence while the ship groaned, pitched wildly and came apart on the rocks. One survivor described how nothing was heard on the chaotic deck except the steadying bark of the commanding officer and the kicking of the horses.

Birkenhead sank 2 miles from the shore. Some soldiers were able to cover the distance, shrugging off their greatcoats and throwing the coins from their pockets, but others were drowned by the weight of their belongings, or were taken by exposure or eaten by sharks. Eight of the nine horses made it safely to land. The Victorian imagination was captured by such valour, and Kipling's poem 'Soldier an' Sailor Too' of 1893 is one of a number of works depicting the incident. The king of Prussia ordered an account of it to be read at the head of every regiment in his army. It is the earliest known example of the 'women and children first' principle being used in maritime evacuation. A lighthouse was later built at Danger Point to mark the uncharted rock.

Other ships built at Birkenhead included the *Ma Robert* of 1858 for David Livingstone's calamitous expedition to the Zambesi, reputedly the first ship formed wholly out of steel. One of the most prolific warships in the American Civil War, CSS *Alabama*, was put together clandestinely at Birkenhead in 1862 for the Confederate Navy; it passed Appleton and co. under a pseudonym and was recommissioned and armed out at sea to overcome British neutrality laws. Aircraft carrier HMS *Ark Royal* was launched from the Birkenhead slipways in 1937, one of five Royal Navy ships to bear that name, which originated with the 1587 flagship that defeated the Spanish Armada in 1588. Expertise at Birkenhead did not stop at ships: bizarrely, some early tube carriages for London Underground were also made there in the 1920s.

A stranger sight for the keepers would have been *Resurgam*, the name bestowed upon a prototype submarine launched from Birkenhead in 1879. Designed by a clergyman, the Rev. George Garrett, *Resurgam* was a central iron drum tapering to massive iron cones at either end, crowned with a modest conning tower. Like an early tank, this steam-powered oddity was hot, throbbing and exhausting to inhabit: altogether it was about 45 feet long and just large enough to stand up in. Though his design was cumbersome and not entirely stable, Garrett was able to convince investors to finance submarines for Russia, Greece and Turkey (he was eventually commissioned as an officer in Turkey's navy), but none of them worked well. When *Resurgam* was being transported through Liverpool Bay down to Portsmouth in 1880 for a Navy trial, problems developed with the ship towing it so the submarine crew swapped over to help with repairs, leaving the submarine unmanned. In their haste they forgot that *Resurgam*'s hatch could only be sealed from the inside. With the hatch left open the submarine quickly took on water and sunk, nearly dragging the ship down with it. Later, in what seems a rather tragicomic life, Garrett lost his savings on a failed farm in Florida.

Such a roll-call of seagoing luminaries (and oddities) brings home how differently British seas are used and perceived today. Michael and I don't know the names of the ships we observe passing us in the darkness; they do not resonate in the way that *Birkenhead* and *Alabama* and *Ark Royal* trembled excitedly in the national consciousness. And while Appleton and his colleagues were integral parts of a fully operational machine, we now camp in a redundant building. For the lighthouse keepers, the lifestyle was cyclical, precisely dictated by the clock: to keep the optic turning, chains and weights slenderly yo-yoing down and up the iron tube, the keeper on shift duty had to complete an exacting pattern of tasks in sequence, like working out a Rubik's Cube. The lenses had to be polished, the clockwork wound, the horizon scanned, the fog bell rung, the watchbook updated hourly, the lamp filled, the windspeed taken, the temperature recorded, the flag hoisted or lowered, the tide ball moved, the brasswork cleaned. Patience and exactitude were of the essence.

If we are explorers, then they were workers with a gravely important job to do, in which errors could be as costly as the *Birkenhead* shipwreck. There is a suggestive tension between the gravity of the job and the purported ribaldry of these keepers' behaviour, which was unheard of on deep-sea towers. Proximity to a depraved shore was too great an influence on the Perch Rock. We feel a flicker of awe for the recklessness needed to neglect such a perfectly worked-out machine. Casting our damp cigar ends over the rail, we go inside to bed.

The medieval chivalric romance *Sir Gawain and the Green Knight* recounts the journey of Sir Gawain through the Wirral (which he finds barbarous) to find the Green Chapel and the Knight therein. During this quest, 'Half slain by sleet, he slept in his armour / Night after night among the naked rocks.' On the uppermost bunk I awake stiffly, marrow-cold, feeling as though I too had slept in beaten metal. I take an inventory: hat, scarf, sleeping bag, Barbour, sweater, fleece, shirt, T-shirt, thermal trousers, trousers, four sets of socks. My mouth and nose are veiled in a dust-mask of the sort you wear when woodworking. The windows are flickering with the distant ripples of the sea, which today is dove-grey and tented with fog. The tower's hide - plasterwork, interlocking Anglesey masonry and thick marine paint - keeps out the fog, but not the February cold. Briefly I think of the others who awoke in these bunks before reporting for duty, which for many must have been their only truly private space. Writing of his time on the Bishop Rock in the 1920s, W.J. Lewis imagined how the woodwork and masonry around his head might hold the psychological residue of his predecessors, like pillows of prior feeling. There is something in that, I think. Lain quietly beside my head might be thoughts of a lover on the shore, hunger, tobacco, or emotional longings to be elsewhere.

We recall our promise to put the tower in order for Doug, but the morning's weather gives us little enthusiasm for the task. Last night's excitement has morphed into a schedule of chores: we have slept off the novelty of adventurers and are now the tower's humdrum inhabitants. The rooms are frigid and unwelcoming and there is no coffee to lift the mood, only the remnants of the whiskey. It would be accurate to say things look rather bleak. I climb down and find Michael in the living room, cold and frowning in a nest of satsuma peel.

The more we discuss the task, the more we realize how ill-equipped for it we are. The kitchen and lantern rooms are imperiously unclean, far beyond what two of us could achieve in a few hours. You would need specialists, and at least a week. The living room and bedrooms in between are rather more approachable, but as they are in a relatively good state of preservation we are reluctant to clean them too vigorously, for fear of destroying some of the more fragile plaster finishes or driving out the old shades of the place. We pull ourselves together and start to clean up the mess we have made – a surprising amount – then move on to sweeping the floors. We open all the windows we can and get air moving through the structure. That we were once housemates helps, as effective housekeeping requires surly instructions and a willingness to criticize each other's efforts. For a poet, Michael is a surprisingly thorough housekeeper. I, on the other hand, can find little enthusiasm for it. After half an hour or so the living room and bedroom have been swept out and returned to how we encountered them. We move up to the lantern. Doug specified that the bird carcasses were to be removed from this space. I sweep towards Michael, who shovels them into an old crate near the door. We gag a bit against the smell. Gingerly we shuffle to the seaward side of the lighthouse as the wind kicks up. Michael has drawn the short straw and heaves over the dead birds; as if from nowhere, a live cloud of screaming gulls swarms about the tower to pursue each feathered skeleton, which has been lifted and flown shoreward by the wind.

We are beginning to think that Doug's suggestion we clean the tower was purely whimsical – he must have known how limited our efforts would be. While making our preparations

10. The bunk beds, 2016

at the fort the previous afternoon we had talked to him about his unusual possessions. The fort is an imposing, triangular building with massive red sandstone walls, pointing out to sea and presenting a flat elevation bookended with squat turrets to the land. There is a large arched opening in the centre and a drawbridge over a small moat. Through this lies a triangular courtyard paved unevenly with old flagstones. Little flights of stairs lead off to gun emplacements and other chambers. It was in this space that we donned our waders and Doug told us how his father had seen a Spitfire downed by enemy action in Birkenhead Park during the Second World War. Years later, the plane having been buried, they both returned with shovels and dug it up, salvaging the powerful and battered Rolls-Royce Merlin engine and lugging it to the fort. This was the start of the building's transformation into a museum of local and military history, which Doug inherited about twenty years ago. The lighthouse came with it, acquired almost by accident. Much of his energies are poured into the fort, curating the exhibitions, putting on gigs (mainly Merseybeat outfits, which feels right – there is much that is Merseybeaten about the fort and lighthouse), and generally keeping the building in use.

Though it stands a little way offshore, the lighthouse identifies visually with the museum and, disused, could almost belong to its permanent collection: less architecture, more artefact. There is a note of ambiguity about its future. A few weeks after our visit, Doug informs me that there are plans emerging to relight the tower as part of a programme of conservation work. The documents he sends suggest the new light will be cosmetic, unsuitable for navigation, and I'm not sure how to feel about this. Would it be somehow inappropriate, like a trivialization of the building's vital former function? The dilemma here is that of all historic buildings that are difficult to access and costly to keep up. Doug mentioned a previous owner's scheme to convert it into a honeymoon suite, making quips about carrying a bride over the threshold and into a keeper's bunk. An alternative use that preserves the tower's character seems unlikely, yet it doesn't seem right to abandon it to nature. Now that it is redundant, the Perch Rock, I think, is a monument to the art of life-saving, an act which continues at the operational rock lighthouses too remote to be seen.

Doug visits only occasionally, usually after winter storms, to check on the state of the rooms. I asked him what the future held for the tower, and a flicker of weariness crossed his face. Doug's ownership of the tower is an anomaly. There are some coastal lighthouses elsewhere in the country owned by private individuals, but these are like any other terrestrial building, only with a large light fitting, capable like other buildings of adaptation and reuse. To own a decommissioned rock lighthouse out in the water is a very different thing. Its design is specific to one purpose that, when departed, leaves a poignant but impractical afterglow. I felt he wanted to say that the tower was a great burden, but for whatever reason he didn't.

At about half past two in the afternoon, the tide slowly creeping out, we see Doug leave the fort across the freshly exposed sand. He ambles across parts of the beach where years ago the remains of Mesolithic round houses were momentarily uncovered by the tide, to the delight of local archaeologists. There was time for a brief dig before the tide eventually erased them. He paces out a line from those round houses to this one, stopping at the lip of the water left around the tower. We have ghosted about enough in the shut-up rooms and holler excitedly down to him from the window, a bit like children sighting a parent. He waves back, amused, as if relieved we have lasted the night.

Interlude: Blackwall

An experimental lighthouse

1866,
BLACKWALL, LONDON

I make my way from East India DLR station along the lip of a dual carriageway roaring with London-bound traffic. Old litter from passing cars is embedded in the hedge and strewn on the footway, without anyone to pick it up. A slip road branches from the carriageway, reaching towards the River Thames. Either side of the road are poorly kept brick walls, steel security fences, corrugated-iron shacks, lifeless windows, no active frontages of any sort. Now and then, I step back from the edge of the narrow pavement as lorries bowl past, up to join the main road.

Around a bend in the river stands an experimental lighthouse, brick-built, diminutive and now rather down-at-heel. Positioned amidst the scrubby industrial districts of Blackwall, east London, rather than ocean swells, it's a little detour in from the sea. Between 1866 and 1988, it was the technological testing-ground for the lighthouses of England, Wales and the Channel Islands. Lantern apparatus for remote rock lighthouses was trialled here, in an environment crowded with homes, offices and everyday occurrences.

I had expected this urban lighthouse to be easier to reach than those offshore, but there is an oddly similar feeling of going out on a limb, even though I have come in from the edges of the country towards its centre. Both share settings - shipping lanes, ring roads - in which people are secondary.

Though their Herculean structures initially command the attention, rock lighthouses owe this daytime form to their night-time function. They are crowned with devices as fascinating as the granite pillars below. Destined for the country's periphery, virtually all of these fittings were forged in Britain's heartlands, in the industrial Midlands and other urban manufactories. Whereas the granite for the towers was dug out of places almost as wild as the sea – the unforgiving landscapes of Cornwall and Scotland – the delicate fittings for the lights were forged in metropolitan settings.

Bearing warnings of the most grievous hazards, the rock lighthouses were unsuited to experimentation, and their remote positions and confined spaces made inconvenient destinations for experimental equipment. It made sense to run trials where the stakes were lower and where the logistics were easier, at coastal lighthouses or inland industrial sites. Or a mixture of the two, which is what I found.

Though light testing and development were not exclusive to Blackwall, I was drawn here because it is the only purpose-built experimental lighthouse in Britain and Ireland. Experiments by their very nature are fleeting, temporary acts, leaving few long-term traces; at Blackwall, the experimental lighthouse serves as permanent evidence. And it has a charisma that compelled me to seek it out, an incongruity shared, in a sense, with my offshore subjects. After all, a lighthouse standing within a city is as arresting as one rising sheer out of the ocean.

Candles burned in the lanterns of the early rock lighthouses. At its summit, Henry Winstanley's strengthened Eddystone of 1699 had a lantern '8 square, 11 foot Diameter, & 15 foot high in ye upright Wall; having 8 great Glass windows and ground Plates for Squares, & conveniency to burn 60 candles at a time, besides a great hanging lamp'. It is not recorded precisely how the 60 candles were arranged within the lantern; presumably in concentric octagonal or circular rings, perhaps chandelier-mounted.

Each 'great Glass window' was actually a large metal grid holding 36 small 'ground Plates' or squares of glass. Glass-making at this time was limited to the production of small, thick panes of glass; the technology to produce larger, slimmer panes would not be developed until the later eighteenth century. Winstanley's 60 candles would have been considerably impeded by his lantern's metal frames and the thickness of his glazing. Saline residue from stormy conditions would have further exacerbated the problem. And situated as the Eddystone was, 13 miles offshore from its supply base at Plymouth, the logistical problems were acute. On occasion, storms held back the supply boat for long enough to almost exhaust the lighthouse's candle supply.

In his lantern, John Smeaton hung a 'chandelier' of 24 candles arranged across two wooden rings, one smaller than the other, suspended on ropes adjustable by a system of gears and pulleys. Watching it lit for the first time from Plymouth, he remarked that it was 'much like a star in the fourth magnitude'.

But candles were a troublesome light source. As it consumes the wax, the flame descends, resulting in a navigational light fractionally higher or lower according to the age of the candle. Repeated across a number of them, especially if lit unevenly and at different stages of consumption, the effect would be like an uneven constellation of small flames. Depending on the quality of the tallow (a kind of fat) or wax in the body of the candle, the flame might smoke heavily or burn dirtily, diminishing the power of the light and fogging the lantern.

It was not just rock lighthouses that suffered from these inefficiencies; the need for clean, reliable and user-friendly sources of light was effectively a global one. Homes, workplaces and streets needed lighting, just as much as the seas. This was a lucrative problem to solve and Ami Argand, one of those who partly did so, was dogged for years by legal skulduggery over the patent of his invention. Argand was an eighteenth-century Swiss chemist, sometime brandy distiller and hot-air balloon pioneer. In 1784, he invented a new style of oil lamp, improving vastly upon existing models that had remained essentially ancient in design and operation.

He found that placing a cylindrical glass chimney over a hollow wick greatly enhanced the draught within, the freely flowing air producing a clean, smokeless flame far brighter than a candle or old-style oil lamp. A rack and pinion mechanism for adjusting the position of the wick allowed the light to be kept in a fixed position, rather than slowly descending as the wick was consumed.

Brightness (or 'luminous intensity') is measured in units of candela, each equating to the flame of a single candle. Just one of Argand's lamps produced a light up to 10 candela in strength, and they would quickly oust candles and fires from lighthouses across the country as the preferred illuminant. For instance, inside the Bell Rock's gleaming new lantern of 1811, 24 Argand lamps were arranged in neat rows on a rectangular metal frame. Attached to each was a brass reservoir holding 24 oz of spermaceti oil, enough for each lamp to burn for eighteen hours (equivalent to the longest night in the Shetland Isles). These 24 Argand lamps held a potential brightness of 240 candela, a great improvement on the Bell Rock's predecessors.

> **catoptric** adj. of or relating to a mirror, a reflector, or reflection [from the ancient Greek *katoptron* 'mirror'].
>
> *OED*

But one naked flame looks much like another. And whatever the quality of the flames, if left naked and unfocused then they cast their rays inefficiently in all directions. Reputedly, some ancient lighthouses used polished stone or mirrors to catch and reflect stray rays back in a chosen direction. Later on, in the eighteenth and early nineteenth centuries, this approach was adopted for lighthouses and became known as the 'catoptric' system.

In the 1760s, one William Hutchinson, a Dock Master of Liverpool, had experimented with placing metal bowls studded with mirror glass behind the flames of the Wirral lighthouses. They looked like inside-out disco balls cut in half. On my journeys in Scotland, I had learned how Robert Stevenson's stepfather, Thomas Smith, had devised hemispherical metal reflectors to enhance the lights of the New Town, and later applied them to Scotland's early lighthouses from the 1780s onwards. Conceived first for Edinburgh street lights, then refined and perfected for stormbound lanterns, the principle has since found other terrestrial applications: for instance, in car headlights.

So Robert Stevenson incorporated parabolic reflectors behind each of his 24 Argand lamps. Each was a sheet of copper with a silver-plate interior, hammered into a parabolic curve, like a shallow dish. A parabolic, as opposed to spherical, curve provides the optimum angle to scoop up all the escaped rays and focus them in one direction. Cumulatively, this gave Stevenson's lantern far greater power than 240 candela, making it appear like a 'star of the first magnitude' in comparison to a single candle.

Stevenson was not the first to employ Argand lamps and reflectors in a rock lighthouse: the system had been previously installed at the first Longships lighthouse of 1796. But that light, and those of preceding rock lighthouses, had been white and static. By the early nineteenth century lighthouses proliferated on and off the coastlines around Britain and Ireland. Many of them showed an unmoving light of the same colour, and sailors struggled to tell them apart.

This raised another problem: however powerful the light, if indistinguishable from others nearby it could create a risk of navigational errors or, worse, shipwreck.

To give the Bell Rock an identifiable light or 'character', Stevenson proposed a light that would alternate equally between red and white flashes. And rather than design a fiddly mechanism to make the lamps themselves flash on and off, he found a simpler solution. While the lamps would remain steadily burning, the frame on which they were mounted would slowly revolve. As each alternate set of white and red lights passed the faraway observer's line of sight, the distance and lightspeed made them appear as brief flashes.

Red glass was installed in front of each of the reflectors on the two narrower sides of the rectangular frame in the lantern room. It was turned by a weighted rope, wound around a drum, that dropped down through a groove cut in the inner walls of the upper four rooms and then through an iron column

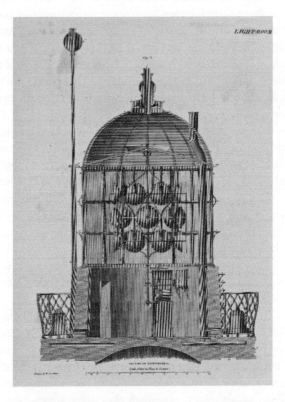

11. A cross-section of the Bell Rock
lantern showing the lamps and
reflectors, 1824

in the centre of the rooms below. Over eight minutes, the mechanism wound itself out and turned the chandelier twice through 360 degrees.

Powerful enough to be seen from a distance of 35 miles, the Bell Rock set a new standard for lighthouse illumination, perfecting not only the lamp-and-reflector technology, but also introducing a new method of identifying the rock lighthouses at night. The ideas quickly spread. In 1810, Trinity House disposed of the candles in Smeaton's Eddystone lighthouse and retrofitted it with Argand lamps and reflectors. Successive new rock lighthouses – Haulbowline, Trwyn Du, Plymouth Breakwater – were designed to incorporate this arrangement from the outset, with the requisite provision for oil stores and route for the winding mechanism inside.

In 1830, John Foster Junior's Perch Rock lighthouse was fitted with a similar arrangement to produce one red flash succeeded by two white flashes, with intervals of one minute between them. Suddenly, all I had seen during our night in that tower begins to make sense. The central, cast-iron tube housing the rope and weights. That rusted clockwork assemblage in the deactivated lantern – it had been the winding mechanism for making the lamps and reflectors turn. Only the lights themselves were absent.

Reflectors had been installed in the majority of British lighthouses, but no sooner was this upgrade completed than the technology was superseded by the work of a man across the Channel. Augustin Fresnel was an ingenious young French engineer and scientist who, while stuck in a dreary job overseeing road-building, conducted extensive researches towards the wave-theory of light. A by-product of these was the dioptric lens, a method of concentrating light into a more brilliant beam than any reflectors.

dioptric adj. 1. serving as a medium for sight; assisting sight by refraction. 2. of refraction;

refractive [from the ancient Greek *dioptrikos*, from *dioptra*, a kind of theodolite].

OED

Instead of mounting the light in front of a reflector, Fresnel's apparatus surrounded it with lenses. Rather than *reflection*, his dioptric lens worked on the principle of *refraction*, gathering the rays emitted by the light and magnifying them into a beam through a circular optic. Ingeniously, a series of concentric rings of annular glass prisms radiating from the central 'bull's-eye' captured stray light rays and directed them towards the central beam, resulting in a light far more powerful than any produced by a reflector, which could only ensnare most, but not all, of the escaped rays.

The Parisian night of 13 April 1821 was cold and clear, with excellent visibility. In a stellar urban display, Fresnel tested his new lens for the first time, alongside two rival reflector systems. They were set up either side of the Paris Observatory and the audience – a large crowd comprising the French lighthouse commission, sailors and assorted bystanders – gathered at the opposite end of the city, on the hill of Montmartre. In her authoritative account of Fresnel's work, Theresa Levitt relates how his new lens 'so clearly outshone its competitors that the [parabolic] reflectors now seemed irrelevant ... a rare chance for France to beat England in technological advancement'. His lens was installed in the Cordouan lighthouse, the oldest and grandest in France, standing at the entrance to the Gironde estuary halfway down the west coast. Consuming half the oil, it cast as much light as 38 of the best English reflectors.

Soon afterwards it was visited by Robert Stevenson, who immediately saw the significance of the innovation and sought Fresnel's advice on introducing the system to Scotland. Mirroring Fresnel's Paris display, in 1833 he arranged for examples of French lenses, prototype English lenses and Scottish reflectors to be erected 12 miles from Edinburgh. Atop Calton Hill in the centre of the city, the Commissioners of Northern Lights watched Stevenson demonstrate the superiority of the

French optics. Under Robert and then Alan Stevenson, Fresnel lenses were gradually fitted to the lighthouses of Scotland.

These public displays of light were dazzling spectacles that brought into the heart of society what had previously been confined to the coasts. They made extremely visible the advances in light-mongering that were being made in both France and Scotland in the early nineteenth century. By contrast, English lighthouses relied on reflectors, variable in quality, often indifferently maintained. As long ago as 1818, Robert Stevenson had visited the first Longships lighthouse off Land's End and found 'ragged and wild-like' keepers who barbequed meat in their lantern room, where the reflectors were dulled with fat and smoke to the point where the light shone brown. This was an extreme example.

Both Scotland and France had the advantage of their lighthouses being under the coherent control of a single authority. Management of English lighthouses, however, was then split between Trinity House and a mixture of private owners, making a unified and consistent degree of illumination impossible. This changed in 1836 when an Act of Parliament was passed to abolish the principle of privately owned lighthouses and give Trinity House the power to buy out their leases. That same year, Trinity employed Michael Faraday as their science advisor. He is today best known for his experiments as an independent scientist, such as his discovery in September 1821 that an electrified wire dangling into a bowl of mercury – a good conductor of electricity – would continuously rotate around a magnet placed in the centre of the bowl. From this came the discovery of electromagnetic rotation, the concept behind the electric motor.

Trinity had first established themselves at Blackwall in 1803, leasing a plot of land at the junction of the rivers Lea and Thames and building a wharf and a few warehouses for the storage of buoys and sea-marks. Among these nondescript buildings, Faraday was given a workshop and improvised experimental lantern, and he was swift to ponder how electricity could be used to power the lights. One of the first systems he tested was an electric carbon-arc light, zapping an electrical spark between two carbon rods connected to the opposing ends of a battery. After two years of trials between 1852 and 1854 he concluded the system should remain in the laboratory, unsuited to a lighthouse. It was too fiddly for the keepers to operate, produced an unreliable light and choked the lantern with acidic fumes from the batteries.

Another system Faraday trialled involved a carbon-arc as before, but fed this time from a steam-powered electromagnetic generator. It had been developed in the late 1850s by Frederick Hale Holmes, a chemistry professor, from Faraday's 1821 discovery of electromagnetic rotation. Holmes had found a method of producing a steady and reliable quality of light between the carbon poles, superior to the erratic sparks of the previous system. Faraday's experiments with the machine at Blackwall showed it produced a light far more brilliant than any naked flame, and resulted in the installation of steam-driven electromagnetic generators in lighthouses at Dungeness and South Foreland on the Kent coast.

Society would not be widely electrified for at least another 50 years, so these were early and pioneering usages of electric light. But although the generating machines were too bulky and cumbersome for immediate application to the rock lighthouses, Faraday's legacy was eventually realized when, in the later twentieth century, electric motors and generators descended from his discoveries were installed in the towers.

As well as his experiments with power, Faraday considered the problem of clarity. Although they burned with clean flames, the oil lamps produced condensation on the lantern glass, affecting the quality of the light. Lanterns, especially those of rock lighthouses, were not really ventilated at all. As the panes of glass were fixed in place, the only source of ventilation was either the door to the balcony or small grilles in the roof. After many visits to English lighthouses, and much tinkering in his Blackwall workshop, Faraday devised a chimney that would expel moisture within the lantern and keep the glass clear while preventing weather from affecting the delicate light. So successful was this invention that it was installed not only in all English lighthouses, but also in the Athenaeum and Buckingham Palace.

Under the impetus of Faraday's experimentation, England's lanterns had nearly reached equilibrium with the dazzling lights of Scotland and France. But, until the 1860s, there were no permanent traces of these displays or designated places for them to occur. They were improvised on elevated points in cities, or, in Faraday's case, a nondescript workshop and hurriedly fashioned lantern. As the lighthouse network grew from the mid nineteenth century onwards, and imperial traffic entered British seas in ever-increasing numbers, the nation's first, and only, experimental lighthouse was constructed by Trinity House at the Blackwall wharf. It was to be an enduring expression of that which had previously been ephemeral.

Late in 1862, James Douglass became chief engineer to Trinity House. He had been born a few miles upstream from Blackwall, at Bow, and he would become one of the most celebrated of the English lighthouse builders. Just then, work was commencing off the Land's End coast on the Wolf Rock, a rock lighthouse that would prove to be a particularly fraught and protracted venture.

At the same time, Trinity House required new buildings at their Blackwall wharf to cope with the pressures of modernizing their lighthouse network and concentrating the power and range of their lights. Despite Faraday's work at Blackwall, a Royal Commission into Lighthouse Administration of 1858 had found that English lighthouses and aids to navigation were still technologically inadequate and woefully administered, the result of the lingering inefficiencies of the mixed-ownership system. There was still much room for improvement.

One of Douglass's first jobs as chief engineer was to design a new chain-and-buoy store that would incorporate a proper lighthouse tower for optical experiments. As the name suggests, the building's other function was to house the great piles of sea-chains and enormous buoys that were brought here for maintenance from the coastlines Trinity House administered. By now a grizzled veteran of their remotest sites, he returned to the Lea Valley from Land's End. It would be a complete departure from the granite towers and remoteness that had been occupying his time.

I find my destination announced by an enormous iron buoy exhibited at a bend in the road with TRINITY BUOY WHARF prominently lettered on the sides. Through a gateway, past a jumble of nondescript brick buildings, and suddenly the wharf opens into a view of the Thames. Skirting the Isle of Dogs to my right, it winds onwards through now-nameless industrial districts, eventually to meet the Channel. Ships still ride at anchor in its throat, but few of them come this far upriver, the larger commercial vessels more easily accommodated at Tilbury Docks. Decline of the Docklands began when imperial trading networks slackened and new cargoes, specifically containers, demanded boats larger than the ancient pool of London could accommodate. Craft on the Blackwall stretch of the river now are mainly Thames clippers, pleasure vessels and tugs lugging great barges of the capital's building materials or waste products.

The first bricks of the experimental lighthouse were laid in autumn 1864. As he was simultaneously occupied with the construction of the Wolf Rock, Douglass must have marvelled at the ease of this build. No seas crashed over the building site; no arduous voyage was necessary to reach it every day; no seasonal violence of the seas prevented the men from working in the winter.

Constructed of brick laid to a polygonal plan, as opposed to stone dovetailed together into a circle, this is a very different kind of lighthouse, owing more to terrestrial methods of building than the swashbuckling engineering of the rock lighthouses. Unlike them, it is not a free-standing tower, but is built into the east wall of a roomy, square-plan brick warehouse with two big triangular gables. Its circular lantern pokes proudly above the rooftop, criss-crossed with diagonal glazing bars and topped with a jovial weathervane.

Originally, the building was designed to have two lanterns, the surviving one at the east end and a now-lost one at the west end. There, Michael Faraday's previous experimental lantern was incorporated into the roof, emerging directly from the slates in contrast to the new eastern lantern, which rose on its own tower. This newer lantern was made in a foundry behind the Bank of England. Appropriately enough, all lighthouse lanterns were themselves fiercely bright at the moment of their creation, the molten state of the iron glowing a profuse red-orange until cooled, tempered and assembled to house another kind of light.

In 1866, the building was completed, a surreal hybrid of warehouse and lighthouse. Today, all survives but the western lantern, which was removed in the 1920s for reasons I cannot identify. Douglass's squat, polygonal tower, crowned with an octagonal lantern, is like an unusual experiment in a different genre. It has a modest brick character absent from its remote, majestic siblings, yet lights ultimately destined for them shone first inside its lantern.

12. A view of the Blackwall wharf showing the new experimental lighthouse, 1868

Experimental displays began flashing into the sky above the capital. On 19 March 1869, the night 'proved cold but very fine and well adapted for seeing lights'. A group of sea-captains and engineers stood expectantly on Charlton Hill in south-east London, mist and pipe-smoke lingering above them. Seen from this vantage, London was like a darkened model of a city, smudged here and there by moisture in the air, but otherwise clear in its details and silhouettes.

Suddenly, as if responding to a pre-arranged signal, strong lights began emitting from a point within the view, pulses of red, green and white light that flew south-east for some distance and printed themselves faintly on the slated rooftops of Charlton and Shooter's hills. For those within range, it must have been as though a strange phosphorescence had invaded their homes, the attic rooms and north brick walls of these suburban houses tinged suddenly with ruby, with emerald, with brilliant white. Looking out at the source, north towards the Thames, an observer would have seen two strong but faraway lights, one changing colour, the other a steady white. They continued to beam for a while, sometimes pulsing regularly, sometimes flashing intermittently. A few hours later, they ceased abruptly.

Two experiments were conducted at Blackwall that evening. The first was to find the right proportion of ruby to clear glass in the design of the lens for the Wolf Rock lighthouse, then nearing completion. No other lights in the vicinity around Land's End shone red, so the Wolf's proposed intervals of red and white flashes would easily identify it in those seas.

But it was not as simple as installing ruby and clear glass in equal measure around the light source. As Stevenson had found when specifying his scheme for the Bell Rock, a red beam is less intense than a white beam because ruby glass filters out all other light apart from the red spectrum. As a result of these differing properties, equal proportions of those glasses would produce unequal flashes of those colours. To properly measure the difference, the engineers rigged up a white light in the western and a coloured light in the eastern turret of the experimental lighthouse. From their temporary observatory at Charlton, just over 2 miles south-east of Blackwall, they could calculate the proportion necessary for red and white flash to show at equal intervals.

While Argand lamps were used for the Wolf Rock trials, the second experiment that evening tested electricity, building on tests conducted by Faraday in the 1850s. To capture and focus all the rays from the electrical light, Faraday had recommended an optical lens instead of a parabolic reflector.

From Fresnel's first designs a sophisticated array of lenses had come into being, ranked in 'orders' according to their size and power, with the sixth order being the smallest and the first order the largest. Comprising thousands of flawless glass prisms mounted on a complex metal cage, these lenses far surpassed reflectors in their scale and sophistication.

That 1858 Royal Commission had been a clarifying moment, exposing just how antique English lights seemed in comparison with the Scottish and the French. Consequently, Trinity House paid greater attention to optical technology and joined forces with Chance Brothers, a Birmingham glassmaking firm that had manufactured all the glasswork for the Crystal Palace in just six months for the 1851 Great Exhibition. From the dizzying range of products displayed therein, Britain had established its reputation as the world's workshop.

French ingenuity was honed by British manufacturing. The Chance workshops were able to achieve the highest quality of glass and efficiency of production, and found in Fresnel dioptric lenses the ideal outlet for their expertise. Among the displays at Crystal Palace was a Chance Brothers dioptric lens, the first of the 2,400 the company had manufactured by 1951. As production mounted, the firm were responsible for a number of innovations to the design, developing a revolving cage-like structure for the lenses to completely envelop the light. They also provided the glass panes for the lighthouse lanterns, including the one at Blackwall.

Returning to that March evening in 1869, a Trinity House delegation including the Deputy Master and its Captains, Dr

13. A dioptric lens on show
at the 1851 Great Exhibition,
London

Tyndall and James Douglass, stood on Charlton Hill in quiet
anticipation. I imagine them, top-hatted and muffled in greatcoats against the chill, consulting their pocket-watches and
peering impatiently into the distance. At the appointed time,
red and white lights beamed from the lanterns of the experimental lighthouse. After several cycles, they deliberated and
agreed that the proportion of ruby to white glass in the Wolf
Rock lens should be 11 to 4 to bring the lights into equality.

Secondly, they observed the trial of an electric generator
and dioptric lens to find the order of lens that best suited an
electric spark instead of a flame. At the International Exhibition of 1867 held in Paris, Trinity House had proudly exhibited
a third-order dioptric lens manufactured by Chance Brothers
and a prototype electric generator. This larger lens was set up
in the western lantern and a smaller sixth-order lens in the
eastern lantern of the experimental lighthouse. Identical electric lamps were placed within each of them connected to the

same generator. The watchers were amazed at the stellar quality of light emitted from their new equipment, and the larger
third-order lens cast it more powerfully than the other.

For later rock lighthouses, only a first-order dioptric lens
would suffice, revolving in a mercury float to eliminate friction in the turns. For the second Bishop Rock (1887), Chance
Brothers manufactured a 'bi-form' first-order apparatus, consisting of two tiers of first-order hyperradial lenses stacked
one atop the other, each tier lit by 8-wick Argand-style lamps.
In fine weather, only the lower tier of lens was illuminated,
producing a beam 40,000 candela in strength. In poor weather,
both tiers were lit, producing an aggregate 230,000-candela
flash. The same arrangement was used for Douglass's Eddystone (1882) and the Fastnet (1904), though the specification of
the latter was more advanced. Incandescent petroleum burners were placed in the centre of the upper and lower tiers of
lenses, which were catadioptric rather than dioptric. Under
this system, the Fastnet's beam was a staggering 750,000 candela in strength, a star beyond any magnitude then achieved.

Blackwall's experiments were interrupted by the Second
World War, when enemy action destroyed some of the work-
shops, though the experimental lighthouse was unscathed.
Lights continued to be shown from it until 1988, when Trinity
House ceased its operations here and vacated the wharf.

A friend of mine used to work for Trinity House at Blackwall in his twenties. Between 1985 and 1987, Clive was an
office junior, responsible for ordering quantities of raw materials for the coppersmiths, the carpenters and other trades
employed in the workshops. He describes to me a hierarchical,
1950s-style office culture, with tea and biscuits, and sherry at
Christmas, women nowhere to be seen.

He worked in the former costing-office, now a nondescript two-storey brick building with concrete lintels over the
windows. From it Clive witnessed the wharf in the final throes
of its maritime business, and the gradual running down of an
operation still Victorian in character. Lights were tested from

the experimental lighthouse, buoys and chains were brought here for repairs, bespoke lighthouse parts were fashioned by skilled tradesmen – James Douglass's workmen would have recognized their methods. For instance, to make a metal lighthouse fitting – anything from a handle to a valve – a pattern maker translated a drawing into a wooden prototype, which was then pressed into a box of wet sand to create a mould, filled with molten metal to create an approximate cast of the part needed.

I fit the buildings I see to Clive's stories of them. The oldest is a former oil-storehouse built in 1836 that now bears a sign saying 'Electricians Shop', where cheeky apprentices ground metal ingots on lathes. Behind it is the Proving-House Range, an extremely long, thin single-storey building built in 1875, designed for laying out extensive lengths of sea-chains, which were tested for strength between two rattling stretching-engines at either end. Nearby is the Fitting-Shop to the north and the Boiler Maker's Shop to the south, both constructed in the early 1950s, two-storey capacious buildings in which much of the manufacturing was done. Contingents of men in overalls ebbed and flowed between these workshops and the canteen, pivoting on the lunch hour, when the tumult of metal-bashing, hooting, rumbling and sawing stopped abruptly, so starkly you could practically hear the sound of downed tools. Yeast from a nearby refinery scented the air, mingling rankly with the odour of Thames mud when the tide was out.

Particularly ingenious were the gadgets made to advertise the presence in the sea of the large, unmanned marker buoys. On some, there was mounted a bell opposed by four hinged hammers, pealing randomly according to the swells below. On others, wave motion moved a plunger through a central tube, pushing air through a whistle mounted above. By night, they were lit with acetylene burners, the raw flame sequenced into semaphore flashes with a mechanism to control the gas flow. Buoys and other navigational aids were brought here from Northumberland, from Wales, from Penzance and the coastlines in between. Lolling in rows on dry land, their giant chains piled into the corners, their immensity echoed that of the sea.

Apart from the experimental lighthouse, what is most noticeable about this place today is the feeling of absence, of great activity slowed to a trickle. By the late 1980s, Blackwall was a mechanical operation in an electrical age. It was cheaper to manufacture components in other locations overseas, and cheaper for those components to be mass-produced and disposable rather than handmade and repairable. For the lighthouse system, these impatient economic forces created the prospect of automation. As long ago as 1965, the Haulbowline lighthouse had been automated, but it wasn't for another few decades that the treatment would be applied to English lighthouses. In 1982, James Douglass's Eddystone became the first of Trinity House's rock lighthouses to be automated; Robert Stevenson's Bell Rock was the last, in 1998. The dioptric lenses were taken from their lanterns and replaced with smaller models or LED fittings. In some cases, solarization removed any trace of the lighthouses' intricately wrought mechanics. Visiting engineers replaced defective parts rather than repaired them. Circuitry replaced gadgetry.

Former industrial districts are now commonplace in London and other major British cities. Usually, their machinery and activities are what give them their visible identity; when these are gone, all that is left behind is a group of nondescript buildings, mute to their former function. The wharf is different in this respect. With its experimental lighthouse, it maintains a link with its nautical past. Just as manufacturing has flowed out of east London, so the deep sea has flowed out of Blackwall. Yet there is just enough remaining to sense the connection, still not entirely severed, between this lighthouse at the core of the nation and the rock lighthouses at its edges.

I stand in the experimental lantern, thinking not of light but of incongruity. Usually, such criss-crossing glazing bars and diamond-shaped glass panes hold uninterrupted views of the sea. But from the Blackwall lantern, I see glossy new developments rising on the south side of the Thames, a sleek cable-car conveying nobody anywhere, the yellow prickles of the Millennium Dome, and suburban London in the far distance. I smile at the sight of Charlton Hill, rising away to the south-east, and think of the eyes of those sea-captains once straining for this lantern.

With their medieval, clannish roots, Trinity House had been slow to embrace the possibilities science offered, especially compared with the innovators of Scotland and France. But the Blackwall experiments showed how the brethren had come to understand the centrality of trials and tests to their lighthouse operations, and had learned to question, to hypothesize (or at least to employ eminent scientists like Faraday to do this on their behalf).

Most fascinating of all is how the experiments were embedded in cities, in Paris, Edinburgh and suburban London, recalling the time when a greater mixture of activity was to be found in these capitals, when hypotheses were tested near homes. Trinity's presence at Blackwall conveys how lighthouse business had been more central to the fabric of national life; now, their main technical headquarters are located less visibly at Harwich in Essex. With the experimental lighthouse at its heart, Trinity's Blackwall wharf brought the heavy sea into the country's capital. A sequence of red and white lights designed for the inhospitable seas around the Wolf Rock first shone over the slate rooftops of Charlton, briefly aligning places that were otherwise leagues apart.

Wolf Rock

A notorious lighthouse

1870,
8 MILES OFF LAND'S END, CORNWALL

'One consolation is that no-one has yet discovered how to build houses on the sea,' wrote an exasperated John Betjeman of new housing sprawling over the Cornish countryside that he cherished. As well as being a poet, he was a seasoned campaigner and author of polemics against such spoilage of places. But as he was a keen architectural critic and acolyte of the Victorian period in particular, I think he would have been delighted to be corrected in this case. By 1934, when he made his comments, nearly four centuries' worth of superlative risk-taking and ingenuity had, indeed, built houses in the sea.

Because lighthouses were positioned so far away from any settlement, the keepers who operated their machinery had to live within them. And, as there was no space on the reefs for conventional outbuildings, their living quarters had to be incorporated into the towers, above the fuel-stores and below the lantern room. Despite the jostling proximity of three men in two or three rooms, their lives are usually characterized as mute and lonely, likened to that of hermits, seemingly the closest forerunners for their idiosyncratic lifestyle.

Out at the country's edges, they worked shifts that were two months long, with relief boats visiting at these intervals to exchange keepers clocking off with those clocking on. The transfer of these men and their belongings was unbelievably precarious, using a breeches buoy, a zipwire on which they were hauled by their colleagues from the rocking boat up to the slippery entrance ledge. The changeability of the sea meant reliefs were often delayed for weeks or even months – it was simply too dangerous to attempt a landing in anything other than reasonably calm conditions. And all this before they had even commenced work.

Their shifts were spent within rooms fitted with cooking ranges, patterned curtains, china crockery, wireless, perhaps a religious text hung on the wall – all the trappings of domestic normalcy. But these couldn't completely disguise the cell-like feeling of the spaces, the curved walls and the strong gales and waves that thudded against them. In many of the towers, every article of furniture was curved to follow the walls, most strikingly the bunks in which the men slept. Sometimes, truly extraordinary rooms were created, like the Strangers' Room at the Bell Rock, with its fashionable rugs, panelling and plasterwork. Such elegance was a surreal thing to find off the storm-lashed Arbroath coastline.

The men had to be all-rounders, capable of dealing with a mercury spillage in one moment and darning a sock in the next. They were trained in housekeeping and DIY as well as in their machines. From dusk until sunrise their nights were divided into watches. In these periods, their sole focus was the light, attending to the complex apparatus keeping the lamp burning and the crystalline optic turning, sounding the fog signal when necessary and watching the sea between times. This they always kept at arm's length, for they were never taught to swim.

These were no ordinary lives on the margins. At the Longships tower off Land's End, keepers and their wives would converse with semaphore flags and telescopes on fine days, the former from the towers and the latter from the cliffs. In her laudable account of that lighthouse, Elisabeth Stanbrook relates how, on the morning of 15 November 1956, frantic flag-waving told one Longships keeper, Bob Eley, that his wife had given birth to a baby girl.

On the Smalls Rock in the early nineteenth century one of the two keepers suddenly died of natural causes, placing the other in a macabre dilemma. With relief a fortnight away, the corpse would putrefy if kept in the tower, yet an improvised sea-burial might look as though he had murdered the man. So, the surviving keeper lashed his dead colleague to the tower's exterior. According to some renderings of the story, heavy weather broke open the improvised coffin, dangling the corpse's arm against the window as if it were knocking to come in. The survivor was found mad by the relief boat when it eventually arrived a week later.

Employed by the lighthouse authorities covering England, Scotland and Ireland, lighthouse keepers had a job for life, a steady progression to the post of Principal Keeper, and afterwards a decent pension. While the role of keeper existed, rock lighthouses were regularly visited and were better known on land among the communities linked to them. But in the late 1980s and 1990s a fundamental change shook this system. One by one, the buildings were converted to automatic operation, the lights kept on by remote control from operating stations on land, their keepers released from service to return to a more conventional way of life.

I tracked down the last of them, men like John Boath and Gerry Douglas-Sherwood, who had once lived at the edge of the kingdom and were now to be found in cities and shires: Edinburgh, Norfolk, Truro, normal places with schools and supermarkets. Though they would deny it, a charisma of distance and extremity still clung to them. Their reminiscences helped me to understand something of the truth about their former lives at the margins, and that rock lighthouses were poorer buildings without them. Regularly ventilated, swept and polished, the air heavy with tobacco, bacon and Brasso, their inhabited phase was their heyday. Since they were automated, the rock lighthouses have led silent, hermetic lives out at sea, clicking their lights on at dusk and extinguishing them again at dawn.

For the majority of keepers, rock lighthouses were notorious postings. At coastal lighthouses, the houses were more conventional, the living quarters not circular but square or rectangular like other terrestrial buildings. Instead of the strange intimacy of three men confined in a granite tower, at the coastal lighthouses keepers lived with their families, in greater semblance of a normal life. Vegetables were grown in kitchen gardens, laundry fluttered on washing lines, and children played idyllically in view of the sea.

None of this domesticity was found on the offshore stations. Such was their notoriety that postings to the towers were at best grudgingly borne or at worst refused altogether. For instance, two men in succession declined promotions to Principal Keeper (the highest possible rank) at the Bell Rock lighthouse, even though to decline such a promotion was to never be offered it again, with the loss of the generous pension and other perks it entailed. This was related to me by John Boath, the man who had become Principal at the Bell Rock in their place. These men, he told me, simply couldn't stand the thought of life inside that rock lighthouse, and chose to end their careers rather than face it. In contrast, John was more sanguine about the privations that came with the role.

(John, incidentally, is made of strong stuff. When keeping a lighthouse in Orkney, he once lost a fingertip in an engine accident and had to be rowed to the Scottish mainland at the dead of night with no anaesthetic to see the surgeon. This he did without complaint.)

Some rock lighthouses were particularly shunned. Among them was the Wolf Rock, positioned 8 miles off Land's End in the Atlantic, where the sea is 20 fathoms deep and regularly feral.

With the rocks of the Longships and the Runnelstone reef, it forms the outermost corner of a hazardous triangle off the Land's End coast. It is one of the rock lighthouses most exposed to the pummelling of the Atlantic. No photographs ever seem to show its surrounding water becalmed. Even in fair weather the sea knots constantly at the lighthouse's stepped foot. Above, swathes of the pale granite are discoloured, as if bruised, hinting at bigger waves held in abeyance. A creamy ring of white surf seems always to surround the rock, like a force field thrown up to repel visitors, or foil escapees.

Although it is not the furthest rock lighthouse from the shore, it was perhaps the most arduous of them to build, with ten years between drawing board (1860) and first lighting (1870). When finished, it quickly developed a reputation among keepers for its sense of incarceration. Rarely could the relief boat get close enough to the rock to exchange keepers clocking on with those clocking off, which frequently extended postings there far beyond the customary six weeks. Apocalyptic storms during Christmas 1947 saw its keepers confined inside the tower from the beginning of December until 15 February 1948, their provisions just about exhausted until an audacious helicopter pilot dropped supplies to them.

Now, as then, the Wolf is a formidable thing to reach. I could find no boats that would motor anywhere near it. Trinity House, the Wolf's operator, was unable to countenance an official visit. So, running out of options, I plotted a less orthodox journey. One of the tower's ex-keepers, Gerry, now lives in Norfolk, about as far from the Wolf as it is possible to be in England. As I couldn't get to the Wolf, I went to see him at his Norfolk home. Our vehicle would be conversation, rather than motion, for a journey in the mind's eye.

Gerry was Assistant Keeper on the Wolf Rock lighthouse between 1975 and 1977, and forty years on I meet him for the first time in a railway station car park. He's a warm, wiry 68-year-old with the sideburns of an avid motorcyclist. He shows me to his van, an ex-Cambridge Constabulary Police vehicle, and we motor along deserted roads in the direction of his home on the Norfolk–Suffolk border. My curiosity is immediately piqued.

When I first made contact with Gerry, I saw an opportunity to sail to the Wolf on his reminiscences. He is the archivist for the Association of Lighthouse Keepers, a society for ex-keepers and lighthouse enthusiasts (somewhat inevitably, I am now a member). I sensed that he held troves of undigitized and unpublished drawings, photographs and information about the Wolf and other rock lighthouses, which, combined with his own compelling experiences, would show me the Wolf more genuinely than if I witnessed it in real time. And I was curious to see what kind of home he had now made in the bosom of the countryside, after years of living at the extreme periphery of the country.

Our drive to his house winds through many East Anglian

14. **Strong waves engulfing
the Wolf Rock, 1971**

villages and market towns. Ancient buildings are everywhere: coaching inns, merchants' houses, hunched alehouses, flint churches, decrepit warehouses, and Gerry seems to know a fact or two about them all. The countryside seeps through the gaps between them, resplendent in autumnal colours, almost displacing the storm-lashed Wolf in my mind.

Along the way, Gerry gives me an overview of his career. Hailing from Eastbourne, on the East Sussex coast, he has ancestral roots in Scotland, East Anglia, Wales, Eire and Berkshire. He had a straightforward schooling but, rather than go to university, he became an apprentice engineer to Volkswagen Motors Ltd in St John's Wood, in London. Afterwards he dallied for a while before discovering, in a careers encyclopaedia, a Trinity House recruitment campaign for lighthouse keepers. Tempted by the variety of places to be posted to and the opportunity to use his engineering skills (engines still make him tick), he applied and entered service in 1970 as a trainee Supernumerary Assistant Keeper (SAK).

Trainees moved around a lot, spending fortnights or months at different stations to learn the ropes. His first posting was at Dungeness, in Kent, a vast, flat geological oddity where the lighthouse warns against a coastline altered constantly by the tide. This was followed by a month at the Trinity House Training School, in Essex, where he learned signal flags, Morse code, First Aid, bread-making and other essential skills. A few of his fellow trainees could only just boil water, so needed to be shown how to keep a house.

There followed a peripatetic sequence of postings to a mix of land and rock lighthouses, as if designed to unmoor a young keeper from a fixed sense of home: the Penlee Point Fog Signal Station in Cornwall, Portland Bill lighthouse in Dorset, Les Hanois rock lighthouse in Guernsey. At the Trinity House workshops in Blackwall, he was trained to operate and maintain basic lighthouse machinery and equipment, taught how to fight fires and operate radio systems, most of which he mastered in the first month of a two-month course. It was at the South Bishop lighthouse, in Pembrokeshire, that he qualified as an Assistant Keeper, his first permanent position. Then, in 1975, he was posted to the Wolf Rock.

Gerry speaks slowly and crisply, without an accent, despite having spent so much time in different parts of coastal Britain where the dialects are many and infectious. When I visit Cornish relatives, I can never stave off the burr that creeps onto certain syllables. But that, perhaps, is a matter of regression in a childhood place. For lighthouse keepers, the nature of their work naturally made them less visible in a community than, say, the vicar. Traversing so many localities, they were really part of an invisible national network; parachuted into places for fixed terms, living mostly on the fringes of communities, they had fewer opportunities to let a place shape their voices. Particularly if their posting was offshore.

After half an hour on the road we pull up by a row of garages on a modern housing estate. I follow Gerry to a small terrace of two-storey houses and we enter the first on the row. A hot-food stand, such as you see in truck stops, swallows most of the driveway and large barrels of sunflower oil and vinegar stand in orderly rows near the door. Gerry explains that it belongs to his co-residing landlord and that four people share the house; he says its suits him well. This house-share reminds him of his lighthouse postings, only without the sense of duty or the circular rooms. You have your own space, but meet and chat in the communal areas, and everybody minds their own business.

Upstairs, his room doubles as his office and the Association of Lighthouse Keepers archive. I have been in few rooms so crammed with information and artefacts. Everywhere there are boxes of documents, scrapbooks, plans, drawings, photographs and books. Upon patterned wallpaper is hung a framed architectural drawing of the Needles lighthouse, in the Isle of Wight, where Gerry was promoted to Principal Keeper, and a framed ALK lifetime-achievement award. He roots through the archive assembled in the nooks and crannies of the room and extracts bundles of drawings and photographs. With coffee and documents, we perch on the edge of the bed and venture out towards the Wolf Rock lighthouse, far beyond these East Anglian walls.

Before the tower was built upon it, the Wolf Rock was said to emit low, elongated howls during storms, the products of high-speed wind streaming through a fissure in the stone. Tradition suggests these grim 'howls' bestowed the name on the rock. I like this story, but struggle to imagine how the fissure would remain free of water in heavy seas, allowing the sound to be produced. It is only my conjecture, but I think there is a simpler, more primal explanation for the name. Wolves have for centuries been quintessential objects of fear; submerged reefs and rocks have similarly menacing qualities. They lurk in sea-scapes, much as wolves lurk in landscapes. To draw the analogy further, there is usually no warning of their sudden and merci-less attack.

Until the eighteenth century, the only scheme for a nav-igational aid on the Wolf Rock was for a wave-rung bell, like the one supposedly placed on the Scottish Bell Rock in the fourteenth century. But Trinity House resisted this 'jingling scheme' on the grounds that idle fishermen would tamper with it, believing the 'musick' scared away fish.

There was one man, though, who was undeterred by the Wolf's notoriety. In the 1780s, Lieutenant Henry Smith, Royal Navy officer and amateur lighthouse builder, had patrolled this stretch of coast in HMS *Squirrel* and knew it well. In my mind's eye, he is a dashing young officer clad in breeches, sharply cut coat and cocked hat, sword and sextant near to hand. He spent some time hustling on behalf of numerous shipowners and merchants before Trinity House granted him a lease to plant a beacon on the Wolf Rock, alongside two other schemes to build a lighthouse on the Longships and a beacon on the Run-nelstone reef nearby.

Despite indignant opposition from Land's End residents, who thought (correctly) that such schemes would deprive them of shipwreck booty, he laid the first stone on the Longships on 18 September 1791. This tower, probably designed by Trinity's architect Samuel Wyatt, was a three-storey affair of local granite. It survived until the 1870s, when it was replaced by a taller, sturdier Longships lighthouse still there today.

History does not precisely record Smith's motivations to build these aids to navigation, but this was the time of privatized hazard-marking, where speculators would obtain leases on hazards and fund the risky construction of beacons and lighthouses in return for the fees levied on ships passing them.

For the entrepreneurial Lieutenant Smith, the year 1795 was momentous: he had managed, with great difficulty, to have a beacon fixed to the Wolf Rock and his Longships lighthouse first shone a light. But the operations ruined him financially. Extraordinarily, he seems to have concluded both of them from the King's Bench Prison in London, where he was imprisoned for debt early in that year. It is with Smith, the first man to mark it, that the Wolf first acquires associations with imprisonment.

While in jail in London, Smith managed his affairs through agents in Land's End and tried desperately to raise a mortgage to pay off his creditors. A dispiriting decade passed, during which he was transferred to the Fleet Prison in London and the sea had felled his beacon (almost immediately after it was put up) at the Wolf, a wrought-iron mast 20 feet high, with a bronze model of a Wolf's head at its apex. Gallingly, his Longships lighthouse began to generate profits but, as Elisabeth Stanbrook explains, Trinity House deemed him unfit to receive the money and diverted it to his extended family instead.

In one of the more unusual episodes in the history of rock lighthouse building, Robert Stevenson called on the lieutenant in prison in 1806. Stevenson had visited Smith's Longships lighthouse in 1801, in advance of building his own Bell Rock lighthouse, and wanted information on how it had been designed and executed. By this time Smith had been imprisoned for ten years, and must have cut a pitiful figure: gaunt and bearded, his once-splendid uniform replaced with prison rags. Although no details of their exchange survive, they sound almost comically incompatible, the reckless, tragic lieutenant on one hand, the fastidious, virtuous engineer on the other.

They strongly disagreed about the possibility of a lighthouse on the Wolf Rock, Smith believing it useless to try and Stevenson coming away muttering, unfairly, that Smith 'had no real capacity for sea-works'. Three years after this testy interview, Lieutenant Smith died in the Fleet Prison on 28 October 1809.

Though the Atlantic shrugged off his beacon there, schemes to mark the Wolf continued to be dreamt up. A large bronze model of a wolf, with cavities to replicate the supposed howls of the rock, was proposed but never implemented. Stevenson's meeting in the Fleet Prison must have lingered in his mind, for he continued to speculate on how the Wolf could be marked. He visited the rock in 1813 and again in 1818, wrestling with the difficulty of the site. Eventually, in 1823, he proposed a stone tower that would cost £150,000 and take fifteen years to build.

It seemed like too much money and time. Other, cheaper proposals were advanced and attempted, such as a cast-iron cone packed with masonry from which stemmed a timber mast with a ball at the apex. Even this simple design took four years to build, being completed in July 1840. The following winter the sea snapped off the mast (oak, 12 feet thick) as though it were a cocktail stick. A new wrought-iron mast was eventually installed in August 1842. That winter, the sea changed tack and *bent* the new mast (7 inches thick) 3 feet out of true, as if it were tired of simply breaking things.

Meanwhile shipwrecks continued to pile up on the Wolf. In January 1855, a French sloop named *Railleure* was sailing from Bristol to Bordeaux, its master Captain Roi an experienced sailor who had made the journey many times before. Despite his detailed knowledge of the waters off Land's End, the ship struck the Wolf at two o'clock in the morning. Five minutes later it sank, but the passing Customs vessel *Badger* managed to save the crew. In 1859, the English smack *Caurinus* was carrying roofing slate from Padstow to Sidmouth when she smashed into the Wolf during a heavy gale. Luckily, a passing vessel named *St Croix* rescued her crew and delivered them to Fowey the next day.

Other crews were not so fortunate. On 16 March 1861, the *Astrea* was carrying Russian wheat and woven mats from Falmouth to Newry (near the Haulbowline lighthouse). At two thirty in the morning she hit the Wolf, but instead of sinking, stuck fast upon it. Hurriedly the crew went for the lifeboats, but the first was carried away by the sea with only one occupant (a Norwegian, who survived) while the second was washed away before it could be boarded. As the sea closed in, their boats stolen away, the crew fled for a small platform halfway up the ship's mast. Heavy seas trapped them there, violently rocking the stricken ship. About two hours later, a fishing boat heard the endangered sailors' cries and tried to get close enough to help them. Suddenly two substantial waves folded over the *Astrea*, drove her off the rock and into the deep water where she quickly sank. There were only three survivors.

A few months later, on 1 July 1861, James Douglass was landed alone on the Wolf Rock. While his companions remained in the boat at a safe distance, he picked his way carefully over the dark and rugged surface, examining the rock. To the casual bystander (though this was not a place to find them), he might have looked like a Victorian naturalist collecting specimens. In fact, he was there to judge the most auspicious place for his masons to hack out a 40-foot circular foundation pit. Below, the waves broke and crashed, and he knew he would not have long before they started to lunge for him.

Eventually he settled on a point in the middle of the Wolf near the old broken-masted beacon. He produced his instruments, and double-checked the gradients. As he had foreseen, the weather changed abruptly and rogue swells began to buffet the rock, preventing the boat from landing to rescue him. Grimly tying a line around his waist, he jumped from the Wolf into the water, and was hauled fully clothed through the chaotic surf. Seemingly immune to the drama of this, he later remarked drily: 'This mode of embarking was frequently re-sorted to afterwards, for getting workmen off the rock, when caught by a sudden change of weather.'

By 1860, Trinity House had built rock lighthouses on the Smalls Rock (replacing the preceding timber structure, completed in 1776) 20 miles off the Welsh Coast, the Hanois Rock at Guernsey (completed 1862), and the first Bishop Rock (1858), the latter being similar to the Wolf in its isolation and exposure. Since Lieutenant Smith had planted his beacon there in 1795, attempts to mark the rock had been skirmishes instead of decisive victories. But, buoyed by their successes on those other tricky sites, Trinity House decided the time had come for a lighthouse on the Wolf Rock.

At this time, their chief engineer, James Walker, was 79. Six rock lighthouses and countless other engineering projects lay to his credit. His Hanois, Smalls and Bishop rock towers were sophisticated renderings of Smeaton's archetype, but with notable refinements. Where Smeaton had sketched the tapering profile of his tower freehand, the curve in the profile of these new towers was compass-drawn, geometrically pro-scribed. That for the Wolf is described by Douglass as a 'concave elliptic frustrum, the generating curve . . . a major axis of 236 feet'. In their lanterns, prismatic lenses replaced candles and reflectors; at their bases, stepped instead of smooth masonry courses hindered waves climbing up the sides. A new lateral-vertical system of dovetailing had been introduced for Les Hanois, which took Smeaton's lateral-only system of dovetailing the masonry to its logical conclusion: stones interlocked with those above and below them, as well as to their sides. Walker designed the proposed lighthouse for the Wolf Rock much as he had the other three towers, and it shares their basic measurements: 116 feet high, 41 feet wide at the base, tapering to 17 feet at the top masonry course; or, as Douglass beautifully put it: 'at the springing of the curve of the cavetto under the lantern gallery'.

But, in his advancing years, Walker was too frail to per-sonally oversee the building of the Wolf Rock. Enter James

Douglass, a 34-year-old Londoner whose rough baptism into rock lighthouse building had been in the heavy weather of the Atlantic. He had helped his father construct Walker's Bishop Rock lighthouse west of the Scilly Isles, a grim and exposed site comparable to the Wolf. In 1862, on Walker's death, Douglass succeeded him as chief engineer to Trinity House.

The Wolf's foundation stone was laid on 6 August 1864. Working only in the summer, the masons had spent the three preceding years hacking and blasting out the foundation pit. As they could only land on the contorted, vertical north-east side of the Wolf, they had to build a 'small' (14,564 cubic feet of stonework) landing-platform before they could begin anything else. The men's safety was prioritized: they were 'compelled' to wear cork lifejackets at all times, and formed their own life-insurance syndicate. But for much of the time the sea would not let them onto the rock to work: in 1862, for instance, they had landed only 22 times between March and September.

Over the next six years, the tower gradually rose. Such was the integrity of its design that the incomplete building survived each winter storm intact, except for that of November 1865. That winter, 34 stones of the fifth masonry course were smashed away by a broken ship's mast tumbling in the surf. Nonetheless, in July 1869, Deputy Master Sir Frederick Arrow set the last piece of masonry in place, aided greatly by a steam-powered crane installed in the upper stages of the new tower (the first use of steam power in rock lighthouse construction). A quick 'topping out' builders' ritual marked this important milestone, followed by a liquid reception on the schooner anchored alongside, where the dignitaries drank the health of the new building arm-in-arm with the masons.

Over the following months they installed the interior of the lighthouse, which was as clever and accomplished as the masonry. Steep, curving gunmetal ladders were lowered into place between the floors. Clocks were hung in every room. Large oil drums and barrels of provisions were hoisted into the lower levels. The penultimate room before the lantern, the service room, became an office, with curved desks and cabinets to hold the log-books, spare components, charts and other essentials. The carpenters built the bedroom in the floor beneath: five bunks arranged on two tiers, with oak-panelled partitions separating them and small cupboards below for bedding and personal effects. All this formed one exquisite piece of joinery, set on a curve to exactly follow the curved granite walls. These sleeping spaces have been known as 'banana bunks' ever since.

This was truly a circular world. The next level down became a living room, with a bespoke cast-iron Cornish range for heating, cooking and washing. Between them, carpenters filled the space with beautifully finished and veneered curved oak dressers and cupboards. Delicate consignments of crockery and tableware filled the shelves and drawers. In the oaken walk-in larder under the staircase, jars and paper packages were arranged on a cool slate shelf. A new table and round-backed chairs awaited their first occupants.

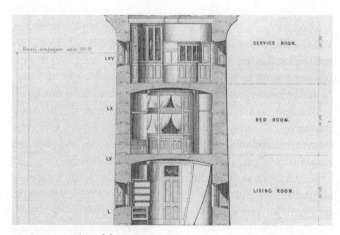

15. A cross-section of the tower
showing the living rooms, 1870

It had been easy enough to get into Haulbowline and Perch Rock. These towers in the shallows required only a modicum of boating, wading and ladder-climbing to reach their innards. But a lighthouse in the deep, like the Wolf Rock, is an entirely different proposition. Until the widespread availability of helicopters, the only way to reach them was by boat, but these sorts of places have few safe anchorages. The sea is never calm enough to risk getting too close, even for local boatmen who know the wrinkles of the hazards like those of their own hands. So, hair-raisingly, the lighthouse keepers and their supplies had to be hauled up a breeches buoy from a boat up to the landing stage of the tower, as follows.

As the boat approaches, the Wolf's gunmetal doors clang open, and the keepers emerge with large sections of steel crane that they hurriedly assemble on the landing stage. This could be the first time in weeks they had walked further than 12 feet – the diameter of the tower's rooms – in a straight line. The relief boat is moored between the rock and a permanent mooring buoy a little way off. On the rock, the keepers cast off the crane rope into the bobbing boat, ready for the first load.

Some stores and belongings are hauled across first, then the keeper clocking on, his torso and feet looped in a bowline. It is an unorthodox start to a working day, dangling above the sea and inching towards the landing stage. As the boat bounces on the swells, the line stretches and slackens, sometimes drooping low enough to immerse him in the sea. If caught by a particularly rogue swell he could be flung towards the rocks. Once he is safely on the landing, the off-duty keeper is sent down the wire, and lowered happily into the relief boat. With the exchange concluded, the ropes are unfastened, and the boat makes its way back to the tender, and the mainland.

To illustrate how difficult this was, Gerry shows me an old Pathé film of an aborted relief at the Wolf Rock lighthouse in 1952. The narrator intones: 'Oil for her generating plants, fresh water for her crew. It's been twenty-nine days since she was last visited, and stocks might be getting low.' I look again at the Wolf. I had not thought of this tower as *she*.

Men clad in oilskins hurry about the deck of a Trinity House lighthouse tender, packing a smaller boat with supplies. The camera cuts now and then to the captain, a lined face above a splendid uniform, who deftly manipulates the engines to keep the ship stationary against the swells. A nervous-looking young keeper clambers in, wearing a primitive 'Mae West' life-jacket chalked with 'WOLF' over a smart uniform. The relief boat is lowered into the water and makes for the rock, the wobbling Pathé camera over the shoulders of the sailors pointed towards the distant tower.

'Across the boiling waters the coxswain's verdict is heard. It's tough when relief is so close at hand, but the spell of complete isolation – that at least will be at an end.' Finding the sea too rough to safely transfer men between the boat and the landing stage, they instead manage to convey a metal canister of letters and newspapers to the tower, on the end of a kite flown from the balcony rail of the Wolf to the relief boat: 'The link with home is unbroken [through the letters], but the prospect of a spell on shore must stay postponed.' With a winsome script and suspenseful score, the clip is very much of its time. But underneath the commentary, the racing wind and surf are plainly audible, and the relief boat seems small and fragile.

These monthly reliefs exchanged keepers who had finished their two-month shift with those who were beginning theirs. They were an opportunity to replenish stores, swap faulty parts, and bring long-craved news and letters from family and friends. For the keeper due his shore leave, it was hard to come to terms with an aborted relief. W.J. Lewis vividly describes the sense of anticipation on the appointed day: 'To keepers on relief day a fine morning is an answer to their prayer . . . joy is sharpened by excitement. It is wonderful to be alive and looking back on the past weary months of exile knowing that in a few hours it will all be over.' Now imagine seeing a squall kicking up and the boat turning back. This was a unique sort of frustration, as powerful as the sea and as difficult to bottle up.

But reliefs were achieved here, just as they were at other rock lighthouses. And for the keepers who had spent two or three months incarcerated on the Wolf, nerves jangled by the wave-quakes against the granite walls and the gloominess of the cell-like rooms, it was relief in all senses.

Visitors, too, had to endure this precarious zipwire act. Frederick George Kitton, a journalist from *Strand* magazine visiting the Eddystone in 1892, described how 'to the novice the process is somewhat exciting . . . I am soon in a position to realise the thrilling sensation of hanging on a rope in mid-air, jerking and swaying over the boiling surf.' In her account of the Bishop Rock lighthouse, Elisabeth Stanbrook writes of a pleasing encounter between two bishops in August 1936. In order to confirm two of its keepers as Christians, the Bishop Rock lighthouse was visited by the Bishop of Truro, Joseph Hunkin, who was hauled up the line in his minister's robes. A photograph shows the bespectacled, smiling bishop suspended in mid-air, his granite namesake looming in the background.

Rigged up on the landing, the crane looks like a giant rod and line, and these transfers were like fishing for men. Only rarely was there trouble landing the catch. Sometimes it was only a slip, such as in November 1894 at the nearby Longships lighthouse, where the line slipped and Supernumerary Assistant Keeper Jackson tumbled straight into the sea. Luckily, he was hauled back into the boat unharmed, though 'well-nigh exhausted, and terribly frightened'. But sometimes tragedy struck. One August day in 1903, Assistant Keeper Sidney Hicks clambered down to the lower part of the Bishop Rock to fasten the mooring rope for the relief boat. As he climbed back up, he slipped on the ledge outside the doorway and fell into the sea. A rogue swell carried him off, and his body was never recovered. Confined as they were in the tower, the grief of his colleagues must have been particularly intense.

Out on these rock lighthouses, keepers placed their lives in one another's hands. This was a far cry from the water-cooler tedium or team-building exercises of conventional workplaces. Instead, there is a certain kind of rapport established among colleagues who fish each other from the surf.

Through the drawings, we enter at ground-floor level. Gerry's description of the Wolf Rock reminds me of Haulbowline:

the bare, darkened granite walls, the dull, mineshaft smells of minerals and oil. The relief crane is kept here, in a large canvas bag dangling from a bolt in the wall. A manhole in the floor covers a 1,400-gallon fresh-water tank. Alongside, under the staircase, is the coal bunker. The heavy gunmetal entrance doors are locked tightily shut by bolts and two large metal stays.

Above this level, traversed by steep iron steps, are the lower engine room and station batteries, the winch room and the upper engine room. He describes these lower rooms so evocatively that I can almost smell them. They are strictly functional, with machines, parts and fuel glimmering in the semi-dark.

But above is the kitchen, the domestic hub of the house. The heart of such a room is its hearth, but by Gerry's time on the Wolf in the 1970s, the original curved Cornish range had been substituted for an angular coal-fired Rayburn. This was part of a programme of modernization in which the Victorian circular furniture was broken up and replaced with rectangular chipboard furniture awkwardly fitted to the curved walls. The loss of these original furnishings, as carefully conceived as the tower itself, was a tragedy. Probably it was reasoned that, by the late twentieth century, lighthouse keepers should no longer have to live like their Victorian forebears. But Gerry's account of the life sounds just as gritty, just as peppered with small discomforts.

Even in the 1970s, the Rayburn was the only source of heat in the lighthouse, and the thick granite ceiling swallowed the warmth before it could reach the bedroom above. For cooking and washing, they used rainwater captured in a tank high up in the service room. Unfortunately, that was frequently polluted by debris from the Rayburn chimney landing on the lantern roof. It could be seen by the way the water turned a bluey-green copper colour when in contact with soap, for the solid fuel they burned was heavily sulphated. Luckily, their drinking water was brought from the mainland, and rested in the cool reservoir at the tower's base. Hot water came from a copper tank on the stove. Sometime after midnight, during middle watch (0000-0400), they washed in the kitchen using a plastic bowl in the sink.

Adverse winds sometimes blew grit and dust back down the chimney and into the kitchen, filling the room with toxic fumes, and sometimes snuffing out the precious fire. Then the keepers would stagger about the circular room, coughing and fanning the acrid smoke out of the windows, having flung open the gunmetal storm shutters. These were normally sealed shut, but had tiny vents letting in small shafts of daylight, and the place was mostly crepuscular as a result. Opening the shutters was risky as waves could quite easily reach up the walls and flood the rooms through any gaps, even on the tower's upper stages.

We study a photograph of the bedroom above the kitchen showing the original bunks. These at least were spared the axe. Gerry explains that he did his best to secure the only bunk with a window, beside which he could settle the pillow and read by natural light. It was common, he says, to be interrupted by the thump of a wave racing over the window inches from his face, 60 feet above sea level. Lying prone was the best way to feel the tower shudder in a storm.

Now and then, my eye wanders to the window of his Norfolk bedroom. Fields roll away from the house and occasionally a car passes sonorously along the road. No waves thump against these windows, but in this room, filled with so many memories, the sea seems to press heavily on the walls.

A door slams - one of his housemates is home for lunch. There is the bleep of a microwave and the tang of a shepherd's pie rises from the kitchen below. Boots clump up the stairs. As we leaf through technical drawings of the lighthouse, I build up a picture of Gerry and his colleagues in a running battle with their workplace.

As well as trying to poison them with sulphurous water, the tower made life uncomfortable for its keepers in other ways. Just below the kitchen sat a pair of generators - one powered the navigational light at the top of the tower and the other the interior lights, water pump and appliances used by the keepers. These ran around the clock, and Gerry describes the sound as a constant *b-b-b-b-b-boom* reverberating through the granite walls. Sooner or later you learned to sleep through it, he says, but perhaps not through the blast of the fog signal, switched on to warn ships away when the lighthouse was hidden by thick fog. This was something like a wind instrument, sounded by air pushed through a reed, for 2.5 seconds at 30-second intervals, perhaps a different sort of howl.

In any case, they were regularly woken by engine failure, the keeper on night watch in the lantern galvanized into life by the sudden dimming and fluctuating of the light source. After rousing the others, two would climb hastily down to the engine room to see what had happened while the third kept an eye on the main light. It was not unusual for them to have to switch the navigational light on to the other, domestic generator, and repair the faulty one in a blackout. Gerry describes the scene without much emotion, but it must have been edgy: two keepers rebuilding a broken-down engine by torchlight, calling up to the keeper in the lantern in the hope that all is well.

I put it to Gerry that the Wolf sounds like a crafty, unforgiving landlord, doing its utmost to keep them on their toes. He agrees that it could be quite a rough life, but is reluctant to anthropomorphize the tower. He is phlegmatic about the extraordinary life that he once led – 'We took a philosophical view,' he says – and shrugs when I ask him about the lighthouse he inhabited being completely engulfed by powerful storms. It reminds me a little of hearing veterans tell their war stories, momentousness bound in understatement. I suspect he's rather sick of being asked.

We talk briefly of his ancient predecessors, such as Dubhan, the Irish monk who supposedly kept a light at Hook in the fifth century, or Richard Reedbarrow, a hermit who maintained a light on the Humber in the fifteenth century. Gerry has great respect for the achievements of these distant figures, stoically burning their lights through freezing fog, storms, rain, covered in ash, eking out meagre stocks of fuel, keeping a warning going for early seafarers. Duty on the rock lighthouses was a form of hermitude, I suggest, fishing for traces of mysticism or romanticism in his career. No, he says bluntly, keepers have always been keepers.

Gerry tells me that, in his time at least, most keepers were atheists and passed their time between watches with sturdy, straightforward hobbies. They made ships in bottles, or studied for Open University courses. Many became ardent naturalists or keen birdwatchers. Somewhat grotesquely, one or two found the time to learn taxidermy. Few seem to have been tormented artists. Such people would never have been employed: lighthouse authorities looked for worldly people with deep reserves of patience and mental stability rather than someone who might be fascinated by a shipwreck.

I ask Gerry what he thinks of Tony Parker's history of lighthouse keepers, for which Parker conducted interviews with working keepers in the 1970s, and which portrays their roles rather less positively. The overall impression there is of a job beset by lonely tedium, and where postings to rock lighthouses were generally dreaded. Boredom was, it seems, not confined to the late twentieth century: when Thomas Carlyle and a companion visited Inchkeith Island lighthouse in 1877, their first impression of its keeper was of: 'a man whose whole speech and aspect said: "Behold the victim of unspeakable ennui".'

Parker spoke to one Principal Keeper who compared himself to 'a kind of clockwork man'. Another was an alcoholic on shore and used his rock lighthouse shifts to dry out. Towers bisected marriages, and frequently ended them. One keeper's wife talked about the gnawing emptiness she felt at the sight of a tower. But, to my surprise, Gerry seems to find these portrayals too sensationalist, remarking that Parker 'didn't talk to the right people'. Perhaps the most revealing moment during our conversation is when he tells me that in his entire twenty-year career as a lighthouse keeper, the Wolf Rock is the only one from which he ever requested a transfer.

*

Until I met Gerry, I thought that the reason for the Wolf's notoriety was the hellish seas that imprisoned the keepers. However, this explanation seemed too easy when I considered that conditions were the same at some of the other rock lighthouses around the British and Irish coasts. Keepers at stations like the Bell or Bishop Rock also suffered delays to their reliefs, and at the Bishop similar heavy weather. Yet they did not have the reputation that characterized the Wolf. There must be something more to this tower. And so there was.

Sometime after he left the Wolf, between 1982 and 1994, Gerry was the Principal Keeper at the Needles rock lighthouse off the Isle of Wight. It was a place he describes as a 'very comfortable station altogether'. In contrast to his three years at the Wolf, his long service at the Needles testifies to the fact that it was a posting he enjoyed. The tower is set into the chalk at the outermost point of the Needles formation, pointing west towards Swanage. Like the Wolf, it was designed by James Walker, but it was completed ten years earlier, in 1859. These siblings differed utterly. Rather than the stormbound Atlantic, the Needles nestles in calmer seas, not very far from the soft Dorset coastline. The landing at this tower was easier, relief more assured.

The Needles' walls are needle-like, rising straight up instead of tapering on a curve. When Gerry first landed there, they enclosed handsomely appointed rooms, with curved oak furniture and other fittings still intact. Instead of the steep, narrow iron ladders at the Wolf, these rooms were traversed by an elegant spiral stone stair. Crucially, they were much bigger: 15 feet in diameter to the Wolf's 12 (though a little smaller in width when the furnishings are taken into account). And above all, they were brightly lit: except for the engine room, there was no need for gunmetal storm shutters at the Needles, where the reflected sparkle of the sun on the water danced on the ceilings of the rooms.

Even the drama and tragedies were differently pitched. The worst thing Gerry saw from the Needles was a ship getting stuck on the wrong side of the Shingles Bank, which was

eventually towed off undamaged by a tug. By contrast, a fellow
keeper on the Wolf Rock heard the Penlee lifeboat tragedy
unfold over his radio set. In December 1981, the MV *Union
Star* suffered engine failure and was blown off course into
Mount's Bay, 8 miles east of the Wolf Rock. The little Penlee
lifeboat, the *Solomon Browne*, rode out into the storm to rescue
the crew, attended by a Royal Navy helicopter. The winds were
hurricane force 12, the seas 60 feet high. All were lost, and the
wreckage of the lifeboat was later discovered along the shore.
Not all of the sixteen crew members were found. In the words
of the helicopter pilot:

'The greatest act of courage that I have ever seen, and
am ever likely to see, was the penultimate courage
and dedication shown by the Penlee when it manoeu-
vred back alongside the casualty [the MV *Union Star*]
in over 60 ft breakers and rescued four people shortly
after the Penlee had been bashed on top of the casualty's hatch covers. They were truly the bravest eight
men I have ever seen.'

With this potential exposure to tragedy, might postings at the Atlantic rock lighthouses have been harder on the
keepers' psyche than those in calmer, landward seas like the
Needles? Gerry's differing experiences on the Wolf and the
Needles suggest this, but also show how much space and daylight mattered. Despite their outward homogeneity, rock lighthouses were variable within. James Walker's design for the
Wolf was strong enough to resist the forces of nature, but the
limited space and light combined with the violence of the surrounding seas made it inescapably prison-like. Later on, taller,
broader towers with extra rooms were built at the Eddystone
and Bishop Rock. Perhaps it had been recognized that a few
extra feet here, another room there, were small kindnesses,
another sort of relief.

The afternoon is wearing on. Gerry puts down the folder
of architectural drawings and picks up another filled with

historic photographs of the Wolf from virtually every decade of its 147-year existence. They show the sea always on the move.

As we leaf through he comments on particular expressions of the waves. He can read them as shepherds can read the clouds in the sky. Two photographs show similarly calm surf. In one, he says, it would be safe to leave the tower and go out onto the landing, but in the other it would be unwise. During his time on the Wolf, he learned to spot rogue swells before it was too late: 'Waves would suddenly appear out of nowhere ... from the landing, you'd see this dark shadow moving across the water, time to get inside ... I've had to jump for it [back into the tower] before now, on several occasions.'

His sea is always reacting with itself. Riplets in one corner of it scale up into frightful waves in another. It's as though he is able to envisage the entire sea in three dimensions, like water in a bath, sloshing to the movements of unseen limbs. We study a photograph of an 'average' swell, where the sea is broken over the rocky contours into complex patterns. He says: 'What I used to like very much was that if you had quite a sea running like this, it reflected light into the building from outside, with the sun shining on the wave-heads ... just fantastic, just like snow, pure snow ... always on the move.'

Then there were the blockbuster storms. One photograph shows the tower almost completely grasped by an enormous mass of water, with only the weathervane peeping above it. Gerry experienced similar conditions during his posting there, the Wolf standing as it does squarely in the path of storms gusting up the Channel. With his usual understatement, he describes the lighthouse's 3,296 tons of masonry shaking alarmingly under this duress.

Speaking to the Institute of Civil Engineers about the construction of the Wolf Rock in 1870, James Douglass relates the first instance of heavy weather experienced by the lighthouse, on 11 September 1869. That day a 'violent gale' struck up from the west, sending 'large quantities of water' over the tower. These were the heaviest seas endured by the new keepers, who observed, 'Although the shock was distinctly felt with each wave stroke, scarcely any tremor was perceptible.' So the Wolf Rock lighthouse did not always shake in heavy seas. Was it slowly weakened through its long service? Gerry thinks the shaking was greatly aggravated by one significant alteration made to the tower a few years before he arrived, which completely changed how it functioned as a building. In 1972, the Wolf Rock became the first rock lighthouse in the world to have a helicopter landing-pad bolted to the top of the tower over the lantern.

A cage of slender steel girders rose in a tube to support a large, circular helideck ringed with safety netting. Like the Wolf's lantern optic, this structure was first assembled and tested at Blackwall on the Thames. Installation of it would be as challenging as the construction of the original lighthouse: though inherently strong, the tower was never designed to take this extra weight. For reinforcement a series of steel rods 16 feet long were drilled into the upper courses of the Wolf's masonry. Because it would not fit under the helipad, the domed cowl of the lantern was sawn off. Working quickly through the summer of 1972, Trinity House contractors assembled the prefabricated structure on top of the Wolf Rock, dangling precariously over the rock and waves below.

It was an ingenious intervention, designed so that the light could shine unimpeded through the bars of the cage, while providing an intermediate catwalk for transferring luggage and supplies between the rooms below and the helipad above. But at the same time, it turned the hierarchy of the building inside out. The Wolf was previously entered through doors at the base, and climbing up through storage rooms, then living rooms, to the lantern above. Inverted by the helipad, the tower was now entered from the top down, through the lantern, meaning fuel and supplies were moved awkwardly through the living rooms down to the stores below. The Rayburn chimney now had a ceiling, which caused pollution of the cooking water in bad weather. Keepers could no longer take the air on the full circumference of the balcony rail.

The first successful helicopter relief added the whir of rotors to the Wolf's soundscape. At a stroke, the helipad ended the drama of boat reliefs at the Wolf Rock. Lighthouse keepers could now be lifted to and from the lighthouse with greater certainty, in a matter of hours. But ultimately, creating a faster and more reliable means of bringing spare parts and new technology to the lighthouse hastened the process of automation. As Gerry says: 'The human side's been taken away, hasn't it? The sole aim of our job was to operate the machinery. Now it's just another box of tricks on the wall. As soon as you don't need the human element there – all the stuff works perfectly OK, probably better than it did – you just don't need humans any more, there's nothing for the staff to do. If I went back there now there'd be nothing for me to do.'

Despite this, and despite the hardships it caused him, Gerry says he would return to the Wolf Rock one last time. I would like to go with him. His attitude to his former residence seems complicated, but he has guided me through the Wolf with care and I am curious to see how the place would affect him now.

The last photograph he shows me is of three men in long gabardine raincoats wearing old-fashioned buoyancy aids: Gerry and his colleagues, about to fly to the Wolf, with their helicopter in the background. This was taken at Penzance heliport in 1976, he says, identifying his colleagues: Principal Keeper Eddie Matthews and Assistant Keeper Tony Bourne. He points to his younger self, long hair blown astray, eyes wrinkled against the wind. Typical, he says, that the photographer decided to take the picture just as they were hit by a squall.

THE CORNISHMAN, THURSDAY, DECEMBER 16, 1976

● THE THREE NEW KEEPERS for Wolf Rock Lighthouse getting ready to take
off from the Penzance Heliport in the Trinity House helicopter to take up their
Christmas duties. This was their second attempt to reach there — the first endeavour to
land at the lighthouse had to be abandoned because of heavy seas. They are (from left),
Messrs. Tony Bourne and Gerry Sherwood (assistant keepers) and Eddie Matthews,
(principal keeper).

16. Gerry (centre) and his colleagues
at Penzance heliport, 1976

Eddystone (II)

A family of lighthouses

1882,
12 MILES OFF LOOE, CORNWALL

By the late 1870s, John Smeaton's third Eddystone lighthouse had become a venerable fixture in the sea. Over the course of a century it had saluted vast numbers of ships plying the English Channel. It stood fixedly in the minds of Plymouth's citizenry, like an outpost of the city distantly visible from its more elevated streets and squares. And it had held generations of lighthouse keepers, each with their own peculiar connection to the shore. Many threads of meaning now ran between the tower and the mainland.

But its tenure on the reef was coming to an end. Shortly after its completion, Smeaton had noticed faint, almost imperceptible tremors when particularly large waves crashed against the structure. Quoted in Mike Palmer's authoritative account of the Eddystone is a letter from one of the early keepers to Smeaton, reporting after a big storm that 'the house did shake as if a man had been up in a great tree'.

Over a century later, investigations found that the lighthouse was shaking more pronouncedly as each winter passed. Nothing was wrong with the tower itself, which by this time was a little dishevelled but structurally sound. Instead, the ledge of the reef on which it stood had been undermined by constant wave action, and it would not be long before it eroded away completely, casting the building into the sea.

Trinity House swiftly proposed to build a fourth Eddystone lighthouse. But they also proposed to demolish Smeaton's tower and unceremoniously dump the stones in the Channel. There was outcry at this. Plymouth's citizens felt strongly that the tower should somehow be preserved – and when Trinity House demurred at the cost, those citizens decided to do something about it themselves. Following much debate, and a series of packed public meetings, a vote was carried to take Smeaton's tower off the reef and rebuild it on land as a monument to its engineer and to the tragedies it prevented during its 123-year operation. A site was found on Plymouth Hoe, where Drake had supposedly played his bowls, a public subscription was raised to pay for the work, and demolition began.

Taking the tower apart was a 'very difficult and tedious operation'. With typical ingenuity, Smeaton had mortared his granite blocks together with an early form of hydraulic cement that set quickly, even when wet, but became almost as hard as the granite itself. The demolition gang had not only to hack through this, but to do it surgically: the intricate interlocking profiles of the granite building blocks had to be carefully preserved if they were to be fitted together again on land.

Today Smeaton's reconstructed tower stands benignly on the Hoe. Only the upper two-thirds – the parts of the tower containing the rooms and lantern – were taken off the reef, leaving the 33-feet-high base there. For a small fee, you can enter, shuffle through the small stone passages and ascend the four stone rooms, the first of their kind when constructed. The rooms themselves are beautifully proportioned, with graceful domed ceilings, although most of the original interiors have long since been lost.

Eventually you emerge up inside the lantern room, a jaunty copper-framed structure with subtly classical decorative mouldings. Smeaton's original chandelier of 24 candles went out a long time ago, and no light was replaced in the re-assembled lantern. Instead, it holds a fine prospect of Plymouth to the north and the English Channel to the south. Much as in Smeaton's time, Royal Navy warships still come and go. You can watch them from the balcony, pacing the circular walkway as the lighthouse keepers once did, while seagulls wheel and scream overhead.

One by one, during that summer of 1882, Smeaton's intricate blocks of granite, now a little worn, began their unlikely journey back to the mainland. Conditions were mostly fair during this project, but the weather was prone to unexpected flourishes, freakish tides, instant squalls. Though technological advances had been made in the intervening century, the sea was only just held at bay, and was still capable of shaking the house.

After the ironwork had been removed from the lighthouse, while the masons were lodged inside, the sea suddenly turned heavy and a strong westward gale sang through the gaps in the partially demolished building. They paused and took shelter, probably in the living room a few floors below, waiting for it to pass. The lighthouse began to vibrate with the increased energy of the waves and one, larger than the rest, struck the building with such force that a tumbler of water was thrown from the living room table and smashed against the floor.

I shiver at this detail, as it transpires that the story of the Eddystone merges with my own. For out of the blue, a few months before my journey to the reef, a distant relative wrote to tell me that he had encountered the Eddystone in the course of his genealogical researches. Remarkably, one of the unnerved masons in that room was named William Nancollas. A master mason from St Austell, he was, according to census records, contracted to work on the demolition of Smeaton's lighthouse. I am descended from him through my grandfather's side of the family, who originally came from St Austell before settling in Looe, half an hour over the Devon border along the south Cornish coast.

An ancient town on steep hills around an oblong harbour, Looe has been a fixture throughout my life. My grandfather was a well-known estate agent and auctioneer in the locality (his most momentous sale being that of an island to a pair of reclusive sisters). Many of his transactions were completed in the Harbour Moon pub on the quayside, and he was known to accept pails of lobsters in exchange for his valuations. My father and aunts were raised in a house named Avalon overlooking the sea, run by my grandmother as a guesthouse. Vivid scenes from our family holidays are imprinted on the place: of seagulls swaggering in sunlit beer gardens, of fishhooks snagged painfully in fingertips, of the rotten odour of low-tide seaweed and of the rusting hulk of the *Naiad*, a shipwreck on the beach. From the bow window of my grandparents' flat, I could see the faraway Eddystone lighthouse, then as now an impossibly solitary and intriguing prospect.

So I made Looe, rather than Plymouth, the jumping-off point for my own expedition to the Eddystone. There is an arrow-straight course between the harbour and the reef, and my aunt found me the owner of the most powerful boat for hire.

Large swells and waves impede us. At our brisk speed, we seem to bludgeon our way through them, slamming into their peaks and dropping into their troughs, motion and impact that send the stomach plummeting. Our catamaran thumps sturdily along, scattering us over the deck and inducing seasickness in Michael. Both he and Roland have rejoined me for this trip to the most seminal reef of them all. We are fragile, however. Last night, we drank with my aunts and uncles in various low-slung medieval inns, concluding with a parting glass in Looe's Angling Club, thick with thirsty fishermen, frequented by generations of relatives. As our table crowded with pint glasses, various fishermen ambled over to advise us that today's weather would be 'fucking awful'. This seemed funny at the time.

Now the choppy sea makes standing difficult, so we brace ourselves in the doorway of the wheelhouse. For Dave, our skipper, these conditions are not that dramatic, but any rougher and he wouldn't have taken us out. We talk about our evening in the Angling Club and he raises his eyebrows. It transpires Dave is on good terms with Billy, the club's owner. Best beer in the harbour, he remarks, but not before encountering the Eddystone.

Dave is a veteran of these seas, a fisherman of 40 years' standing, at first on commercial trawlers before owning boats of his own. *Mystique II* (a successor to an earlier boat of his) was built for him in Plymouth about a decade ago. Now Chairman of Looe Harbour Commissioners (which manages the harbour's activities), he still fishes commercially and runs

expeditionary trips such as ours. We talk briefly of my relatives in Looe, whom he knows only distantly, although he was
at college with one of my aunts. It was there that he was first
taught the history of the Eddystone, and the idea of a rock lighthouse on a syllabus intrigues. In their audacity and innovation,
these building schemes would be fine ways to teach engineering, and their stories would hold the attention of even the most
wandering minds. Certainly, it is the stories, rather than the
facts and the dates, which Dave chiefly remembers. He cheer-
fully rattles off a schoolboy's account of the Eddystone that is
true in spirit rather than details.

Roland and I peer around the wheelhouse door at Michael, who cuts a forlorn figure. He slumps on a pile of ropes,
clinging to the gunwale, head in the crook of his elbow. All we
can do is pass him water. A sharp boat-hook on a pole stands
over him like an ill omen. Dave's diagnosis is curt: only dry land
will cure him of his seasickness. Lucky, then, that ours is only
a three-hour round trip. We must be back by 11 o'clock, before
the tide drains out of Looe harbour and blocks our return.

A few moments later our speed slackens. No land is visible in any direction. Overhead, great areas of metallic cloud
compete for prominence against fairer, bluer sky. Daylight fluc-
tuates accordingly. Dave proclaims that we've made good time
and reduces the engines to a rasping gurgle. Ahead, our destination looms up in the spray-flecked windows of the wheelhouse.

A dark column of Victorian masonry rises massively
from the reef, so tall that it seems to lay claim to the sky as well
as the sea. Shuttered windows stud the length of it, relating
the position of the internal floor levels on the weather-beaten
exterior. Narrowing as it rises upwards, the tower is crowned
with a cylindrical cage of steelwork, a wide-brimmed helipad
and a rack of solar panels, modern additions that complicate
its architectural form. Laid down on the waves, the tower's
shadow appears like a rippling pathway towards the base.

When it was 'opened' by the Duke of Edinburgh in 1882,
this fourth Eddystone tower stood as a monumental exhibition of Victorian engineering and manufacturing. It was in

every way a refinement of previous designs. Royalty descended on Plymouth, and a lavish celebration was held in the town's Guildhall. A flotilla of naval vessels performed manoeuvres in the English Channel. What the new Eddystone lighthouse represented was nothing less than imperial power and benevolence. No finer building had yet been raised out in the ocean.

Designed by James Douglass, then Trinity House's chief engineer, the new Eddystone lighthouse was largely built by his son William, resident engineer on the project with Thomas Edmonds. William Douglass implemented his father's work beautifully. Twice as tall as Smeaton's, with double the number of rooms, exquisite circular furniture and a powerful glass optical lens instead of candles, the Douglasses' tower was built upon Smeaton's Georgian blueprint and thoroughly 'improved' it in the manner of the Victorian age.

It quickly drew visitors. In 1892, the journalist Frederick George Kitton spent three days in the new Eddystone and related how 'during holiday time there are cheap excursions from Plymouth to the lighthouse by large steamers.' During his time there, he saw one:

> crowded in every part with its living freight. When it comes within a hundred yards of the rock, we on the gallery signal to it by dropping the clapper of one of the two large fog-bells, which is responded to by a vigorous waving of handkerchiefs on deck.

Now we drift on the currents at more or less the same distance. Around our boat surf breaks in foaming bands over the barely hidden reef; currents formed by deeper elements manifest themselves as churning patches of surface water known as eddies. It's a visual explanation of the Eddystone's name: the sea literally eddies around the stone. A vortex of flows, counter-flows and upwells make boating dangerous within the reef's orbit. Occasionally, Dave returns to the wheelhouse to adjust our position, but it is a mark of his seamanship that he does this only infrequently, exactly attuned the behaviour of the water.

We take the opportunity to fish for pollock. Our lines fall into the water, dragged down quickly by ingot-shaped weights. Dave shows us how to regulate their descent by placing our thumbs on the spooling reels. Roland and I stand to starboard, rods over the gunwale, as we drift over the reef for pollock; Dave roams the deck in the background, advising and instructing. When you feel it go slack, he says, it's hit the bottom. Wind it up slowly, then cast off again. Keep a steady rhythm. Down and up, down and up.

I picture my lure sinking down through the fathoms. Rising up from the seabed, the top of the reef is almost like the summit of an underwater mountain. Around such hazards, marine life is plentiful, because the vigorous currents surrounding them create a microclimate in which many species thrive (except shipwrecked sailors, perhaps). I picture my tackle sinking past fluttering kelp, bulbous anemones and sponges, reclusive lobsters and through great shoals of fish swarming about the rocky stack.

The line slackens. I peer down at the velvet-dark sea, following the thin thread out of sight. My weight and lure have settled untaken, on some unseen shelf of the reef or on the seabed proper. As I wind back up there is momentary resistance, the line being toyed with by fish or catching on ledges of the reef. I wonder idly whether fragments of the earlier, destroyed Eddystone lighthouses snag my ascending hook.

I bring forth nothing from the depths, no catch, fish nor fragments of lighthouse. Roland's first attempts are similarly unsuccessful. As we cast down again, the boat temporarily becalmed, Michael rises from his pile of ropes. Seasickness still grips him tightly; he is as white as the fibreglass deck. I wince as Dave exclaims: 'Bloody hell, you're dying!' With this, Michael makes for the gunwale and addresses the sea once again. Dave fetches him more water, and with a worm of guilt I return to my rod and the prospect of the lighthouse (I need to pay attention, as I don't know when I'll be here again).

Rock lighthouse building had come far since Smeaton's time. New methods had nullified some of the dangers.

Sulphuric acid was used to remove the seaweed and other matter from the reef, rendering it cleaner and less slippery. A large, circular brick structure called a cofferdam was built around the construction site, enabling the masons to work in the dry with steam-powered tools. A powerful steamship, the *Hercules*, rapidly transferred the stones of the new lighthouse and the workmen to the reef from Plymouth. And by the late nineteenth century, the Establishment had taken a close interest. Where Smeaton risked his life to lay his own foundation stone, that of the fourth Eddystone lighthouse was laid in grander, less rackety circumstances by the Duke of Edinburgh, on 19 August 1879.

But it remained perilous. At one point during the build, a taut chain snapped, striking William Douglass from the ledge on which he was working so that he tumbled 70 feet towards the exposed reef below. Miraculously, a large, freak wave leapt up and caught him just before he hit the rocks, cushioning his fall so that he suffered only a terrifying soaking rather than death or shattered bones. Given the Douglass family's spectacular lighthouse pedigree, it's tempting to think the sea was moved to catch him out of respect.

By that time, rock lighthouse building had become a family business. As the towers grew more refined, so the ability to build them became concentrated within a few families. William and his father, James Douglass – Sir James after the Eddystone's completion – were not the only members of that family to raise towers offshore. James had helped his father, Nicholas, and brother, William, build the first, ill-fated Bishop Rock lighthouse south-west of the Scilly Isles. Both boys were baptized into a niche career, frequently swimming through rough waters to the boat when work concluded. William Junior's drenching, though fearful, was nothing new in the Douglass dynasty. Elsewhere, many of the Irish lighthouses were built by George Halpin Senior and George Halpin Junior, although almost nothing is known of them.

We know rather more about the four generations of Stevensons who monopolized Scottish lighthouse-building and built magnificent towers out in the North Sea. Robert Stevenson's Bell Rock paved the way for his sons Alan, David and Tom to build their own towers, the finest of which is Alan's Skerryvore of 1844. Another, the Dubh Artach rock lighthouse, was engineered in part by Robert's grandson Robert Louis Stevenson. Happily for us, literature stole him from this dangerous profession.

It wasn't just engineering that ran in families. Over the centuries, dynasties of lighthouse keepers came into being. Among the most notable of these was the Knott family. George Knott, of the sixth generation, kept the light at Smeaton's Eddystone and made a very fine cork model of it, a painstaking work as exact in its details as the original building. Generations of Cunninghams have looked after Haulbowline and still do so.

My own personal connection with the towers is hardly dynastic, but it illustrates the reach of these towers across the generations. At the Eddystone, the trend is particularly acute. The towers on this reef are a legendary family of buildings, the design and demise of each generation influencing those of the next. In the wider sense, this is true of the towers nationwide: all share a common ancestor, Smeaton's third Eddystone lighthouse.

Near where we fish, the base of Smeaton's tower juts out of the sea, far more substantial than I had expected. Douglass's tower is the one that had transfixed us when we arrived here, but I now find myself more preoccupied with these remains. Their survival out here is a testimony to the quality of Smeaton's design and construction, and furnishes its successor with a singular context. You could come here with no knowledge of the story and reasonably deduce that the one tower grew from the other. It is remarkable that such architectural layers should persist, barnacle-like, in this liquid place.

Weathering has blackened the stonework and streaked it with green stains, but it seems otherwise remarkably sturdy. What's left is the bottom third of his tower, wide at the base and narrower as it rises. It looks uncannily like a tree-stump, a fitting simile, given the influence of oak trees on Smeaton's design. Rungs climb up one side, now leading nowhere, but originally giving access to the entrance. An iron pole sticks mysteriously out of the top. A cormorant alights and flaunts its wings, and I think about my ancestor, who was here before me.

17. Smeaton's and Douglass's
towers juxtaposed, 2017

Suddenly, the ends of our rods arch violently as the lines are tugged downwards. Both mine and Roland's lures have been taken at once, sending Dave into paroxysms of excitement. Steady, steady, he cries. Reel in just as you were before. Whatever it is on the end of my line struggles to get away. We hang on and stiffly wind in, watching the sea eagerly to identify what we've caught. All is featureless until the sight of a beautiful silver pollock develops in the water.

In the end, we catch three: two for the barbecue, and one which we present to Dave. As he readies *Mystique II* for our departure, we find we have drifted around the reef so that Smeaton's base is almost hidden behind Douglass's tower in the foreground. Dave tells me that this is a handy way of navigating back to the harbour. If you line them up like this, he says, you have a course that points approximately north-north-west: a straight line back to Looe.

Gesturing to the bank of screens and dials in the wheel-house, I ask Dave whether he actually uses the lighthouse for navigational purposes. He pauses for a moment. No, he says, but I use it as a warning. If it weren't there, skippers would give the reef a wide berth, even with their GPS systems. It seems significant that Dave, a fisherman all his life and a prominent seafarer in Looe, should say this. The presence of the tower and the light give certainty. Of the many layers to modern navigation – analogue and digital, observational and technical – the tower and the light might seem like relics of an earlier time, but for Dave at least they remain a fixture.

Apart from the occasional encircling gull, there are now no signs of life from the tower, no smoke issuing from a stove-pipe, no bustle behind the storm shutters. The building seems to brood, as though unused to visitors. It's been a long time since keepers fished with long lines from the lantern gallery, waving to boatloads of sightseers. About the only palpably human touch is an accidental spillage, a long, fuchsia-coloured streak striping the masonry downwards from the seventh-floor window. Fruitlessly I speculate what, if anything, it signifies.

Magnificent though it is, this latest generation of the Eddystone family was less of a pioneer than its ancestors on the reef. Although constructed with the most efficient tools then developed and wrought of the finest masonry, metalwork and glassware then available, the tower was built from the hard-won principles established by Winstanley, Rudyerd and Smeaton. It was less of an exhilarating gamble than those early towers had been. Designed with the comfort of these precedents, the fourth Eddystone was cushioned by imperial resources against failure.

Yet there were still pioneering advances to be made. In 1982, when exactly 100 years old, Douglass's tower became the first of the English rock lighthouses to be automated and de-manned. Like its predecessors, it had opened a new chapter in the story of these buildings, but one marked with poignancy and ambivalence. Men lost their jobs. Centuries of offshore living ended where it had begun.

More recently, scientists have monitored the tower to understand just how rock lighthouses can shake in storms without collapsing. Perhaps because their survival would seem, *de facto*, to prove their resilience, no one had sought to understand just how these massive buildings survive such extremes. Apart from some nineteenth-century studies by the Stevensons, very little scientific investigation had been done to quantify the stresses on the towers.

So, in winter 2013, the Eddystone was chosen by the University of Plymouth as the site of an experimental study. Sensitive instruments were deposited in the lantern to record the impacts of the waves on the tower. Wave-heights were measured from a monitoring buoy anchored a little way off from the reef. That winter, the Eddystone endured the severest storms in 50 years. On land, violent weather demolished the coastal railway tracks at Dawlish in Devon, flooded seaside towns and generally harried south-west England, echoing if not equalling the Great Storm that obliterated the first Eddystone lighthouse in 1703.

According to the instruments, the Eddystone's granite structure easily withstood these storms. Although vibrations were recorded, the tower's structural integrity was unaffected. Reassuringly, no weaknesses were detected in the tower. It has aged well.

Using the data from the Eddystone study, scientists were able to calculate the size and force behind the kind of wave needed to bring down the tower: 17.5 metres high, with a force of 21,141 kilonewtons, a wave equivalent to a wrecking ball weighing 2,155 tons. Such a hypothetical wave, the scientists drily remarked, is impossible in the English Channel – at least for the time being. But in the context of climate change, rising sea levels and stormier oceans, rock lighthouses may have to contend with far stronger forces in the future. If the Eddystone is anything to go by, it seems they could comfortably handle anything short of an apocalypse.

Remarkably, this was unknown to their original engineers, who designed and built the towers according to precedent rather than physics. With no detailed studies of wave-loading then available, those Victorians had founded their towers solely on weight and hope. So important were their projects that they were entrusted to men with bonds running deeper than any contract. Blood, it seems, is thicker than seawater.

Bishop Rock

A distant lighthouse

1858 AND 1887,
32 MILES OFF LAND'S END, CORNWALL

I run, puffing and directionless, along curved and sloping roads embanked with wild garlic. No soul stirs in the hedgerows. I run up steep inclines to hills crowned with old lookout towers, facing towards America. Small birds hop and wriggle in the roadside dust, scrubbing their feathers clean. I run below an infinite blue sky unrolled, cloudless, with the sun's heat clasping my bare neck.

In my mind, as I run, are the builders of the Bishop Rock lighthouse. Far removed from the mainland, these men clung like limpets to unforgiving nodules of granite. Atlantic swells regularly crashed over their godforsaken building site, but they clung on with the help of harnesses bolted deeply into the rock. Even the tools were tied down. They ate limpets, too – in their grim quarters on a nearby islet, because storms frequently halted their supply chain. Limpets and barnacles chiselled from the waterline, gull's eggs reluctantly thieved from nests: on this poor fare, they summoned the strength to build a tower at the extreme end of the kingdom.

For a moment, I pause at a crossroads. An unattended stall bears fresh eggs and an honesty box. As I catch my breath, I map the courses of the dry-stone walls interlacing the fields. Then off again, this time along a road that, breasted, reveals the sea unrolled below, marked with the wiry profiles of white breakers. I run down towards the cove, but think warily of the return distance. Without intending to, I have jogged to the other end of this island. I have run out of land.

Britain does not run out at Land's End, though the name given to Cornwall's toecap, and the sight of its gnarled cliffs yielding to the Atlantic, feels final. Instead, there is one last landfall

28 miles south-west of the mainland: the Scilly Isles, an idyllic archipelago of five inhabited islands – St Mary's, St Martin's, St Agnes, Tresco and Bryher – and countless uninhabited islets. Irregularly shaped, randomly clustered, they are like a geological encore before the ocean.

As you sail through them, the parts of the archipelago seem to move together and apart like stage-sets, closing some views and opening others. This way, I had caught fleeting glimpses of the Bishop Rock lighthouse, the tower's profile disappearing and reappearing between headlands and islands in an oddly crowded seascape.

Navigation here is some of the most exacting in British waters. Outcrops of rock crumb the stretches of water between the larger islands. To the north, east and west of the archipelago there are minefields of rock formations, of all shapes and sizes, some submerged, some visible. Around the Bishop, the seas are not featureless planes of water, as you might expect so far into the Atlantic. It marks the westernmost point of the Western Rocks, a nasty geological trap on the approach to the Scillies and the English Channel. This sector of sea is one of the most lethal in Britain's waters. As Cyril Noall put it in his inimitable *Cornish Lights and Shipwrecks*: 'Deceived by the strong and treacherous currents, misled by fog, or driven helplessly before the fierce Atlantic gales, hundreds of vessels have come to grief upon them.'

My family and I are staying in a cottage on St Mary's, the largest of the islands. The boat from Penzance, *Scillonian III*, docks in its harbour and the Scilly airport perches on one of its higher hills to the south. Incomers from either source are then distributed by boat to the other, smaller islands. Though we have visited only three, they are all said to possess surprisingly individual characters, given their similarity and size. Run feudally by a long-established family, Tresco, for instance, where the main draw is a beautiful botanical garden, comes across as haughty and well kept. On the other hand, St Agnes, the smallest and south-westernmost of the inhabited islands, is a sleepy fusion of the pastoral and the nautical, with tightly winding lanes, a disused lighthouse and a church with a bell recovered from a shipwreck.

It is often said that the Scilly Isles seem not quite part of the United Kingdom. Visually and socially, they are settlements in miniature. Everything is on a smaller, more human scale: small towns, small roads, small communities, small talk. Their terrain is mostly low-lying, and the sea is everywhere you look. Boats bustle in all the harbours and boatmen come and go on the active quaysides. Every pub is ornamented with nautical ephemera, but sincerely, as though for the taste of the locals rather than the tourists. Overall, the mood is of a tiny principality, or a water-republic.

Partly this is because the islands are heavily fortified. As a potential staging post from which to attack the mainland, the Scillies were heavily equipped with batteries and gun emplacements from the Elizabethan period onwards. Because the pace of modern development has been far slower than on the mainland, these fortifications still dominate the islands' silhouettes, especially when observed from the sea. The most prominent is the Star Castle on St Mary's, built on the eastern headland by Sir Francis Godolphin in 1593 to dispel another Spanish invasion. Even the old lighthouse on St Agnes incorporates four small gun ports at first-floor level.

Today, the 28 miles separating the Scilly Isles from the mainland does not seem very far. Yet this distance swells out of proportion and defines them. Storms can hold back deliveries of groceries and banknotes, and sever the submarine telephone lines. Travel to the mainland is just expensive and lengthy enough to rule it out every day. Perhaps more than these practical aspects, the Scillies feel as though they have been quarantined from mainland economic forces. Property development is virtually non-existent; the towns are little-changed assemblages of buildings from the seventeenth century onwards, while prime fields with gorgeous views remain untouched. Past centuries are thereby quickly evoked. On the quayside at St Mary's, the age of creaking galleons is easy enough to conjure up.

Prehistoric monuments proliferate across the islands, deepening the sense of distance. Ancient burial chambers, standing stones, field systems and villages bristle nakedly all around, easily read and comprehended in their landscapes. At Halangy Down Ancient Village, on the north headland of St Mary's, the walls and passageways of Iron Age roundhouses lie open to the sun. On the tiny islet of Nornour, a place that seems barely capable of supporting life, there are traces of pre-historic roundhouses and a farm. On my morning run, I paused at Bant's Carn, a prehistoric burial chamber. Sunlight pierced its walls. I crouched low on its threshold, and the thousands of years between myself and its buried occupant did not seem very far at all.

Four miles west of St Agnes, out in the Atlantic, stands the Bishop Rock lighthouse. At a total of 32 miles south-west from Cornwall, it is the furthest rock lighthouse from Britain. Of all these stations, it is the starkest and most exposed, braced against the Atlantic and not much else.

My father and I follow a coastal path that loops along small, sickle-shaped beaches towards the harbour. Gusts of sea-breeze come in now and then, tasting of minerals, iodine, salt, ozone. The day promises to be a fine one. We are on our way to the quayside on St Mary's, bringing crab sandwiches and chocolate biscuits for sustenance. Though it is mid-morning, and mid-April, the sun is slowly coming to the boil. We arrive early and queue for our tickets at a single-cell granite kiosk, built prob-ably as a harbourmaster's or Customs office, and now a place from which the boatmen do business.

Chalked hastily on a blackboard is the legend: 'Bishop Rock lighthouse, nature watching at Annet + Western Rocks', at £17 per ticket. This isn't a trip that can be run very often – bad weather frequently cancels it for weeks at a time – so there is much interest and it swiftly becomes oversubscribed. But these are enterprising boatmen. When our boat, the *Avocet*, becomes laden to the gunwales with tourists, another, the *Parallel*, is swiftly drummed up to take the rest.

A wiry, freckly skipper in wraparound shades and his younger assistant direct us down the granite steps to the boat; they handle the masses like indifferent farmers corralling livestock. The assistant sports a black eye and cuts to his face; briefly I daydream about a fistfight between rival boatmen on a darkened quayside. My father nudges me, indicating some of our fellow passengers. A portly gentleman in red corduroys with roving eyes. A feline, elderly German man travelling solo, but easily netting new friends. Retirees in deplorable hats, sensible clothing, cameras, waterproofs, rucksacks, sunglasses, meditative expressions, some murmuring. A game of bridge might break out at any moment.

We leave the harbour sedately, motoring south-west towards St Agnes. The boatmen retreat from the deck up onto the open-air bridge safely away from us. They remain up there for the rest of the trip, tersely communicating via a PA system.

Passing St Agnes, the smallest of the five inhabited islands, the skipper drawls a commentary about its lighthouse. One of the first to be established by Trinity House, in 1680, it was erratically kept, and though a useful aid to navigation in the immediate locality it was unable to prevent ships running onto the Western Rocks. In 1911, it was superseded by a more useful lighthouse on another headland, and has since become just a squat white landmark, earning a measure of distinction through age.

Annet, our first stop, is an uninhabited islet to the west of St Agnes. It is the barest scrap of land, consisting of two low-lying grassy hummocks on bedrock, barely 50 paces from one end to the other. We draw near, and the boat sways as people rush between gunwales for a glimpse of a porpoise or an elusive breed of bird. Seals cluster on rock shelves, and in the sunlight their oily skins have the rainbow sheen of spilled petrol. They pose shamelessly for the cameras. From his lofty vantage above us, the skipper drip-feeds sightings through the PA system, as though he can make the fish and fowl appear when he wants.

Sunlight glitters down upon all available surfaces; faint starbursts of light come up from the black depths to the bottle-green shallows. Our engines are cut to the quietest hum, and the sea is incredibly calm beneath the hull. I recall the verse from Coleridge's *Rime of the Ancient Mariner*: 'Day after day, day after day, / We stuck, nor breath nor motion; / As idle as a painted ship / Upon a painted ocean.'

Misshapen growths of rock loom ahead to the south-west, the beginning of the Western Rocks. Having motored through open stretches of water between islands, the *Avocet* now embarks on a fiddlier course, threading between tight clusters of rock. As we round the last part of Annet, heading south-west, the Bishop Rock lighthouse springs up on the horizon, slightly larger this time, before disappearing behind a rock in the foreground.

Surrounding the boat are 300-million-year-old outcrops of granite, scaly with weed and dribbling with broken water. I was surprised to learn that they all have names, some of which the skipper lists through the PA system: Gorregan, Trenemene, Crebawethan, Melledgan, Gilstone, Hellweathers, Rags, Rosevean, Rosevear. The names seem as ancient as the rocks themselves, relics of a forgotten tongue (which is close enough, as they derive from Cornish, a language once close to extinction but now, happily, enjoying a revival). But why name such isolated, primeval outcrops? Perhaps it was an attempt to claim ownership over, and thus neuter, the remote and dangerous.

The Bishop Rock lighthouse reappears and disappears among these ancient shapes. We thread towards it now through impossibly narrow channels, where the rocks are almost close enough to touch from the gunwale, and across viscous stretches of water oozing above submerged ledges. We marvel at the skipper's ability, for this can't be easy navigating. My father remarks how it's different for us, with an engine that can be instantaneously switched between forward and reverse. In the days of sail and steam, when it was much harder for ships to abruptly change direction, it would have been fatal to be ensnared here.

We dawdle by some outcrops and hear of shipwreck. Pausing near a formation called Pednathise Head, the skipper

18. The distant Bishop among
the Western Rocks, 2017

tells us how, on a February night in 1977, a French trawler, *Enfant de Bretagne*, got into difficulty in heavy seas around the Western Rocks. A giant wave scooped it up and dropped it on top of the Pednathise rock, where it stuck fast. Having heard the trawler's distress signals, the Scilly lifeboat came to the scene and shot flares into the night sky, illuminating the stricken trawler and the faces of the terrified crew in the bows. But then the flarelight expired, the lifeboat's spotlight malfunctioned, and the trawler disappeared. In the seething darkness, the lifeboat crew heard the dreadful rush of a heavy sea about to fall. Just before it did, the lifeboat wriggled through a narrow channel and escaped. Commendably, they returned for a second rescue attempt, but there was no sign of the *Enfant de Bretagne*. It had vanished, the wreckage and the bodies were never found, and the sight of those anguished French faces under the flarelight must have haunted the lifeboat crew ever since. They were given a silver medal for trying.

In just a few centuries, thousands of lives were lost in this seascape. We pass the Outer Gilstone, where in 1707 Admiral Sir Cloudesly Shovell's flagship HMS *Association* went down with the pride of the British fleet, having made a catastrophic navigational error.

In October that year, fifteen magnificent warships commanded by Shovell were returning, laden with wounded soldiers, from a failed attempt to defeat the French and Spanish at Toulon. From Gibraltar they had sailed up the Spanish coast, and ran into ugly conditions in the Bay of Biscay. Disorientated by storms, they approached the mouth of the Channel in the belief they were somewhere safely west of Ushant, a little island off the French Breton coast; navigation at this time was little more than informed guesswork. In fact, they were much further north than they realized, heading straight towards the Scilly Isles, closing in on the Western Rocks at nightfall.

Like racehorses falling at a jump, four ships of the fleet successively ran aground on the hazards. HMS *Association* collided with the Outer Gilstone Rock and sank in five minutes. HMS *Firebrand* struck the Outer Gilstone too, but was lifted off by a wave and managed to limp away before sinking in Smith Sound nearby. HMS *Eagle* bounced off the Crim Rocks and then went to pieces on the Tearing Ledge. And HMS *Romney* struck the Bishop Rock itself, going down with all hands. The combined death toll was over 2,000 men in a single night. Quiet reigns over the *Avocet*, and for several long minutes there is only the white noise of the ship-to-shore radio ticking eerily from the wheelhouse.

But as catastrophic as the wreck of the British fleet was, it would be centuries before a lighthouse was built on the Bishop Rock. Instead, the tragedy led to the government of the day establishing a Board of Longitude and launching a prize for demonstrating the most accurate means of determining longitude, the lack of which was believed to be the cause of the disaster. It was just too difficult to build anything so far out to sea. For the time being, the distance was insurmountable.

Unsurprisingly, signs of human life out here are few. An exception is the barren islet of Rosevear, slightly larger than the other formations, where a ruinous stone building grimly hangs on. Its roof has vanished, leaving only the partially collapsed triangular gables, but we can see that it is of a rectangular plan, with regular windows and doors, like a bothy on a Scottish mountain. Who could possibly have lived here, and why? Given the onslaught of the Atlantic, the building's presence is scarcely credible. Our disbelief is deepened when the skipper tells us it dates from the 1850s, meaning it has clung on here for over a century. It was meant to be a barrack during the construction of the first Bishop Rock lighthouse. To avoid lengthy journeys to and from St Agnes, Rosevear was settled by the labourers, masons and lighthouse engineers. This was its first, and its last, inhabitation. I marvel at the thought. It's one thing to live this far out in a strong stone rock lighthouse, but to live in a barrack of this terrestrial design, unfortified against tall waves, must have been truly dicey.

We leave Rosevear and the Western Rocks behind, motoring over more open waters towards the Bishop. If mapped, our course would look erratic, at once linear, looping and zig-zagging, as if plucking up the courage to make for the remoteness of the ocean. Now, after all the glimpses of it between islands and rock formations, the lighthouse is constantly in view. We quicken our pace.

There are various theories about why the Bishop Rock is so named. One is that, before it acquired a lighthouse, the formation strongly resembled a bishop's mitre. Another is that men with the surnames Bishop and Clerk were wrecked there in the seventeenth century – around the Bishop Rock are a few smaller rocks, which are sometimes termed the 'Clerks'. But according to Elisabeth Stanbrook, the name first appears in an administrative document of 1302. Written in crabbed and clerkly Latin, it records how the rock was used as a place of execution: two Scillonian women charged with theft were taken to the 'Maenenescop' (Cornish for 'Bishop Rock') and left there to be drowned by the tide.

By 1849, the Bishop Rock was about to begin saving lives, rather than taking them. Trinity House seem to have been galvanized into action to mark the Bishop by a flurry of disastrous shipwrecks on the Western Rocks in the 1840s: the passenger liner *Thames* in January 1841, with only four survivors; the wheat-carrying *William Proben*, lost on Melledgan in February 1841; the schooner *Douro*, wrecked on Crebawethan with all hands lost in January 1843; the schooner *Challenger* in November 1843, which went to pieces on unspecified Western Rocks, and from which the crew narrowly escaped, managing to row to Bryher with only one oar.

The first design for the Bishop Rock was unusual: a skeletal cast-iron structure, like a climbing frame. Such a lighthouse – iron-framed instead of masonry – was an experiment on an exposed site of this kind. Rather than crash against a stout mass, the sea would dissipate its force between slender stilts. The principle had worked well for 85 years on the Smalls Rock, off the Pembrokeshire coast, although there the structure was wooden (and very cramped, with only a two-room cabin for the keepers provided atop the stilts). Iron-framed lighthouses had also worked successfully at more sheltered locations off the Lancashire coast and in the Thames estuary. Perhaps the deciding factor was that it was far cheaper than building a masonry rock lighthouse (£12,500 instead of £36,000), especially on the Bishop Rock, the sheer distance of which steepened the cost of men and materials.

But it was a false economy. At the start of February 1850, a colossal storm mauled the Scilly Isles for three days. When it had abated, Hugh Tregarthen, Trinity House's Scillonian agent, peered forebodingly from the window of his house on Tresco, perhaps knowing in his gut what he would see. Where there should have been a skeletal profile on the distant horizon, he instead saw nothing: the sea had demolished the unfinished lighthouse.

It had been a dreadful miscalculation. The existing stilted iron lighthouses stood in sheltered locations and were nowhere near as exposed as the Bishop's position facing the wide Atlantic. This failed attempt to bridge the distance with economies was a salutary lesson that, for the business of rock lighthouse construction, there was to be no skimping on cost. Trinity House rallied for a second attempt, determined to surmount it properly. James Walker, their engineer, returned to the drawing board. This time, they would make something in stone.

Until now, Walker had designed only two rock lighthouses: Trwyn Du (1838), marking the entrance to the Menai Strait, and Plymouth Breakwater (1844), squatting on the giant barricade at the entrance to Plymouth harbour. Both of them are stocky towers in comparatively benign positions. As demonstrated by his first, iron-framed design for the Bishop, Walker was inexperienced in locations of such exposure.

This time, he designed a more conventional stone tower. As with the previous attempt, operations on the rock were managed by Nicholas Douglass, then in his fifties, assisted in the physically demanding parts of the job by his sons James and William, both in their twenties. The available working surface was impossibly small and constrained, with the masons dangerously close to one another's tools. A chasm had been bored for the enormous foundation stone, which could only be laid with someone down there to guide the stone into the precise setting. Fearful of the obvious risk of being crushed to death, the masons refused to do it until 'a Douglass' – probably James – went down there first as an example to the others.

Nothing shielded them from the Atlantic as they worked. Frequently ambushed by swells, they clung on to one another with a grip 'so intense as to sometimes cause flesh wounds'. Oddly, one man seemed to have enjoyed it: the Scillonian poet Robert Maybee, who in 1855 worked as a labourer on the light-house. He wrote chirpily of the experience: 'It was a very pleas-ant summer and I was pleased with my employment.' But he had worked only one summer on the rock and he was, after all, a poet.

It took the men eight years to raise and light the tower. Construction was beset with all sorts of problems: quarrels with Augustus Smith, the local landowner (quaintly self-styled 'Lord Proprietor of the Isles'), droughts in the granite supplies, and tinkering with the design by the committees of Trinity House (who ordered that the tower should be enlarged halfway through construction). Rather preposterously, Trinity House censured the men for working on Sundays, showing the illu-sions these grandees had of the build. But they relented when it was explained to them that the unpredictable weather meant every day counted.

On 28 August 1857, the last stone boomed into position; on 1 September 1858, the light first pulsed from the lantern. Weighing nearly 3,000 tons, a granite lighthouse 147 feet high now crowned the Bishop Rock. Trinity House was jubilant at this success, but its jubilation was not to last.

A storm in 1860 split the cast-iron lantern dome, tore away the 250 kilogram fog bell and brass entrance door, and shook the lighthouse to such an extent that the keepers' crock-ery spilled out of the cupboards. In 1874, a truly ferocious storm raged on the Western Rocks, with winds blowing at hur-ricane force and waves rearing 70 feet high. Lens and lantern glass were cracked, swathes of external masonry were fractured, and the lighthouse quaked severely. After this, a futile attempt was made to strengthen the tower, bolting it together inside and out with thick iron ties. But under storm after storm, the lighthouse became increasingly bedraggled. Fissures appeared in the exterior of the building; the faces fell from the granite blocks, the stonework exteriors becoming more like patchwork.

Brutal weather was the main factor, but it could be that the structure was inherently weakened by Walker's decision to mortar and peg the stones together, rather than dovetail them into an unbreakable mass. The situation called for a drastic structural intervention.

So, in 1882, James Douglass (by then Walker's successor as engineer to Trinity House) drew up proposals for the fortification and enlargement of the Bishop Rock lighthouse. Rather than demolish it, Douglass proposed to encase Walker's beleaguered structure within a heavy granite overcoat, dovetailed firmly together. At the base, he introduced a colossal granite drum, with perpendicular sides instead of tapering to part the waves. At the top, he built the lighthouse upwards by a further four levels, with a new double-height lantern at the apex. Inside, Walker's rooms survived in the lower half of the structure, but the old entrance was filled with bricks and buried in the new granite drum at the base. Douglass sought weight. Nearly all fittings were to be of gunmetal. All the extra granite raised the weight of the masonry to 6,000 tons; the lens optic alone weighed 6 tons. The total height of this 'second' Bishop Rock would be 167 feet, making it the tallest rock lighthouse then built in the kingdom.

With an existing structure from which masons could dangle in harnesses, this second build would not be as arduous as the first. Douglass and his men benefitted, too, from technological advancements, utilizing much of the steam-driven equipment employed on his fourth Eddystone lighthouse, completed in 1882. They started on the Bishop that year, and completed the work in 1887. But even though this second project was marginally easier, the sea here lost none of its power to terrify. Looking down from the top of the tower as they finished the lantern, one man remembered: 'As the waves receded for the next onslaught, it was like looking down into the jaws of hell.'

The encasement and growth of the existing tower was a novel scheme. By thriftily reusing the masonry structure of Walker's lighthouse, Douglass saved money and time. It was an intriguing early act of preservation: Walker's 1858 tower nestles, Russian-doll-like, within Douglass's edifice of 1887. Rather than one building succeeding another, like the four Eddystone lighthouses, here the old work evolved into the new, the first Bishop Rock becoming the second, the result not clearly one lighthouse or another, but a metamorphosis of the two.

That it has taken a battering is at once obvious, for the Bishop Rock is by far the most weathered of the rock lighthouses I've seen. Everywhere, the stonework is discoloured and pitted, laced with orange and reddish stains where internal rust has gradually percolated through the granite. Blackish wave-marks smear the lower parts of the tower like camouflage. Weather has shaded the granite every kind of grey, from elephant-hide to cumulonimbus. Originally bottle-green, many of the storm shutters have completely lost their paint, as though grit-blasted off.

However, to my father it is a thing of beauty, a perfect lighthouse soaring straight up out of the water. I see his point. It is mightily sized – the great drum-like plinth alone is absolutely colossal – but rises with acute grace from a tiny rock, no more than a toehold in the sea.

So completely does it fill the view, 167 feet of granite thrown up to the heavens, that our senses, already warped by our journey, struggle to process the spectacle. Out here, the stories of its build seem fictional. The lighthouse stands like the finale of a conjuring trick before the method is revealed. Without prior knowledge, it's impossible to deduce from the sight alone how it could possibly have been constructed. At many of these sites, traces of the workings have been left behind: the little railway at the Bell Rock, the landing-quay at the Wolf, and most obviously the remains of Smeaton's tower at the Eddystone. Here, there is nothing to betray how the trick was done.

A helipad at the top indicates the current means of entering the structure, but the old entrance is still visible below. Steps up from the waterline are notched into the scaly pink granite. You would gingerly climb them up to the plinth, where a short flight of rungs leads to a narrow ledge encircling the rest of the tower. You might pause here, glancing back at the sea swallowing and regurgitating the steps below. Then, you must summon the nerve to traverse a longer series of rungs going up to the blistered entrance door, over 40 feet above sea level.

These steps and rungs are about the only features on a domestic scale. Otherwise, what impresses most strongly here is the impersonal scale of the engineering, the feeling of sublime intervention into nature. So overwhelmingly vast and monolithic is the Bishop that it is hard to think of it as a mere building. Rather, like a suspension bridge or dam, it is a pure expression of structure and tonnage, conveying a sense of great forces harnessed and manipulated.

Abstracted by these qualities, the tower's age feels indeterminate. It is barely two centuries old, which pales against, say, the eight centuries' standing of Norman churches in the English countryside. Yet weathering has blurred the joints between the stones, making it seem as though hewn from a single rock. It has the timeworn sense of having withstood great forces. It feeds off its primeval setting. Viewed with the misshapen Western Rocks over which it presides, the scene is of an upright stone amidst collapsed and illegible forms, strangely reminiscent of prehistoric sites on land.

It is ancient in one particular sense. Much of the granite that forms it was quarried from Bodmin Moor, in Cornwall, out of a deposit formed between 330 and 272 million years ago (it cannot be more precisely dated). Each of the Bishop's stones might have been dressed in the 1880s, but they are far, far older in origin. And there is a sense of destiny about this granite. It began life as fluid magma, first pushed up from the Earth's core, then cooled over millennia. As it solidified, it became a structure of interlocking mineral crystals, like the interlocking pieces of the lighthouses, as though the stone itself was meant for this purpose.

A tangle of wires and cabinets up in the lantern, together with the turning lens, are a reminder that the Bishop still operates. Like the other towers it is uninhabited, and now probably uninhabitable. Indeed, I've met the people who fly out here to maintain this equipment, to ensure the lens never falters and the bulb never fails. For them, it is a grim station to service. Once, when the tower was besieged by the Valentine's Day storms of February 2014, these engineers were thrown from their beds by the impact of the waves on the walls. They spoke of awful groanings and crashes emanating from the Bishop's depths as the storms intensified.

About half a mile beyond the lighthouse are the Retarrier Ledges, scene of the disastrous wreck of the *Schiller* in 1875, one of the finest transatlantic steam liners of the age. She was en route from New York to Plymouth, entering the English Channel, when thick fog cloaked the Bishop's light. For some reason, the Bishop's fog bell went unheeded, and the *Schiller* drove straight onto the Retarriers at low tide, which were fully exposed for maximum carnage. Of the 254 passengers and 101 crew, only 45 survived. The lighthouse keepers could only ring their fog bell in anguish as they watched the ship broken on the ledges from the windows of the tower.

Shipwreck greatly declined after the first flash of the light here in 1858. Indeed, as lights first flared on other dangerous hazards around our coastlines, shipping disasters once seen as almost inevitable were averted. It was as though each new rock lighthouse incrementally tamed the sea. In the Bishop's case, the surrounding waters were particularly dangerous, and taming them was a great coup.

But the subsequent wrecks of the *Schiller*, the *Enfant de*

Bretagne and numerous others near the lighthouse show that, however sublime our interventions, the sea unleashes forces beyond our control. As the skipper concludes the tale of the *Schiller*, there is a new potency to the retreating Bishop, a potency of success intermingled with failure. On that fateful night in 1875, this powerful presence was powerless to help.

The Bishop continued to shake in storms, despite Douglass's campaign of work. One of its keepers, W.J. Lewis, described the experience in *Ceaseless Vigil*, an astute and lyrical memoir of his time in the lighthouse service. Lewis was stationed there in the 1920s, and his vivid account of being stormbound in the tower illustrates just how alarming conditions could be: 'the whole structure trembled with the impact – a queer sensation beyond accurate description, and one which calls for strong nerves . . .'

Our expectation of a building is that it will be secure and immovable. To suddenly doubt the protective qualities of 6,000 tons of granite, particularly standing far out to sea, must have shaken the psyche. To witness the rattle of a cup and saucer for the first time must have been a nasty shock. But there was no choice but to bear these ordeals stoically, or resign from the service (and the job security, pension and other benefits it entailed, comparatively rare for the time). Like communities living on fault lines, keepers on stations like the Bishop had to live in a state of psychological readiness for these seaquakes. I cannot imagine it ever got any easier to endure them. Lewis recounts:

> The tower seemed almost alive as it danced on its foundations, unable to retaliate but only to stand firm and dance out the tune . . . I stood now at one of the top windows watching the huge waves sweep in from the Atlantic, heaving their volume towards the lantern and lashing over the top. The sea suddenly struck under the gallery coping with such force that the lens was partially lifted off its mercury bath

before dropping back and splashing the mercury like a shower into the lantern. The vibration was so terrific that it took two of us to replace new mantles on the burners as they were shaken off . . .

Storms of such intensity are rare and may be experienced only once in a lifetime. After this storm an inspection by qualified engineers was carried out on the base and the equipment of the lighthouse and not the least thing was found out of place.

That a tower like the Bishop can 'dance upon its foundations', as Lewis so beautifully put it, defies logic, confounds the senses. That its structural integrity is unaffected by this movement – as the recent Eddystone study seems to indicate – only deepens the sense of mystery. This surreal behaviour shakes our concept of a building, and gives these mighty structures an unexpected vulnerability.

No one speaks of the Bishop as we cover the distance back to St Mary's. Conversation ebbs among our fellow passengers, who seem ready to return to harbour. Instead of retracing our course through the Western Rocks, we bypass them to the north and motor through a large, clearer channel called the Broad Sound, for a safer progress through the sea. By this point, my father and I long for beer.

With the sun at its zenith I smear suncream on my cheeks like a cricketer. A hipflask brought against cold weather remains capped, the whisky too sun-warmed through the pewter. I eat absent-mindedly, still digesting all that we have seen. My father remarks how lagoon-still the waters were, the meekest Atlantic he has ever experienced (and he was brought up on the Cornish coast), despite the Bishop being in a sector renowned for its death-dealing waves. The sea was deceiving us, he felt; only it lulled us not into a sense of security, but one of disquietude. It glittered like the Caribbean, not the Atlantic; the sun burned fabulously overhead.

At these distant latitudes, the senses are heightened, perceptions sharpened. Reason is left on the quayside. We were not alone in our observations. Lewis had this to say about night watch (which he termed 'graveyard watch') in the Bishop's lantern room:

> Keeping watch has an extraordinary effect on the mind. There is time to think and for the imagination to play with thoughts. One finds oneself in this way fully prepared to believe in wholly unreal happenings and beings, and sound different from the usual lantern noises can cause a moment of terror. Some weird noises are heard which seem to have no origin, or anyway it is never known what caused them. And once on a very dark night when very few stars were visible and the low surrounding rocks were wrapped in dark I saw suddenly a brilliant shining pool. It looked like a huge diamond set in ebonite. Its light was dazzling and mysterious and there seemed no explanation. The pool was one of many I found on that part of the rock the next morning and in no way was different from its neighbours.

I thought of how ready I had been, in the mess room of the Haulbowline lighthouse, to believe in the hauntings that had resulted in its consecration. I remembered my musings about Norse deities placated from the ornamented, half-tide balcony – beliefs and speculations that had seemed ridiculous back on the mainland. But out at the Bishop, placed in a similarly extraordinary setting, this mindset seemed entirely possible again. That night, Lewis attempted to find an explanation for what he had seen:

> I trained a telescope and night glasses on it and found I could see everything in the pool quite clearly. My theory was that the pool was in the direct line of a particularly bright star's beam and that it received the light from one direction and reflected it in another. But it is only a guess.

Otherworldly events cluster here. In 1907, a schooner

with seven masts and seven sails, like a distorted hallucination of a ship, was wrecked on the nearby Shag Rock. In 1849, the first ill-fated Bishop Rock lighthouse was visited by the aptly named Lady Tower, an aristocrat, who sketched it merrily from a boat. Later, on the islet of Rosevear, inhabited by Douglass's workmen, a grand ball was once held when construction was nearly finished. In his biography of Douglass, Thomas Williams describes how:

> [t]he sheds were all cleared of their contents, brilliantly illuminated, and decorated with bunting, and, at the expected hour, the visitors arrived in innumerable boats. Dancing was kept up until early morning (when the guests rowed back by moonlight) to the accompaniment of the barrack band, led by James Douglass, who played well on the flute.

A remarkable event, given this islet is a wind-scoured, wave-struck hummock of scant grass and bedrock, just about field-sized. Working alone on Rosevear one day, a blacksmith heard ethereal music from a source he couldn't identify. He thought (or perhaps hoped) that it might somehow be the labourers returning from the lighthouse, so he continued to work his forge, expecting to see his colleagues scramble up the hill at any moment. But only hours later did they materialize, long after the music ceased, which the blacksmith described as 'not of this world'.

I think of Gerry, the phlegmatic ex-keeper of the Wolf Rock. He would have no truck with such talk. For him, there was nothing fantastical about lighthouse keeping, the structure, or the distance from the land. He was armoured against visions; Lewis positively revelled in them, despite claiming that he was 'not a romancer'. Indeed, Lewis seems to have been something of an exception to the general sobriety of most keepers, who spoke of their extraordinary circumstances as though they were perfectly commonplace.

But there is nothing ordinary about a place like the Bishop. Rock lighthouses are inherently surreal ventures. Mirage-like to a distant observer, but mountain-like to a close spectator, theirs is a strange duality, a quality of mystery alongside mastery. That a building can frequently dance upon its foundations is perhaps the most surreal aspect of all.

During my previous expedition to the Eddystone, Dave had suggested getting a photo of me with hand outstretched in such a way that I appeared to be holding Douglass's tower between thumb and forefinger. We spent an inordinate amount of time attempting to do it, trying to line up my hand with the lighthouse at the correct angle, but the sea had rolled too much under the catamaran's hulls, eventually foiling our photoshoot.

Our whimsical efforts there made the deeper point that it is difficult to position yourself in relation to these towers. Whatever the approach, there is always a distance between you and the lighthouse. Having travelled all the way to the Bishop from the distant mainland, I could not press my hands against the cold masonry, or lean up against the tower's flanks, as I could with most buildings on land. The boat could only get as close as the skipper dared, meaning final contact was never achieved, and the tower remained maddeningly out of grasp.

In prehistory, the Scilly Isles were a single landmass, split by rising sea levels into their present assemblage of isles and islets. This explains the apparently odd locations of some prehistoric Scillonian settlements. For instance, the islet of Nornour seems an unlikely place for a farm, but not if it was once a hillock of the larger island.

A central plain, which originally joined them all together, was flooded by rising sea levels by the sixth century AD, shortly after Britain ceased to be part of the Roman Empire. In some places, this plain is only just under water; at very low tides it is possible to walk between Tresco and Bryher. Indeed, as late as the Elizabethan period plains of salt marsh still joined some of the islands.

This inundation of the land may largely have happened in antiquity, but from it emerged folklore still known and recanted today. The segue from Isle to Isles could well have

19. Steps up to the Bishop Rock,
2017

produced the fable of Lyonesse, the drowned country somewhere west of Cornwall, where King Arthur is said to have slain
Mordred. Various locations have been posited for Lyonesse,
but one of the most persistent claims is that it lies beneath the
tranche of sea from Land's End to the Scilly Isles. There might
be a grain of truth to the theory that the Scillies were once
joined to Britain. At Wherrytown beach, near Penzance, low
tide exposes fossilized tree stumps, traces of an ancient forest
that was growing in the Bronze Age.

Wherrytown was also the location of a singular intervention into the sea. As well as the ancient tree stumps, low
tide here exposes curious rock formations: long dykes of 'elvan'
stone, which is a composite of quartz, feldspar and porphyry.
Lying about 240 yards offshore, they are reachable on foot when
the sea has retreated. Now, these unnamed formations are
nondescriptly dark and seaweed-strewn, but in the eighteenth
century, they sparkled with rich veinlets of tin ore. Miners
came to hack them out, but soon exhausted the surface deposits
and stopped visiting, deterred from further excavation by the
twice-daily immersion of the rocks by the tide.

But not Thomas Curtis, a miner 'of humble circumstances' from the Cornish mining town of Breage. In 1778, at
the age of 57, he began excavating the rocks to get at the rich
submarine seams of tin indicated by those veinlets that had
already been quarried. In doing so, he sank the Wherry Mine,
the world's first offshore mineshaft.

As with building a rock lighthouse, he could only work
between tides in the summer months. To hold back the sea,
he constructed a 20-foot high wooden turret around the mine
entrance, waterproofed with fat and pitch and buttressed with
iron. Three years later he had burrowed deep enough to find
the tin, and began extracting. The mine quickly became profit-
able: in 1792 alone, £3,000 worth of tin (over £400,000 today)
was brought up.

The wooden shafthead held back most of the sea, but it
still leaked into the mine. Before each shift could begin, the
miners spent up to two hours emptying seawater from the

workings with ropes and buckets. After six hours, the sea came into the workings once more. Though the men bailed efficiently the most they could empty was four gallons per minute; the sea could not be fully resisted.

In 1794, a visitor to this extraordinary venture related that it was:

> seventeen fathoms deep, that the sea continually drained into the workings, and that the roar of it could distinctly be heard. The descent is by means of a rope tied around the thighs, and you are let down in a manner exactly the same as a bucket into a well, for the water is more than knee deep in places.

This submarine mine was the inverse of a rock lighthouse like the Bishop. Rather than building upwards on a wave-swept hazard, Curtis burrowed downwards, creating void instead of structure. The dark glitter of tin at his mine's end was the obverse of a navigational light. But eventually the mine failed. A ship adrift in a storm demolished the wooden shafthead, and the sea raced in and closed the mine up.

A chancy and opportunistic project, the Wherry Mine stood only a few hundred yards out to sea, close by the safety of the shore. Perhaps this comparatively short distance made the Wherry miners complacent about the sea's power, satisfied to risk their ramshackle structure for the sake of whatever profit they could make before it was overwhelmed. As indicated by their constant bailing of the workings, this was an operation on borrowed time, in a space only temporarily annexed from the waves.

The lighthouse is a very different endeavour. Despite being the most seashaken of houses, it has prevailed against the sea. Great distance shaped it; the instantaneous destruction of the first, iron-framed attempt demonstrated cost-cutting and opportunism were foolhardy out here. As each mile mounted, there was a corresponding increase in the need for solidity and sublimity. By 1887, we had risen to the challenge posed by this distance, erecting an enduring monument, a withstanding stone.

We stake comparatively tiny claims in the waves; in turn, rising sea levels claim huge tracts of our dry land. Of course, this is an ancient contest: such inundations cost our prehistoric ancestors their farms, their field systems, their shrines, their homes. We share common ground with them in this, for the sea levels continue to rise, putting our own holdings at risk. But on the Scillies, the sea has not yet rubbed out our Bronze and Iron age ancestors: their standing stones immortalize them.

In their time, the Bishop Rock stood much more prominently out of the sea than now (and, coincidentally or not, the Bant's Carn burial chamber is aligned to point towards it). Today, most of the original rock is submerged, but the drum-like base of the lighthouse currently rises fully above the level of high water. Not for long. Slowly, over the coming centuries, the rising sea will creep up the base and swallow rung after gunmetal rung of the old entrance ladder. As it does so, it will flood the remaining parts of the low-lying Scilly Isles, covering the fields and extinguishing the settlements.

At 167 feet, the Bishop Rock lighthouse is taller than the highest Scillonian hill (Telegraph on St Mary's, at 157 feet). When the rising seas have completely engulfed the monoliths of our ancestors, the distant Bishop Rock will become the last stone standing above the waves.

Fastnet

A vital lighthouse

1854 AND 1904,
8 MILES OFF WEST CORK, IRELAND

Suddenly, I hear the cry 'Ditching! ditching! ditching!' and I make a mental note of this additional piece of jargon – meaning 'We're crashing' – and file it away next to 'airframe' for helicopter and 'whisks' for rotors. 'Brace! brace! brace!' cries a voice from the cockpit. Shuddering downwards fast, I brace as we hit the water with an impact that jolts me out of this absurdly inopportune thinking. Jostling and bumping into the guy next to me, I grope for the large escape handle with my left hand and for the circular buckle securing the four seat straps with my right hand, as we were trained. Water seethes into the cabin, levelling with my knees, then with my chest, and I draw in the biggest breath I can muster just before it reaches up for my throat. The machine overturns, plunging us into burbling darkness; I keep my eyes closed tight and my breath held fast.

Strapped into a capsized helicopter, I have never been this disorientated. Water has run into my nostrils and is plumbing my sinuses. But I must recall my training and act on it. Luckily, as we went down I had lunged towards the window – my escape hatch – and I now sense in the black that it's to my left. Refraining from deploying my EBS compressed-air breathing apparatus, I feel the air-pockets pressing in my lifesuit, yearning to float me upwards in these changed conditions. I'm on the point of releasing my seat straps when I remember that without an opening through which to escape I'll be buoyant and thus trapped.

As I pull down on the emergency handle the window comes ajar and I easily bat it away. My right hand goes to my strap-buckles and I twist them loose. Lunging for freedom, I become aware that my shoulders are almost too broad for the window opening. I get my head through, but the lifesuit and lifejacket snag repeatedly against the inner face of the airframe. Bugger. Breath almost out, I realize like a fool that the opening is taller than it is broad, so I corkscrew 90 degrees clockwise and sail sweetly through, the air in my lifesuit urging me up towards the surface, the air in my lungs clamouring to be replenished. I come up spluttering, deploy the lifejacket and strike out for the raft. As I climb up out of the training pool, the instructor claps me on the shoulder and says, 'For a writer, you held your nerve well.'

West Cork, Ireland, perishingly early on a February morning. Overhead, the rotors whine and gather force just like they do in films. We crackle with anticipation, clad in yellow flight suits and lifejackets, belted tightly into the cabin. Neilly smiles, and Dave raises his hands in mock supplication. The noise from the rotors becomes tremendous and we don headphones with intercoms to speak to one another. 'Here we go, lads,' says the pilot, as we are plucked from the ground with a wobble, rising with deceptive slowness until we dangle 1,500 feet up. Then we surge ahead, nose slightly dipped, rotors angled forward, West Cork in miniature below us, the sea rippling in front of us.

This is a bird's-eye perspective to have of the sea. Neither floating on its surface nor far removed in the clouds, we glide halfway between the points from which most people see it. We fly over numerous small islands, and I watch the last of their beaches pass underneath us, a frontier crossed.

Below, the water is lively, writhing, rising and falling in patterns too complex to take in at this speed. Sheets of aquamarine sea are covered in thousands of white scribbles, written by the gusts touching the surface. We bank to the west and the Fastnet appears in the starboard window, a great jagged hump with tiny flights of steps and level surfaces sculpted into the rock, like the exposed workings of a mine.

At the centre of the rock, the black base of the first lighthouse built in 1854 hangs on against the weather. It had been part of a cast-iron tower that rattled so much in heavy seas that it was condemned and dismantled. Its successor grows arrestingly from the Atlantic side of the rock, its foundations merged deeply into the base. Finished in 1904, the second Fastnet lighthouse is the last of the great rock lighthouses and is pitch-perfect in its form and details. Even from this airborne perspective, it has an obvious flawlessness, studded with bottle-green storm shutters and crowned with a white lantern. Between it and America there is nothing except breeze and water, and it looks gallantly into huge seas.

This vision of the lighthouse in the helicopter's safety glass is like a photograph about to be made real. We describe a perfect circle around the tower, as though attached to it by an invisible thread. As we hover, the pilot asks Neilly if it's OK to make a landing. A square concrete pad with a faded yellow 'H' advertises the landing-place. It looks a terribly small target for the pilot to take aim at. Surf only bothers the lower parts of the rock, safely below the halfway mark, so Neilly gives the all-clear. We draw a little way out to sea, turn around and begin a linear descent, the pilot steadying us against the winds. As we get closer, details spring out: explosive plumes of surf crashing against rock formations, gulls gamely riding the restive thermals, the shimmering slickness of the helipad. Despite the gusts, the pilot puts us down very gently, with a slight wobble as the helicopter settles on its runners. He keeps the rotors spinning and stays in the cabin, ready to take off quickly if the sea abruptly worsens.

Neilly flings open the door and noises swarm into the cabin, the surf below thundering and the rotors above roaring. We disembark gingerly, for no railing guards against the drop from the helipad, and the winds are strong and buffeting. Sea stretches for miles in every direction, blue far out and milky around the shards of the rock. Neilly grasps me by the hand and leads me away from the helicopter to a sheltered corner in the lee of the old lighthouse's base, a giant iron drum coated with black, cracked tar. Holding hands like the odd couple, we walk with difficulty against the wind. He leaves me there for my own safety and returns to help Dave unload the gear. Together they lumber over the baggage, tools, fuel and water drums and pile them next to me. Spray-painted a slick blue and orange, the helicopter looks alien against the primeval rock. When everything is offloaded, Neilly gives the thumbs-up, and the pilot draws the helicopter upwards and, with a returning wave, suavely veers off towards land.

There isn't any time to lose because the helicopter is returning with more cargo to unload. We lug the things down to the blockhouse underneath the helipad, a large, reinforced building where the diesel for the lighthouse is stored. It doesn't look like anything much, but it was here before either lighthouse, originally constructed in the 1850s as a barrack and workshops for the men building the first tower. Somehow the simple brick, iron and timber structure has clung on, though the weight of the concrete reinforcements for the helipad surely helps.

With rubber seals around the wrists, ankles and neck, our flight suits help keep out the wind. While waiting for the helicopter to return, we walk about. The Fastnet lighthouse is built into the south-west, Atlantic-facing part, where the rock is strongest. Angled diagonally, the other end of the rock points landward to the north-east; this is where the helipad and blockhouse stand. The topography is unusual: the rock's highest point is the middle, a third of the height of the lighthouse tower and level with its fourth floor. We stand there with the sun on our faces and the wind trying its best to usher us from the rock into the sea. Suddenly Dave exclaims and points skywards. I can see nothing at first, then just about make out the black dot of the helicopter returning.

I stay well back while it's unloaded for a second time. When it departs for good, Neilly seizes me by the hand and bawls 'Welcome to the Fastnet!' over the roar of the surf. We carry all the gear down to the blockhouse, and rest there awhile.

After shedding our flight suits and slipping them onto old coat hangers, we make our way down steps and across a puddled causeway to the lighthouse. Hefting a sledgehammer, Neilly leads the way with his shoulder set to the wind. Ahead, the green gunmetal doors are shut fast and secured with thick golden bolts. Last opened a few months ago, the bolts have stiffened in their housings. After fiddling with the padlock, a few blows from the sledgehammer unlimber them and a door leaf falls inwards with a clang. Neilly beckons for us to move quickly; we get inside just as a thick cloud of sea-spray hisses past the entrance.

You might describe this part of the building as the lobby, though no lobby ever looked quite like this. We are in a granite chamber with blocked windows, illuminated by fluorescent lights mounted on the ceiling. An iron column pierces the centre of the space; an iron stairway curves upwards to a room from which emanates the roaring drone of a generator, like machine-gun fire. Much of the bare granite walls is masked with various pieces of kit: cable trackways, snaking pipes, steel cabinets, fuseboxes, a water pump, and many other things of unclear purpose. And as with the lobby of a house, random items have gathered here: cagoules, ear defenders, a broom, a battered pair of shoes, a hacksaw. With the noise of the generator is the hot smell of constant motion, its ceaseless operation keeping the internal air moving, with the result that the tower is not as stale as most shut-up houses.

The first thing Neilly does is lever up an iron manhole cover in the stone floor. Beneath it is a dark void, a chamber as big as the room in which we stand, but subdivided by a wall with ladders clamped to either side. He shines a light through the opening, and sees water tremble and shimmer under the torch. We have water, he remarks, with something approaching relief. All of our drinking, cooking and washing water laps in this tank. We had ferried out extra drums against the possibility of a diminished supply, but Neilly seems satisfied that we will have enough for the week ahead. With the staccato roar of our power source above, the water tank proclaims our independence from land. To live on a rock lighthouse is to be intimate with the sources of your necessities.

We do not climb up into the lighthouse straight away. Neilly decides that it would be best to first return to the blockhouse and haul over our belongings, our food, Dave's tools and a few drums of water, just to be safe. Leading the way each time, Neilly halts us now and then at the doorway, just before waves spray past. He is able to read the swells coming in from the Atlantic, and knows when one is likely to overtop the causeway. Though they all look as one to me at the moment, later on he will impart some of this knowledge.

Our goods are safely, if damply, piled into the entrance room of the Fastnet. One by one we heft things up the curving ladders, all seven of them, to the kitchen. Climbing through the tower, we pass copper-bright rooms in which generators growl; mustily dark chambers in which woodwork bunks gleam; spartan white spaces flickering with dials and switches; then finally we are up into the penultimate floor, the kitchen. Sunlight pours in through three windows spaced around the walls; a door gives out onto the tower's lower balcony. We open it and a fresh sea-breeze surges into the tower, counteracting the smells of hot metal, oil and iron. On the eighth floor of the lighthouse, below the lantern, this kitchen is remarkably homely and well equipped. All the white goods you would find on land are here, with the exception of a dishwasher, only they are arranged in a circle following the walls. A circular table is placed in the middle, with an iron column piercing the room, a continuation of the one I had seen at ground-floor level. A VHF radio, blue coils of rope, binoculars, anemometers and compasses give a nautical gloss. A blue, white and pink mosaic floor immediately snares my attention, abstract, fan-like patterns radiating within coloured borders. Laid when the lighthouse was built, it is unexpectedly decorative and exquisite. As with the Bell Rock's Strangers' Room, and the cast-iron reliefs at Haulbowline, I ponder the motive for this luxurious flourish so far offshore.

The door onto the balcony points north-east towards Cape Clear Island, the nearest landfall. I step out and grasp the rail, roughly 130 feet above the sea. Parted by the tower behind me, twin gusts of southwesterly wind meet again in my ears. Below, there is a good view of the old lighthouse stump, the helipad, and the general plan of the rock. Around it, a white sea churns and stirs itself, with individual breakers leaping out and fizzing into spray. The tower's long, midday shadow falls on the water, pointing north at the distant mainland.

To live on the Fastnet for a week was the coup I had been seeking. By my reckoning, five nights in this tower would teach me more about rock lighthouses than I could ever amass from the decks of boats, through binoculars from headlands, from archives or from recollections, however pungent and detailed. It was an opportunity to get beneath the skin of a great deep-sea light comparable to the Eddystone, the Wolf, or the Bishop, all of which I had encountered in powerful ways, but with actual physical contact unattained. Above all, I hoped to gain a glimmer of empathy with the lost race of lighthouse keepers who had lived in these extraordinary buildings, by stepping into the curvatures of their lives.

A maintenance visit was scheduled for the end of February. Knowing the significance of the Fastnet to a venture like mine, my contacts at Irish Lights booked my passage on it without demur (to their eternal credit). But first, there was training to undergo, preparations to make. I learned how to escape from a helicopter if it crashed into the sea, an essential prerequisite even for writers. Somewhat oddly, this took place at a facility on a Norfolk airfield with twelve Trinity House technicians. As well as being a fortifying experience, it was a visceral reminder of the risks still faced by today's lighthouse engineers.

In the week preceding the trip, I planned what I would eat down to the last porridge oat. Five days' worth of meals had to be taken out there, packed into a single large rucksack along with everything else that I needed. Acting as my own quartermaster, I decided it would be a spartan regime: porridge flavoured with salt for breakfast, cheese and biscuits for lunch, grains, greens and lean cuts for dinner. Luxuries included coffee and chocolate. Ambitiously I packed a copy of *Ulysses*, reasoning that an extraordinary setting might help me breach this extraordinary book. All non-perishable foodstuffs I sourced in London, leaving only the perishable goods to buy in Ireland. In this kind of planning, I walked in step with the lighthouse keepers themselves, who had had to take all their provisions with them, and plan their diets in this military style.

In Ireland, the night before the helicopter flight, I had a last supper of Guinness, fat scallops and asparagus. Afterwards, I walked along the quayside to my lodgings with a rising sense of apprehension. What had seemed like a fantastic adventure in the run-up started to feel like an intimidating venture. I had no idea who I'd be spending the week with, how many of them there'd be, and how well disposed they'd be towards an English writer underfoot. I recalled my immersion in the capsized fuselage, and the nerves mounted even more.

I needn't have worried. Upon arriving at the helipad on Monday morning, I found Dave in one of the outbuildings making his preparations. An affable fitter from Wicklow, thirty-something and bearded like a privateer, Dave had an easy disposition that augured well. He had been a fitter in the Irish Lights for most of his career, as his father had before him. Between extravagant founts of tobacco vapour he told me of his task, and the reason for this trip: overhauling a generator, which involves taking it completely to pieces and fitting it back together again with new components. It seemed a simple enough endeavour, so I asked him why he needed five days to do it. You'll see, he grinned.

Out at the helipad, an orange windsock stirred lazily. A lithe pilot dressed in navy overalls with gold epaulettes inspected every inch of the helicopter, which looked reassuringly modern and functional. Various people came and went, assembling drums and containers, taking readings from instruments, and piling our belongings on the weighing-stand. Then, a tall, broad-shouldered figure arrived, with wiry grey hair and a seafarer's bearing. This was Neilly.

He pumped my hand vigorously, seemingly relieved at my appearance. You need to be able-bodied, he explained, there's a lot of lifting and climbing to be done. He had not known much about me, and had speculated about my fitness (I later learned some previous visitors had not been very agile).

We joked about my Greek-sounding surname, and he remarked that he was glad my English was good, as we'd be doing a lot of talking over the next week.

But there was little time for it at this moment. The three of us put on our flight suits and watched the requisite safety video. We loaded the gear into the back of the helicopter. Neilly took me aside and told me what to do when we touched down on the helipad (keep out of the way, essentially). I was pleased to be going with him and Dave, solid, worldly characters who seemed as though they wouldn't spoil at close quarters. Conversely, they seemed half amused to be chaperoning a conservationist. We trooped in our costumes to the airframe, and the orange windsock pointed encouragingly out to sea.

On Tuesday morning, I awake to the muffled burr of the generator a few levels below. A beam of sunlight slants through the storm shutter, striking the iron column in the centre of my room (as there are only three of us, we each have our own). Swells boom distantly against the foot of the lighthouse below. I reach out to the curving masonry of the wall, which is not stone cold as it had been at the Perch Rock, but infused with residual warmth. This is a living building, I think to myself. I lie there sleepily for a little while longer, then swing out of the bunk and search for my shoes on the delicate mosaic floor. Remote scuffling from above tells me the others are already up, and I climb the steep, curving ladders in search of them.

They sit quietly at the round table in the kitchen, which is brilliant with sunlight and prospects of the sea. I pour coffee and a glass of water, which tastes not unpleasantly of the granite tank in which it rests. After a cordial breakfast, we discuss what is to be done with the day. Dave will begin his disassembly of the generator, about which he seems a little preoccupied. I don't blame him. The previous evening, he had described the scale of the task: over 1,000 components to be dismantled and placed in careful order, documented with a smartphone camera, ready for reassembly. In a circular room cramped with other machinery, this is not as easy as it sounds. The components range in size from the engine block down to the tiniest rubber gasket, all of them slippery with oil. Just one missing piece is all it would take to scupper the work, and I can now see why he needs five days.

We must support him however we can, says Neilly, after he goes downstairs to begin. I agree, and ask whether any chores need doing. He explains how he usually begins his time on the Fastnet by giving the place a good sweep, but seems dubious about me helping him. You're under no obligations, Tom, he says emphatically. After a little debate, we resolve to sweep the place out together. My real motive is that housekeeping requires close observation, and is therefore a good way to study every inch of the lighthouse. I finish my coffee and we begin.

It's about ten in the morning. We start up in the lantern room above the kitchen. It is breathtaking, especially on so fine a day: a triple-height space, mostly glazed, in which a colossal biform lens slowly turns. On each of its four sides, concentric prisms of glass radiate outwards from a central bull's eye, held within an intricate frame. The arrangement is repeated again above, so there are eight faces in total. This is the first original lens I have seen working *in situ*. Moved by a little half-horsepower motor, it turns seamlessly, sitting in a frictionless mercury trough. Though it weighs 6 tons, the whole arrangement can be moved with the pressure of a little finger.

I sweep dust into piles that Neilly shovels into a refuse sack. We find a rhythm and get the job done quickly, descending through each level of the lighthouse. There is much detail to admire, most eye-catchingly the mosaic floors, present on all but a few of the levels. Neilly remarks that Italian craftsmen were brought to Ireland in 1904 just to lay them. There is a theory that the failure of the first Fastnet lighthouse so embarrassed the commissioners that they were determined to build its successor perfectly, inside and out, whatever the expense.

Other details are subtler. I admire the cast-iron treads of the ladders and the elegance with which they meet their landings. Neilly enthuses most about the gunmetal windows throughout the tower. Stopping by one on the landing between floors, he explains how it works. Two hinged lights open inwards and meet at the centre, where they are secured by a vertical revolving bolt that engages with studs in the frame to make them weathertight. In the stonework above, a thoughtful indent has been carved to receive the bolt when fully open. The two lights close seamlessly, such that Neilly says a piece of paper would be neatly sliced in two if placed between them. The rectangular, globe-ended handle that operates this mechanism fits satisfyingly in the hand, and is secured with a neat little hasp. Over a century after the windows were installed, they work perfectly.

From top to bottom, the order of the rooms runs: lantern, kitchen, service room (annexed as a bedroom by Dave), first bedroom (Neilly's), second bedroom (mine), bathroom, upper engine room, lower engine room, entrance. We have swept out seven floors when we encounter Dave in the racket of the lower engine room. There are three generators in the lighthouse, one in the upper engine room (No. 3) and two in the lower (Nos 1 and 2). Painted a dark green, bulbous and circular on one end and boxy and square at the other, they look like small steam locomotives with the wheels removed. Pipes lead from them into the walls. Only one of the three operates at once, powering all the appliances and the navigational light; the other two are there as failsafes.

They do a lot of work. No. 2, currently active, has been operating continuously for something like 10,000 hours, so Dave decides to switch over to No. 1 to give it respite. After some yelled discussion, he and Neilly move gingerly around the machinery to the blinking switchboards. They signal to one another, Dave presses a button, and suddenly the tower slumps into darkness and silence. A softer standby light falters on, then, after a pause, No. 1 revs crazily and the tower shivers back to life.

By now it's midday. Lunch is bread, cheese, onions and ham, taken at the round table in a fresh sea-breeze. I insist on doing the washing-up, despite the others' protests; the sink is below a window that looks out onto nothing but the infinite

Atlantic, a view to make a banquet's worth of plate-scrubbing possible, even worthwhile.

Afterwards, Dave descends back to the depths of his workplace while Neilly and I ascend up to the bright lantern. He prowls the space with a clipboard, reading dials and gauges. Unlike Haulbowline, converted to solar, electrical operation, the Fastnet still belongs to the diesel, mechanical age. As with the engine rooms below, there is an extraordinary cacophony of modern pipework, cabling, steel cabinets and other technology necessary to operate the lighthouse automatically. Punched through walls and ceilings, the installations have been done as sensitively as possible, yet they crowd the surfaces of the rooms and cloud their original forms.

We reflect that all this clutter is required to do the job of three keepers. When the Fastnet was manned, and unaltered, it was a simple, elegant machine. The lens was turned by a clockwork mechanism that relied on weights on chains housed in the iron column descending through the lighthouse. Keepers wound and rewound it, lit the paraffin burners at dusk, and snuffed them out at dawn. They logged the weather and monitored the state of the lighthouse. Their judgement and initiative overcame problems and emergencies. Now all this is done mechanically. It occurs to me that the sheer volume of gadgetry and servicing replacing three people demonstrates just how precisely designed we are.

As the day winds down, the weather winds up. In the kitchen, the VHF radio crackles with a Small Craft Warning and a Gale Warning from Valentia coastguard, meaning a force 8 gale is blowing, and the sea is expected to be rough. We eat our dinner to the sound of the winds getting higher around the walls. Tired out by the day's labours, we all retire early. I try to make a dent in *Ulysses*, but can't, so pack it safely into the bottom of my rucksack, where it will remain for the rest of my time here. Tomorrow, if the sea has abated, Neilly has promised to show me around the rock, to get a good view of the tower from the outside. Inside, the bedroom has the feeling of a stronghold, enclosed by massive granite surfaces like a circular castle keep. But shortly after I turn out the light and close my eyes, there is a distant, ominous crash above the noise of the generator. It was the sea rushing against the lighthouse, and I swear I felt a tremor.

Breaking the sea due south of Ireland's tip, the Fastnet occupies a critical navigational position. It was the last thing Irish emigrants saw as their ships slid out of the eastern ports for America, bequeathing it the name 'Ireland's teardrop'. Conversely, it was a more jubilant prospect for those coming the other way, being the first thing encountered by Ireland- and Britain-bound American shipping after the void of the ocean. Latterly, it has become the centrifuge around which racing yachts annually swing as they compete out of Cowes; a slicker boat race, sponsored by Rolex, over much different emotional swells.

This important approach was unmarked until 1818, when a land lighthouse was constructed on the south cliffs of Cape Clear Island, between the mainland and the Fastnet. It would transpire to be a poor siting. As I saw myself from the Fastnet's balcony one foggy morning, the upper reaches of that island and its lighthouse can be rendered completely invisible by mist, a phenomenon that would have disastrous consequences. On a hazy November night in 1847, the American packet vessel *Stephen Whitney* was wrecked off nearby Crookhaven. Fog had concealed the Cape Clear light, causing the captain to miscalculate their position and sail straight onto the coast. Of the 110 people on board, only eighteen survived. A few days afterwards, the *Cork Constitution* reported:

> An awful calamity has taken place on our coast. Ninety-two fellow creatures have been hurried into eternity, and the friends who were watching to welcome their arrival are plunged in mourning and woe. Since the wreck of the *Killarney*, we have had nothing so afflicting on the Irish coast. The vessel was one of

those noble liners for which the communication between Liverpool and New York is famed . . .

Then unmarked, and lying 4 miles further out in the Atlantic
than Cape Clear, the Fastnet Rock was a much more effective
location for a lighthouse. In response to the *Stephen Whitney*
disaster, the Commissioners of Irish Lights spent six years
building one here, from 1848 until 1 January 1854, when its
light first shone. This was a cast-iron tower designed by George
Halpin Junior, the son of the Haulbowline's builder, George
Halpin Senior. As with his father, there is little information
available about Halpin the younger; as with Haulbowline,
there are few details of the construction of this first Fastnet
lighthouse, but it was an odd arrangement. The three-storey
iron tower contained only the fuel stores and the light itself –
the keepers' living quarters were provided in a narrow, rectangular single-storey building jutting out from the tower's base.

The whole thing was too weak and, despite reinforcement with more cast iron in the 1860s, the commissioners
knew that it would not last. It shook too pronouncedly in heavy
weather, and a lighthouse of the same design on the Calf Rock
was destroyed in 1881. How they ever thought it would be ad-
equate is a mystery, especially given the failure of the first iron
Bishop Rock lighthouse in a location of similar exposure. So, in
the 1890s, they condemned it and plotted the construction of a
new granite tower, such as those then completed on the Wolf,
the Eddystone and the Bishop rocks.

William Douglass, brother of James, had been appointed
the commissioners' engineer in 1878. Having helped build the
rock lighthouses at Les Hanois, the Wolf, and the Great Bass-
ess reef off the Sri Lankan coast, he distilled his experience
on these projects into a superlative design for the Fastnet. As
the evidence of the windows and other fixtures demonstrates,
every inch of the building was masterfully treated.

By this time, bitter failures and mercurial successes had
elevated rock lighthouse building to a prodigious science. All
the lessons learned on previous towers shaped the Fastnet: a

tapering silhouette of the best Cornish granite, a stepped base to sunder the waves, lateral and vertical dovetailing of the masonry, gunmetal storm shutters flush with the curved exterior, gunmetal fittings to weigh down the tower as much as possible, steam-assisted construction gear (on a custom-made ship named *Irene*), and a first-order biform optical lens with a range of 27 nautical miles. Indeed, rarely have the words 'first-order' been so fitting a description for a building.

On Wednesday morning, Neilly and I heave open the gunmetal entrance doors and venture out onto the causeway. As promised, he is showing me around the rock and we have a few hours to explore it before the sea becomes too rough for safety. He potters about, peering over ledges and inspecting surfaces proprietorially. The air is leaden and fog has made visibility extremely poor, completely cloaking the horizon so that our rock seems a solitary, enshrouded outpost.

Strictly speaking, there are two parts to this hazard: 'Big' Fastnet and 'Little' Fastnet, separated by a small channel, but part of the same outcrop below. It consists of hard clay slate of the Lower Silurian age, approximately 430 million years old. We roam around 'Big' Fastnet, where the lighthouses and helipad stand, and Neilly points out places where strong waves have splintered, fractured and fissured the rock. It's chilling to see this evidence of the sea's power. During one storm, an especially potent wave sheared off a huge chunk along the grain and dropped it onto the helipad, gouging it considerably. He shows me a long fissure near the causeway that has widened since he was last here. All over the rock, there is a contrast between these wild, unworked textures and the more formal surfaces and steps hacked out by the Fastnet's builders. Much of the workings survive: the causeway, a landing-quay, a rusting, dismantled iron derrick to unload cargo, and the iron rails of a tramway for moving blocks of stone.

Towering over these defunct workings is the end result. Fastnet is the biggest rock lighthouse of them all, 177 feet high (10 feet higher than the Bishop), 52 feet wide at the base (10 feet wider than the Bell). Each stone of the lighthouse is precisely carved and set. The joints between them show little sign of wear. Each junction between the gunmetal fittings and masonry looks immaculate. Trace amounts of rust and wave-stains aside, the tower is in perfect condition. It is as much a flawless work of construction as a masterly design.

As we study the details, Neilly tells me much of this perfect execution was down not to Douglass, but to another man. In the many photographs of the Fastnet's construction, one figure constantly appears: a stocky, moustachioed fellow in a bright white coat, like a scientist, posing with the men and hawkishly overseeing the operations.

This was James Kavanagh, a master mason from Wicklow and the foreman in charge of the building of the Fastnet. He was a man in whose fabulous singlemindedness there is some-thing of the early Celtic Christians who fashioned hermitages on remote islands around Scotland and Ireland (one, Skellig Michael, was established in the seventh century AD and lies relatively close to the Fastnet off the Kerry coast). This was not because he was superlatively devout himself, but because he lived like them – as his own gaoler on this unforgiving rock.

Kavanagh insisted on setting every interlocking piece of the tower himself, from the burly foundation stones to the delicate cornice at the top. While others hauled and craned the stones to the rising tower, he saw them home with his own hands. He had a dedication to the perfection of this build that amounted almost to mania. From 1896 until 1903, he refused to go ashore while construction was underway, living in a small barrack with his men, who sensibly went home regularly on ro-tation. Only when operations ceased for winter would he prise himself from the rock.

In the diesel store under the helipad, Neilly levers up a trapdoor in the floor, and we descend into a series of dark cata-combs hacked out of the clay slate. Light filters dimly through small glass blocks in the walls, revealing that these spaces are partially formed out of brick, timber and iron beams. Con-structed in the 1890s, they were the barracks and storerooms that housed the Fastnet's builders. It is very surprising they haven't been washed away, I say to Neilly, and he shrugs. We pause in the corner of one room, and he points to an apparently featureless, slimy section of wall against which some pieces of timber are propped. Under torchlight, I discern the profile of a bricked-up doorway. This, he says solemnly, was Kavanagh's hole.

He drove his men hard, but fairly. Rising at dawn, he made them swab out this barrack against lice and infections, and after breakfast worked them until dusk. He threw himself into the work alongside them, sharing all the dangers, the only concession to hierarchy being this small alcove, now sealed off, to which he occasionally retired and slept.

It is difficult to understand quite what drove him. Was it simply the satisfaction of seeing a job well done, or was there something else? Certainly, it must have taken a lot to keep him from his wife and family in Wicklow, whom he saw only in the winters during those years of the Fastnet's construction. It could have been about making his mark with a stellar project, though he was already advanced in his career and acknowledged as a master mason by this time. Or it may be that Kavanagh initially approached this job as though it were any other, but that slowly the atmosphere of the Fastnet and the magnificence of the venture began to work on him. Perhaps he came to think of those unusual, interlocking masonry pieces as his own puzzle to assemble, whatever the personal cost.

But those photographs of him show few outward traces of mania. Instead, they correlate with the workmen's testimony of a charismatic man, stern but affectionate, leading from the front and tackling this weighty venture with a lightness of touch. You can almost hear him corralling and bantering with his men, cussing them, berating them for their mistakes and praising them for their successes.

Kavanagh set the last stone on 3 June 1903, at the age of 47. With seven years of ascetic living pent up inside him, he took ill soon afterwards and was sent ashore. A month later, on the day of his wedding anniversary, apoplexy struck him dead. Tragically, he left a wife and eight children, the youngest

20. James Kavanagh (far left in the
white jacket) building the Fastnet,
*c.*1902

of whom was not yet twelve months old. Flying her colours
at half-mast, the *Irene* transported his body to Wicklow. Four
coastguards carried his flag-draped coffin along the quayside
and through the streets. Over a thousand people followed the
great man home.

Time to be going, says Neilly, as the weather begins to
shift. Quickly the fog clears and the windspeed increases. Spray
threatens to overtop the causeway and we scurry to safety
inside, our exploration of the rock concluded for now.

Climbing up through the tower on our way to the balcony, we pause in the upper engine room to watch Dave at work.
Clad in a white boiler suit, he crouches bodily over the partially
disassembled generator as though wrestling with it. It is an intimidating sight. On a large, improvised table beside him, hundreds of pieces are arranged in neat rows, annotated in marker
pen. Like Kavanagh, he has his own puzzle to assemble, though

of a very different scale. With the other generator below roaring loudly, he doesn't notice us, and we leave him in the depths of his concentration.

Up in the kitchen, Neilly unhooks his anemometer from the wall and shows me how to measure the windspeed out on the balcony. It is blowing at 42 knots, which registers at Force 9 on the Beaufort scale of wind force. This sounds dramatic, but Neilly seems unbothered by it. During his stint as Fastnet attendant, he's seen far stronger winds and taller waves. Even so, during my time on the Fastnet the windspeed seldom drops below Force 8, described in the scale's accompanying text as 'generally impedes progress'. For most of the time, it keeps us inside the tower, walking in circles, and ascending and descending the levels like the old clockwork mechanism that once turned the lens.

On Thursday lunchtime, we receive news that our departure has been shifted from Friday to Saturday. It seems the winds are forecast to be too strong for the helicopter, which can safely fly at windspeeds of up to 50 knots. Neilly and Dave are phlegmatic about this, and seemed to expect it, though they are hardly overjoyed. Despite the advances made from the days of boat reliefs and zipwire, it is still impossible to fully guarantee arrival and departure times. I feel a glimmer of empathy with the keepers. Things about this business I had taken with a pinch of salt now seem acute. This charismatic marooning is now tinged with yearnings for home and halcyon weather. And, as confirmation of our relief cannot be given until half an hour or so beforehand, we are kept in a kind of slow-burning suspense for the rest of the visit.

No matter. We talk of how another day was a gift for Dave, who can use it to conduct extensive tests when he finishes rebuilding the generator. As we end lunch – the remains of the previous evening's chilli – I ask him how it's going. 'Tom,' he says circumspectly, 'I'll know when I press that button and the thing starts.' It seems a tall order for him to have bear this responsibility on his own, with no technical backup should any problems arise. But he is quite composed under the pressure, and disappears back to the depths.

I spend time up in the lantern room. At some point during our stay, Neilly had discovered a crack in one of the windowpanes, and that morning we had carried a kite-shaped replacement pane up there ready for the glaziers. Despite the brilliance of the sunshine today, the sea is running high. Neilly shows me how to interpret the swells coming in from the Atlantic. They march in from the ocean in rows, sometimes offset, sometimes in line, and every fourth one seems to be larger and break more heavily than the others. This is how he calculates when it's safe to move around on the rock and to and fro on the causeway. For him, it's an innate kind of understanding, derived from a lifetime's scrutiny of the sea.

Neilly was raised on a farm near the sea on the Mizen peninsula, West Cork, which can easily be seen from the Fastnet on a clear day. After a number of different jobs, he joined the Irish lighthouse service as Coastal Tradesman, repairing and redecorating lighthouses across Ireland. As with Dave's mobile role as a fitter, the work was peripatetic; in the evenings, both of them exchange stories of strange sights and escapades on far-flung Irish headlands. Four of them grappling with a furious seal on a beach to free it from a painful piece of wire mesh. Running for cover as the skies were blotted out by thousands of migrating gannets, dropping guano like Lancaster bombers. Odder still, finding a quantity of spring rabbits had invaded the paint stores and covered themselves in pink pigment, so that one man thought he was having visions as they gambolled pinkly in the fields. They worked with some strange fellows too, such as the man who when on duty ate only pig's trotters *confit*, and when off drank only imperial quantities of port.

They call this life 'on the coast'. It comes with heavy responsibilities: care of the nation's lighthouses, which must work without fail, and their remoteness means there is often no recourse to headquarters. In such a vital navigational function, there is little room for error even in the smallest jobs. But this is counterbalanced by a greater autonomy and a special, simpler texture of work now lost to most of us. It is the privilege of working in extreme surroundings, distilled to the elements, handling power and moving parts, surrounded by stone, water and air. What they do is so appealing because this kind of mechanical, practical work has increasingly faded from view for most people. Working 'on the coast' seems to have a richer, more elemental texture to it than any office job, and both men grimaced when I told them about mine.

From the lantern, Neilly and I scan the horizon for ships. During my time here so far, I haven't seen many, save a few bar-shaped silhouettes of tankers on the horizon. At the moment, the sea looks too rough for all but the larger vessels, but we spot a bright red trawler struggling to port. Though it moves slowly, it's hypnotic to watch, swaying and dipping on the swells, larger waves rearing behind and shunting it forwards. It looks desperately small out there. Though the name of the vessel eludes us, Neilly thinks he recognizes it from Baltimore, a small harbour near his home. He says he thinks it will make it back, but there is a note of worry in his voice. I watch it until I can't see it any more.

It is dangerous not to fear the sea, he emphasizes. He tells me how his wife, Jackie, is a cox on the local lifeboat, and has seen first-hand the havoc the sea can wreak, how boats too easily get into difficulty. Possibly we understand it less now that digital instruments steer us to our destinations and back. He believes we are too insulated by safety measures, that we take the sea for granted. At his local pub near the harbour, amateur yachtsmen used to enter proudly wearing pristine nautical gear, flippantly proclaiming that they were men of the sea. This levity so bothered the regulars that signs had to be erected to stop them. Among more experienced salts, to lose your fear of the sea is to place yourself in greater danger. Neilly has spent time on trawlers, and tells me that few trawlermen can swim. Why would they bother, he says. They know what their chances of survival would be in the frigid, heaving Atlantic.

Their world is bounded by the gunwales of their trawlers, not to be crossed under any circumstances.

With that, he claps me on the shoulder and heads downstairs to help Dave. I sit with my back to the ladder between the lantern's gantries, the massive lens turning silently beside me, looking out over the Atlantic. A formation of gulls rides around the tower. Here, in their element, I realize they are beautiful things, poised silently on the thermals, a far cry from the squawking, chip-stealing reprobates of harboursides.

I had time, from the elevated perspective of the lower balcony and lantern, to study the sea, really look at it, and watch it behaving in a way you don't really see from the shore. It breaks around the reef in repeating patterns that reflect the submerged geology around the rock's waist. There is a point to the south-west, in the path of the Atlantic, where the sea gathers itself up and splinters over a submerged reef on a long, horizontal plume that looks like the scaly neck of a giant beast. On a smaller piece of rock nearby it breaks into a perfectly contained white cloud, always the same size and shape. Engulfing the Little Fastnet, the sea falls back and dribbles in thousands of streams down crevices that will deepen over the centuries. Here, you get something of the sea's eternity – rising, falling, swelling, calming, dousing and rinsing and thrusting against the rocks in myriad ways, a lazy, beast-like play of motion that will never end.

It teaches me that, if and when their day of reckoning finally comes, there is another use for rock lighthouses. It's so obvious that I wonder why it didn't occur to me until now. Simply, they are fine observatories from which to contemplate the sea.

Late on Thursday afternoon, Dave completed his puzzle. I was porpoise-watching on the balcony when Neilly called up to say the power would temporarily be off as they switched to the newly reassembled generator. Rather than go down to watch the proceedings, I decided to stay out of the way, reckoning that this moment of truth would be stressful enough for Dave without an audience.

Their yelled conversation floated up from the tower's depths, mingled with unidentifiable noises. I sat at the round table in the kitchen and waited. Suddenly, the power drained out of the room, the fridge ceased to hum and the lights were extinguished. Outside, the weather was grey and noncommittal, barely illuminating the darkened kitchen through the windows. Time passed. I peeled a satsuma, and began to worry for Dave. Had he mislaid a tiny piece of the puzzle? Was the machine refusing to cooperate? Unused to the silence in this normally noisy tower, I drummed my fingers on the table, paced in circles around the kitchen, fiddled with my binoculars and my notebooks.

But then, the silence was chased out of the lighthouse by the glorious racket of an engine gunning and bursting into life. The lights sprang on, my phone showed charge, and the appliances quietly awoke as electricity flooded the cables throughout the tower as sap rises through a tree. Dave and Neilly came upstairs, jubilant, and pronounced the trip a resounding success. I felt privileged to be there with them. There was wistful but unfulfilled talk of the need for celebratory whiskey.

Fastnet was the last of the great rock lighthouses to be built. When it was finished in 1904, all the hazards around Britain and Ireland then considered to need such a lighthouse had been marked. With their awe-inspiring logistical challenges, these hand-made granite towers were enormously expensive to build. Ill-fated experiments with other materials, most notably iron for the first Bishop and Fastnet, showed that granite was the surest and best approach in this period.

As time moved on and technology developed, newer methods made it possible to place navigational aids offshore in positions where no rock existed on which to build. Newer, cheaper materials began to be used with more certainty. In 1918, a squat, drum-like concrete tower was built on land, towed out into the English Channel and sunk on the Nab rocks, to replace the Nab lightvessel. In the 1960s, a concrete tower was sunk on an underwater platform prepared by divers on the Kish sandbank in the Irish sea, replacing the Kish lightvessel. In the 1970s, a similar method was used to place the Royal Sovereign lighthouse platform out in the English Channel.

These later offshore lighthouses are ingenious works of engineering. But they don't have the charisma of the rock lighthouses. I would not classify them as such. They are utilitarian in design, machine-made, and all very different in appearance. They lack the exquisite workmanship of the truer rock lighthouses like the Fastnet, the gruelling strain of building them exemplified by men such as James Kavanagh, and the miraculous quality of such stupendous achievements in less advanced times than ours. From the Bell Rock of 1811 to the Fastnet of 1904, this family of granite towers are the quintessence of lighthouses. In their magnificence, they are the truest buildings of them all.

On Friday, our last day in the Fastnet, I spend time lingering in the rooms, making videos and taking photographs, trying to drink in as much as I can before we leave the next morning. We begin to wind down our presence here, restoring the lighthouse to its uninhabited state. When the work is done, Neilly and I sprawl around the kitchen table, counting down the hours, while Dave checks and double-checks the engines below.

Our talk turns towards the future. As well as being the last and arguably the finest to be constructed, Fastnet is one of the last diesel-powered, mechanical lights. Neilly reckons its solarization is not far off. This would remove the generators and miles of cabling and pipework covering the internal walls and mar the fine exterior of the lighthouse with solar panels.

One form of light fuelling another is a pleasing idea, but this solar way of operating is largely invisible and intangible. I find the generators, piping and cabling in the Fastnet affecting because they give the lighthouse a visible identity as a working thing. Moreover, the miles of copper piping have been skilfully wrought, carefully skirting original features like the mosaic floors. They now seem part of the building, a layer of its being rather than a crude overlay. If its initial clockwork operation represents a first phase of the lighthouse's life, this mechanical operation represents a second, a valid part of the building's narrative that shouldn't be erased. At Haulbowline, virtually all traces of the mechanical phase had been ripped out, and my understanding of the lighthouse's functional history had consequently been poorer. Far from being static, unchanging works of engineering, rock lighthouses have phases of development much like terrestrial buildings. In this sense, they have lifespans that will only be curtailed if they cease to function.

In a pleasing twist, I discovered that it was Dave's father who installed much of the pipework in the 1970s. Spending five days and nights with Dave and Neilly on the Fastnet demonstrated that the story of rock lighthouses did not end with the removal of their keepers and conversion to automatic operation. The work of Neilly, Dave and others like them is a continuity of attention, of care and maintenance of these buildings, albeit less visible and more peripatetic than the daily ministrations of the keepers. In the 1980s and 1990s, the newly automated lighthouses were described as 'unwatched', and the same might be said of the work that continues on them today.

As the Fastnet was automated in March 1989, Neilly was made its attendant. In a sense, his role replaced that of the keepers'. The last keepers, he tells us, couldn't believe the lighthouse would function without them. On their last night, convinced that they would be reprieved at the eleventh hour, they continued to perform their duties in the lighthouse, attending to the light and keeping the watches, even though it had already been automated. In his authoritative work on the Fastnet, James Morrissey recalls the haunting suggestion of its last Principal Keeper, Dick O'Driscoll, that once the keepers had left for good the Fastnet should revert to its original Gaelic name, *An Charraig Aonair*, 'the rock that stands alone'.

Lying in my bunk on Friday night, I realize how fitting an end this is to my journeying. From the Bell to the Bishop, each rock lighthouse has spoken differently: as a pioneer, as a monument, as a mystery, as a ruin, as a home, as a distant monolith. Buildings are given identities and meanings by people, so it is remarkable how, in their periphery, little-visited rock lighthouses should have such vibrant characters. But it was with the Fastnet that I had perhaps found their essence. More than any of their other guises, these buildings have a unique inner life of their own. They are not static, but age and change idiosyncratically to suit our demands of them. Most remarkable of all, they thrive under tougher weathering than that borne by any other sort of building. In this, rock lighthouses stand together, not alone.

Epilogue

In Salutem Omnium
('For the Safety of All')

Motto of the Irish Lights

Just before midnight, on Garrison Hill, my wife and I settle down on a bench under the walls of the old Star Castle. After dinner we decided to walk up here, through the quiet streets of St Mary's, to inspect the darkness for the beam of the Bishop Rock. On the way, our footsteps sounded crisply in the empty streets and the empty beaches swished softly with the sea. It is not yet drinking-up time, and the only signs of life come from the orange glow of the pub windows. Now and then, we nip from the pewter hipflask I took out to the Bishop a few days earlier, but which remained capped on the boat's hot deck.

Night-time visibility is excellent in the Scilly Isles. The settlements on the islands are not large enough to taint the sky with light pollution so the stars shine down unimpeded. On our bench, we tip our heads back and admire the constellations. Tonight, Orion's Belt is particularly vivid, and we spot the Plough and a few others. Being Londoners, we're not totally confident in our identifications; in the capital, there are few opportunities for stargazing as a purple veil of pollutants hides them from view. Here, they shine piercingly and unfamiliarly overhead.

We look back down at the dark horizon, remembering why we're here. It is pitch-black, so I can't tell for certain, but I believe we face roughly south-west, towards the Western Rocks and the Bishop. But, unexpectedly, a battery of other lights litters the seascape in this view. They wink quickly, out of sync with one another, combining to form no rhythm of flashes but a cacophony instead. Which one is it, Josa murmurs, and I confess that I have no idea. I realize I am ill-prepared for this night-time excursion, because I have failed to properly research the Bishop's characteristic: the identifying signature of its light.

Something tells me that the Bishop is not among the lights we initially see. There is harshness and flatness to them that is characteristic of modern LED technology; I suspect they come from newer buoys and poles marking hazards in the channel of sea between St Mary's and St Agnes. LEDs are well suited to such navigational aids because they are long-lasting, require little maintenance and are capable of great brightness (the same reasons they are frequently used for street lights). However, they lack the depth of older light sources such as the prisms and filaments of the rock lighthouses.

But, as we stare into this other constellation, one particular light differentiates itself from the rest. Two white flashes, one quickly succeeding the other, then a period of darkness. I say white, but the colour is warmer, yellower. It does not have the diamond brightness of the stars or the brittle whiteness of the LEDs. Each of the flashes perceptibly swells and diminishes, coming as though flung over a long distance. It can only be the Bishop Rock.

We strain our eyes for it, trying to ignore the LEDs dancing in front of it. After a time, the Bishop's two flashes come again. They seem to imprint themselves on my retina, leaving behind a fading yellow tunnel, a far more lasting impression than the modern lights in the foreground. This is a more venerable light of awesome range and power.

Up in the Bishop's distant lantern, the rotating prisms capture the rays and hurl them to us as flashes. With a brightness of 60,000 candela and a range of 20 nautical miles, its hyperradial optic is original and one of the finest to have been made. And the passing of the Bishop's rays through the old glassware gives them a beautiful golden depth.

We admire this quality, especially compared with the later technology winking alongside it. I think of my expedition to the tower a few days before, when even up close it had seemed as mysterious as a standing stone. Now, from a distance, in the dark, it feels strangely knowable. Seeing the Bishop's light is like seeing its pulse, its animating spirit. There is the feeling that at last the tower is communicating. From that old tower, there come two white flashes, every fifteen seconds, cutting decisively through the younger lights.

Our thoughts stray to the future. No one seemed to know what the next phase of the rock lighthouses' story would be, or would entertain the idea that, one day, these towers could be redundant for navigational purposes. Perhaps it is an emotional thing, like refusing to countenance the death of a loved one. But technology advances at incomprehensible speed. That they should cease to operate seems unthinkable – such is the feeling of permanence they radiate – but it was once unthinkable that they should ever be de-manned and automated.

Yet, for now at least, there is enough shipping in British waters to warrant their continued operation. Skippers James and Dave both told me how they navigated by them. What safeguards them, perhaps, is the certainty they offer. Whether standing by day or flashing by night, rock lighthouses are the last failsafes. Satellite navigation is very efficient, but it is not immune to failure, being vulnerable to cyber-attack or even damage from space debris. Rock lighthouses may shake in storms, but they remain as fixed points, warning of hazards in the fluid sectors of the world.

Josa passes me the hipflask and I take a long pull. For a moment, I take my eyes off the Bishop and examine the flask in greater detail. Mostly circular in shape, with smooth rounded edges but for the small neck and cap, it fits snugly, satisfactorily, in the palm. Moonlight glints on the polished pewter. This flask is a reminder that this has been a journey through a circular world. I kept finding the shape everywhere: in the ground plans of the towers, the design and motion of their lenses, the shape of their flashes, even in the itinerary of their keepers, bound fast to the clock.

Without end or beginning, the circle connotes infinity, and since prehistory it has influenced the designers of earthworks and structures. Stone circles of varying ancient pedigrees litter the British landscape. Circular stone towers survive from the late Iron Age in the form of Shetlandic brochs, still standing to a remarkable height. Their purpose seems to have been a combination of the domestic and the defensive. Later on, in medieval Ireland, over 50 stone round towers were built in the vicinity of churches and monasteries. Various theories have been proposed as to their existence, although it is generally accepted that they acted as bell towers or places of refuge in war. The juxtaposition of their circular forms with nearby places of worship is apt. Both reach, literally and figuratively, for the divine, another association the circle has had since antiquity. You might, perhaps, see the rock lighthouses as the latest in this lineage of circular buildings. Of all our stone circles, they are certainly the youngest, but they seem to have the strength of millennia compressed inside them.

At that experimental lighthouse in Blackwall there is now a curious installation. Instead of a light, the lighthouse now houses *Longplayer*, a musical composition intended to last a thousand years that began playing on 31 December 1999. It was the brainchild of Jem Finer, the Pogues guitarist who co-wrote the Christmas song 'Fairytale of New York' with Shane MacGowan.

Longplayer occupies the upper storeys of the old buoy warehouse joined to the tower, and discreet speakers filter the sounds through the octagonal interior and lantern room. The sound installation is recordings of Tibetan singing bowls, hundreds of them, played in sequences and then randomly programmed together. Many of the circular bowls are on display in the roofspace of the adjacent buoy warehouse, beautiful beaten bronze vessels. Classed as 'standing bells', they are played by striking or rubbing the rim with a padded handle. Arranged by the computer, the sequences produce a mesmerizing fluctuation of tone and pitch beyond accurate description, especially when married to the sight of the deserted Thames through the panes of the lantern room.

It is a soundscape of chimes, akin to the seascape of lights emerging at dusk to seafarers around Britain. From tower to tower go strong beams, crossing darkening seas. *Longplayer* challenges us to remain interested, to keep the inclination to maintain our interest as the centuries pass, measuring the value we place on endurance. I feel the fate of this circular orchestration is somehow intertwined with that of the rock lighthouses. After all, the chimes resonate in the lantern where their lamps and lenses once flashed.

My journeys have shown how the rock lighthouses can have surprisingly variable traits and associations, from fame to obscurity, from ruin to bright functionality. But as I found at the Bell Rock, at the outset, they all share one overriding characteristic: they are navigational gifts for the safety of all. In an increasingly fractious and cynical world, the rock lighthouses emit an unprejudiced message of fellowship. To renege on this, to let the lights go out, would be a worrying gesture. If there comes a time when we allow the Bishop and the other towers to fall first into darkness, then into the waves, it will say a great deal about us. Maintaining them perhaps maintains our generosity of spirit.

As its prestige ebbed following the World Wars, Britain learned to treasure its history, particularly the physical traces of it. Antiquarians have been rediscovering and studying ancient ruins from the eighteenth century onwards, but it was in the twentieth century that movements were formed, legislation passed, organizations like the National Trust born and buildings saved for the nation. At about the same time, we became castle-goers, rather than seafarers, a nation keen on its old conquests and enthusiastic sightseers of its monuments to them. This has shown no sign of abating: our history has become part of our coinage in the world, and our appetite for historic buildings and places only grows.

Castles are visited by millions each year, yet some of the most interesting strongholds we ever built were never on land. Lighthouses embody an altruism which saw us illuminate the seas for everyone, but they also have associations with more discredited, imperial elements of our history. As sensational and instructive as any terrestrial building type, these sea-shaken houses are a kind of unseen, marginal part of Britain's heritage. And they hold a quieter story: the social histories of the communities linked to these offshore towers, the keepers, seafarers and families who once formed their hinterland, one that has been fragmented but, as I found at the Fastnet, not yet totally lost.

Josa nudges me out of these speculations and I hand her back the flask. It's gone midnight, and we decide to return home. She gently tilts the flask to her lips, and again the moonlight catches brightly on the pewter. As if in response, and with stellar strength, two old, bright flashes come shooting out of the distance.

21. Dusk at the Bishop Rock,
1932

The rock lighthouses of Great Britain and Ireland and their dates of construction

Eddystone - 1698, 1708, 1759 & 1882

Smalls (1) - 1776 & 1861

Longships (2) - 1795 & 1875

South Rock (3) - 1797

Bell Rock - 1811

Haulbowline - 1824

Perch Rock - 1830

Trwyn Du (4) - 1838

Plymouth Breakwater (5) - 1844

Skerryvore (6) - 1844

Needles (7) - 1859

Skervuile (8) - 1860

Les Hanois (9) - 1862

Blackwall (London) - 1866

Wolf Rock - 1870

Dubh Artach (10) - 1872

Chicken Rock (11) - 1875

Oxcars (12) - 1886

Bishop Rock - 1858 & 1887

Beachy Head (13) - 1902

Fastnet - 1904

Bell Rock

12

6
10

8

3

11

Haulbowline

4

Perch Rock

1

Blackwall

Fastnet

7

13

2

5

Bishop Rock

Wolf Rock

Eddystone

9

Notes

Eddystone (I)

The *Mayflower*'s captain's words are quoted in Adam Hart-Davis, *Henry Winstanley and the Eddystone Lighthouse* (2003). Henry Winstanley's description of the 'very fine bedchamber' appears on one of his engravings (late seventeenth/ early eighteenth century), reproduced in Hart-Davis's biography.

Bell Rock

The Notice to Mariners is reproduced from Robert Stevenson's *An Account of the Building of the Bell Rock Lighthouse including Details of the Erection and Peculiar Structure of the Edifice* (1824). All subsequent quotes from Robert Stevenson are also taken from this, apart from his comment about the commissioners ('should neither sit . . .'), an extract from his correspondence which appears in R.W. Munroe's *Scottish Lighthouses* (1979). R.M. Ballantyne's words appear in his book *The Lighthouse: Being the Story of a Great Fight between Man and the Sea* (1865). Further reading includes Bella Bathurst's *The Lighthouse Stevensons* (1999) and David Taylor's *Bell Rock Lighthouse: A Reference Site* (http://bellrock.org.uk).

Haulbowline

Alexander Nimmo's sailing directions are from an unpublished document (1821) held at the National Archives. Alan Stevenson's description of Haulbowline is from his *Account of the Building of Skerryvore* (1848). The Trinity House representatives' description ('a fixed light with twenty 25 inch reflectors . . .')

appears in an unpublished Trinity House minute book of 1869. The description of Haubowline as a traditional smuggling route and the quotes relating to the incident involving William Sweetman are from unpublished, declassified MoD files relating to Carlingford Lough in the 1970s, held at the National Archives.

Perch Rock

Rose George's insightful investigation into modern seafaring is *Deep Sea and Foreign Going* (2013). Bella Bathurst's *The Wreckers* was published in 2005 and Hugh Hollinghurst's *John Foster and Sons: Kings of Georgian Liverpool* in 2009. John and Diane Robinson's detailed *Lighthouses of Liverpool Bay* came out in 2007. The sniffy quote about New Brighton ('few readers would care to be recommended . . .') is taken from *Round the Coast* (1895), an album of photographs now available on line (http://www.thornbury-pump.co.uk/ Coast1895/contents. php?thepage=58). The lines from *Sir Gawain and the Green Knight* are from Brian Stone's Penguin translation (1974).

Interlude: Blackwall

Winstanley's description of the candles of his 1698 lighthouse are from one of his own engravings (late seventeenth/early eighteenth century), which appears in Adam Hart-Davis's biography, mentioned above. John Smeaton's words are from his 1791 account of the Eddystone, published in *Eddystone Lighthouses* (1882). Theresa Levitt's *A Short Bright Flash: Augustin Fresnel and the Birth of the Modern Lighthouse* was published in 2013. The description of the night of 19 March 1869 ('proved cold but very fine . . .') is from a Trinity House unpublished minute book of the same year.

Wolf Rock

The John Betjeman quote is from the introduction to his *Cornwall: A Shell Guide* (1934). James Douglass's descriptions and comments are from his paper on the Wolf Rock, given at the Institution of Civil Engineers in 1870. Elisabeth Stanbrook's account of life on the Longships is from her *Longships Lighthouse* (2016). W.J. Lewis's comments on the keepers' sense of anticipation on relief day are from his *Ceaseless Vigil* (1970). Frederick Kitton's words are from his account *A Visit to the Eddystone Lighthouse* (1892). Tony Parker's oral history of lighthouse keepers is *Lighthouse* (1975). The helicopter pilot's comment on the Penlee lifeboat tragedy appeared in the *Plymouth Herald* in 2017 (https://www.plymouthherald.co.uk/news/local-news/solomon-browne-remembered-946384). A comprehensive account of the lighthouse is given in Martin Boyle's *Wolf Rock* (1997).

Eddystone (II)

The Mike Palmer quote is from his *Eddystone: The Finger of Light* (2005). William Douglass writes of the 'very difficult and tedious operation' in

his paper on the Eddystone for the Institute of Civil Engineers (1883). Frederick Kitton's words are from his account *A Visit to the Eddystone Lighthouse* (1892).

Bishop Rock

All W.J. Lewis quotes are from his *Ceaseless Vigil* (1970). Cyril Noall's words are from his *Cornish Lights and Shipwrecks* (1968). Elisabeth Stanbrooks relates the encounter of the two bishops and the use of the Bishop Rock as a place of execution in *Bishop Rock Lighthouse* (2008). Robert Maybee's words ('It was a very pleasant summer . . .') are taken from her book, as is the 'jaws of hell' comment from one of the men who worked on the building. Thomas Williams's description is from his *Life of Sir James Nicholas Douglass* (1900). The quotes about the Wherry mines are from Sir Arthur Russell's article 'The Wherry Mine, Penzance, its History and its Mineral Productions', *Mineralogical Magazine* 205, Vol. XXVIII, 1949.

Fastnet

James Morrissey's account of the Fastnet is *A History of the Fastnet Lighthouse* (2005). The report from the *Cork Constitution* appeared in the *Belfast Newsletter* on Friday 19 November 1947.

Acknowledgements

Of the lighthouse world, this book could not have been written without the help of Phil Lawlor, Mick O'Reilly, Rory McGee, Barry Phelan, Arthur Ward and Sean Cunningham (all of or with Irish Lights), Kirsten Couper, Doug Darroch and Dave Bond. I am particularly indebted to Neilly O'Reilly and Dave Purdy for their hospitality and good humour on the Fastnet. John Boath, David Taylor, Gerry Douglas-Sherwood and Clive Cornwell all gave generously of their time in agreeing to be interviewed or proofreading parts of the manuscript. Neil Jones and Malcolm Johns (of Trinity House), Allison Metcalfe, Carol Morgan and Elisabeth Stanbrook all provided valuable insights.

Just as supportive have been my fellow Planning Officers at the City of London Corporation, and particular thanks go to Kathryn Stubbs and Annie Hampson. My former tutor Judi Farren-Bradley patiently oversaw this enterprise to begin with, while my tremendous agent Carrie Plitt helped it towards realization. At Penguin, my talented editor Cecilia Stein made this book the best version of itself, and the perspicacity and sharp eyes of Rebecca Lee and Claire Peligry were crucial in honing the text. My thanks, too, to Helen Conford, Matt Hutchinson, Ingrid Matts, Jim Stoddart, Richard Green, Francisca Monteiro and Chris Wormell for their enthusiasm and artistry.

In the field, Michael O'Mahony and Roland Ellis were sources of fine companionship and photographs (and from Michael also came wise counsel on the manuscript). Family and friends – too numerous to all name – kept the whole thing afloat. Special mentions must be made of Nick Hayes, Conor O'Brien, Max Decharne, Peter and Karlien McNamara, Tom Garwood, Matthew Cooper, Richard Parish and the Burness and Nancollas families. They now all know more about lighthouses than they would probably care to, and for that I thank them deeply.

And finally, my profound love and gratitude to Josa, for being both a rock and a light in the making of this work.

Image Credits

The individual and organizations listed below kindly gave permission for the following illustrations to be reproduced in this book:

Trinity House: 1 and 3; *Stormy Landscape with shipping close to the Eddystone Lighthouse* (3) was painted by Admiral Beechey in 1874. National Library of Scotland: 4, 6 and 11; 4 and 11 are details from drawings published in Robert Stevenson's *Account* (1824). National Archives: 7. Michael O'Mahony: 9 and 10 (© Michael O'Mahony). Mary Evans Ltd: 12 (Illustrated London News © Mary Evans Picture Library); first published 18 January 1868. Morrab Library, Penzance: 14 and 21. Institute of Civil Engineers: 15; this drawing was published as an appendix to James Douglass's paper on the Wolf Rock, given at the Institute in 1870. *The Cornishman* & Cornish Studies Library: 16; first published in The Cornishman, 16 December 1976. National Library of Ireland: 20; this photograph was part of a series taken by Sir Robert Ball (1840–1913), Scientific Adviser to the Commissioners of Irish Lights.

Photographs 2, 5, 8 17, 18 and 19 are the author's own.